A Life with the Printed Word

John Chamberlain

Regnery Gateway
Chicago

Published by Regnery Gateway
360 West Superior Street
Chicago, Illinois 60610

Library of Congress Catalog Card Number: 81-85567
ISBN: 0-89526-656-3

For Tanya, Liz, Margie, Chris, Ben and Johnnie Jr.

Contents

Introduction

L ate one afternoon in the fall of 1955, on the eve of the appearance of the first issue of *National Review*, something people more loftily situated would have called a "summit conference" was set in New York City, for which purpose a tiny suite in the Commodore Hotel was engaged. Tensions—ideological and personal—had arisen, and the fleeting presence in New York of Whittaker Chambers, who had dangled before us in an altogether self-effacing way the prospect that he might come out of retirement to join the fledgling enterprise, prompted me to bring the principals together for a meeting which had no specific agenda, being designed primarily to reaffirm the common purpose. As I think back on it, two of the five people present at the outset were born troublemakers. To say this about someone is not to dismiss him as merely that: Socrates was a troublemaker, so was Thomas Edison. But troublemaking was not what was primarily needed to distill unity, and so things were not going smoothly, one half hour after the meeting began. And then, when it was nearly six o'clock and I thought I detected in Chambers a look of terminal exasperation, John Chamberlain came in, a briefcase in one hand, a pair of figure skates in the other. He mumbled (he usually mumbles) his apology.... He had booked the practice time at the ice rink for himself and his daughters.... The early afternoon editorial meeting had been protracted.... The traffic difficult.... No thanks, he didn't want anything to drink—was there any iced tea? He stole a second or two to catch up on Whittaker's family, and then sat back to participate in a conference—which had been transformed by his presence at it. When a few days later Chambers wrote, he remarked the sheer "goodness" of John Chamberlain, a quality in him that no man or woman, living or dead, has ever to my knowledge disputed.

At the time a sharp difference had arisen, not between me and John, but between Willi Schlamm and John's wife, Peggy (RIP). Schlamm viewed the projected magazine as a magnetic field professional affiliation with which could no more be denied by the few to whom the call was tendered, than a call to serve as one of the twelve apostles. Poor Peggy would not stand for it: John was serving then as an editor of *Barron's* Magazine and writer for the *Wall Street Journal*. Before that he had been with *The Freeman*, before that with *Life*, before that *Fortune*, before that the *New York Times*. In each of these enterprises he had achieved singularity. He had two daughters not yet grown up. How could anyone reasonably ask that now, in middle age, he detach himself from a secure position to throw in with an enterprise whose working capital would not have seen *Time* magazine through a single issue, or *Barron's* through a dozen, and whose editor-in-chief was not long out of school?

I like to remind myself that I did not figure even indirectly in the protracted negotiation, respecting, as I did, not only the eminence of John Chamberlain, but also the altogether understandable desire of his wife for just a little economic security. But Willi was very nearly (nothing ever proved that conclusively shocking to Willi) struck dumb with shock. That was one of the clouds that hung over that late afternoon discussion, in which Willmoore Kendall exploited every opportunity to add fuel to the fire, principally by the device of suggesting that for *some* people security means *everything*; the kind of thing John did not wish to hear, among other things because it so inexactly reflected his own priorities—he was concerned not with security, but with domestic peace.

So it went, and in one form or other the tensions continued, though they never proved crippling. John settled the problem by moonlighting—as lead reviewer for *National Review*. But I learned then, during that tense afternoon, the joy of a definitively pacific presence. Ours might have been a meeting to discuss whether to dump the bomb on Hiroshima; and John Chamberlain's presence would have brought to such a meeting, whatever its outcome, a sense of inner peace, manliness, and self-confidence.

There are stories he does not tell, in this engrossing autobiography; stories about himself, and this is characteristic. Bertrand de Jouvenel once told me, in a luncheon devoted to discussing our common friend Willmore Kendall, that any subject at all is more interesting than oneself. Actually, I am not sure that this is so, because some people know no subject thoroughly other than themselves, but with John Chamberlain self-neglect is not an attribute of manners, but of personality. When *National Review* started up, he would come in to the office every week (it was then a weekly), and sitting down in whatever cubicle was empty, type out the lead review, with that quiet confidence exhibited by sea captains when they extricate their huge liners from their hectic municipal slips to begin an ocean voyage. After forty-five minutes or so a definitive book review was done; and he would, quietly, leave, lest he disrupt the office.

In those days "the office" consisted of six or seven cubicles, each one with desk and typewriter. Most of NR's top editorial staffers, from the beginning on, have served only part time—James Burnham, Willi Schlamm, Willmoore Kendall, Whittaker Chambers, Frank Meyer—so that although they would, week after week, always use the same office, at any given moment at least one cubicle was unoccupied, though seldom the same one. A young graduate of Smith, age 24, four or five months into the magazine's life complained to her classmate, my sister, that the repairman who came once a week to check the typewriters had not once serviced her own. No one was more amused on hearing this than John Chamberlain, the delinquent typewriter repairman, who that week, servicing the typewriter, had written a marvelously illuminating review of the entire fictional work of Mary McCarthy.

I never saw him, during the thirties, slide into his chair at the *New York Times* to write his daily book reviews, many of them masterpieces of the form. Nor at *Fortune*, returning from two weeks on the road to write what he here calls a "long piece," which would prove the definitive article on this or that intricate problem of management or labor. Or at *Life*, presiding over the editorial page which was Henry Luce's personal cockpit, from which he spoke out, through John, to God and man in authoritative, not to say authoritarian, accents: but I declined to believe that in any of these roles, or in any of the myriad others—as professor at Columbia, as dean of journalism at Troy State University in Alabama, as a book writer, or columnist—John Chamberlain ever did anything more disruptive than merely to greet whoever stood in the way, and amble over to wherever the nearest typewriter was, there to execute his craft: maintaining standards as high as any set by any critical contemporary. Because John Chamberlain could not ever sing off key. And the combination of a gentle nature, and a hard Yankee mind, brought forth prose of which this book gives a representative sample. The voice of reason, from an affable man; unacquainted with affectation; deeply committed to the cause of his country, which he believes to be co-extensive with that of civilization; and certainly, with that of his two girls by his first marriage, and his son—a budding young poet—by his second, the enchanting Ernestine, to whom he went soon after Peggy's untimely death.

In this book Chamberlain seeks to bring the reader quietly along, that he might reexperience the author's odyssey. He does this, characteristically, without pushing or shoving; as if to say—at any point—that if the reader desires to hew to a different turn in the road, why that is all right by Chamberlain; although the probability is that, if the reader will reflect substantially on the data, he will in due course come around.

The data!

We are all familiar with autobiographical accounts of ideological explorations, some of them wrongfully exciting. John Chamberlain's is surely the most soft-throated in the literature. As a young man who had demonstrated his prowess as a critic (William Lyon Phelps called him the "finest critic of his generation"), as a political thinker manifestly addicted to progress, he wrote his book *A Farewell to Reform*, in which he seemed to give up on organic change, suggesting the advantages of radical alternatives. But his idealism was never superordinated to his intelligence, and in the balance of that decade of the thirties, and following that of the forties, Chamberlain never ceased to look at the data, which carefully he integrated in his productive mind. Along the line (he tells us) he read three books, so to speak at one gulp (how many books has he read, reviewed, during his career? Or better, Has anyone read, and manifestly digested, more books than John Chamberlain?)—and the refractory little tumblers closed, after which he became what is now denominated a "conservative," though Chamberlain prefers the word "voluntarist." The books in question, by the three furies of modern libertarianism—Isabel Paterson, Rose Wilder Lane, Ayn Rand—provided the loose cement. After that, as he shows us here, he ceased to be surprised by evidence, now become redundant; evidence that the marketplace really works, really performs social functions, really helps live human beings with live problems.

This book is a story of that journey. Its calmness and lucidity, its acquiescent handling of experience, free of ideological entanglement, provokes in the reader the kind of confidence that John Chamberlain throughout his life has provoked in his friends. That he is that to them—a friend; but that in no circumstances are the claims of friendship so to be put forward as to run any risk of corrupting the purity of his ongoing search, through poetry, fiction, economic texts, corporate reports, and—yes, seed catalogues—for just the right formulation of what may be acknowledged as the American proposition, by which an equilibrium of forces breeds the best that can be got out of the jealous, contentious, self-indulgent, uproarious breed of men and women that have made so exciting a world here, giving issue, in one of America's finest moments, to a splendid son, who here has given us his invaluable memoirs.

WILLIAM F. BUCKLEY, JR.

Chapter 1

I t was the hippie summer of 1970. A tall, muscular kid had been looking over my decrepit barn in the field across the road. He approached me tentatively as I went out to get the mail. He had been a construction worker on a project that had just been completed, he said, and had nothing at the moment to do. He lived in a crowded in-town area, and had no place to run his dogs. Would I let him bring the dogs out to run in my field? And would I mind if he and a couple of his friends were to use the barn as a meeting place while the dogs were having a romp?

There was such a wistful quality to his appeal that I did not say no. His story about living in the inner city, which he expanded upon, seemed symptomatic, even though I discounted much of his talk about the young not being consulted about making the rules that were supposed to govern them. Before he left we had a deal: he would keep the barn in good order and would permit no smoking by his friends in what was the remnant of a haymow.

Of course, it all worked out badly. The boy, John Oliva, meant well, but, as the hot summer progressed, with the young literally swarming all over the United States to new Woodstocks and whatever, he couldn't control his friends. The word went around and they brought other friends. On one bad night, when a rock festival had been advertised for a ski slope in the not-too-distant township of Middlefield, Connecticut, the barn, in my absence, was the dormitory for kids who had come like lemmings from as far away as Vancouver in Canada and North Carolina in the U.S. It was pretty much of a mess. The good that was to come out of it was that my dance-teacher wife, who had always looked upon the barn as a possible dance studio, decided to go ahead with her own project if only to save the structure, with its ancient, wood-pegged beams, from having to be wrecked as an eyesore.

What had possessed me to give John Oliva (who later died trying to hop a freight in Nebraska) *carte blanche* to use my field? I can only say that I was the victim of a comparison that may have been all wrong but that seemed valid at the moment. As I talked to John Oliva at the mailbox I kept thinking

1

how free the world was in the early years of the century, before World War I. I was born in 1903, the year in which the Ford Motor Company was first incorporated and the Wright brothers flew the first airplane. In those early years, we knew the internal combustion engine as a rare marvel; it had not yet overrun the landscape and choked the cities, or led to unwinnable wars in which young men were drafted to no discernible purpose.

Part of my young life was spent in the inner city of New Haven, on Park Street, a respectable neighborhood that was on the edge of the Oak Street slum. But in summer—and indeed for some winters—we moved to Morris Cove on the east side of New Haven harbor. The curious thing is that life seemed just as free in one place as the other. In his memoir, *Starting Out in the Thirties*, Alfred Kazin, a first-rate literary critic but a sometimes careless reporter, has pictured me circa 1934 as a standard-product New England middle-class rebel from a bourgeois furniture manufacturer's home. Aside from the minor error of confusing furniture manufacturing with retailing, the idea of presenting me as class-dominated when young was a little startling. Park Street Yankees—and there were few enough of them—went to Webster School where they were "integrated" (though we did not know the word) with the swarming Italians from Oak Street and Jews from Spruce Street. We were taught by Irish women who put their souls into their work: one of them, a Miss Kelly, conducted me with a firm clutch on my shoulder from the third grade back to Miss Lynch in the second grade as a disciplinary measure, and only let me return to her class when my father, who was divorced from my mother, promised better behavior (and a more seemly supervision from my grandmother, a harassed lady of infinitely good heart and unconquerable permissiveness) in the future.

If Lynwood Tower, Ray Montgomery, and I were Park Street "wasps," we had few other playmates who were in that category. We had a gang, the only qualification for membership being that one could not be Italian. I remember the names, even though I am not certain of the spellings: there was John Sinyoski, a Pole; Pritchard Clew, the son of a Negro preacher; Lester Zimmerman, a German; Abie Silver, a Jew; Willie Murray, Irish; Gordon Swebelius, a Swede whose father was to become a famous gunmaker in World War I. Tower, Montgomery, and I were the "Anglo-Saxons" in the group—I had not yet digested the fact that my mother, Emily Davis, was mainly Welsh. Our mission in life was a protective one; we kept together in order to resist what seemed to us the animosity of the clannish Italians, who may have had a legitimate reason to dislike us for preying on their parents' shops for the Clix and Piedmont cigarettes we smoked in an empty lot kitty-corner to Webster School. Occasionally we had Homeric clashes at the corner of Oak and Park, using garbage-can covers for shields and hurling rocks that, luckily, never connected to cause any serious injury.

In spite of the names we called each other (wop, guinnie, squarehead, mick, yank), we did not really take our differences seriously. It was a rough democracy, not yet poisoned by that over-sensitiveness that makes it a matter of "racism" to tell an ethnic joke. I suspect that my experience was similar to the childhoods of many another "wasp" in the cities of southern New England in the days when the melting pot was really effective. In later years it struck me as extremely significant that the names along the fashionable Ridge Road in the Hamden suburb of New Haven were mostly Italian. Eventually the Italians went Republican, taking the play in City Hall away from the Irish who dominated the city when I was growing up. As for the Irish, we minority yanks admired them inordinately. They were the boys with the imagination. I paid tribute to them in a foreword I wrote many years later to James T. Farrell's *Studs Lonigan*, thereby incurring the enmity of an old friend, Dillon Toole, who fancied I had insulted the "lace curtains" among them in my partiality for the more hearty of the breed.

The point of going into all this is that northeastern America, after the turn of the century, was the freest society that one could possibly imagine. We lived in an "inner city," but we used our legs—and bicycles—to get out of it at will. We scoured the West Rock ridge for chestnuts (the trees had not yet been blighted), and Gordon Swebelius and I had a regular routine of taking a trolley to the shore to pick up periwinkles, oblivious to the cruelty of taking them home to backyards where there was no salt water.

At Morris Cove, the freedom of the city was compounded. We lived in a house fronting the harbor next door to my birthplace. My grandfather, whose hobby was sailing up to the time of his untimely death at 60 of angina (he would have lived if he had had the benefit of modern medicine), had left an old catboat-rigged craft in the backyard. The boat, which showed daylight through its seams, was a challenge. We went to work on it with oakum and putty, making it seaworthy up to a point. From then on we lived in a state of perpetual warfare with my grandmother, who would stand on the shore beckoning to us to come home as we set out for City Point across the harbor or for the breakwaters at the harbor's entrance. In between prodigious acts of bailing, my friends and I became passably good sailors, although, lacking a cabin boat, we never went in for cruising as my grandfather, father, and Aunt Betty had done before me.

The freedom of the water was matched by a corresponding freedom in the swampy back country between Morris Cove and East Haven. My grandfather, before his death, had carried me piggyback over all the trails past what we called the Turtle Brook (in reality, the beginnings of Morris Creek). Ray Montgomery, a constant visitor from New Haven, and I collected diamond-back and speckled mud turtles for a "farm" of thirty-six of the reptiles, all of whom escaped one night when someone carelessly opened the door of their cage. We knew the value of wetlands long before the ecologists started a belated movement to save them. Alas, the environmentalists came too late to preserve the swamps along Morris Creek. They are now filled in to make the Tweed-New Haven Airport, and I can never leave from there to go to Washington without nostalgic twinges of a memory that left me open to John Oliva's plea for running room for his dogs many years later.

My father married again when I was eleven and my sister Mary was nine. The problem with a new marriage seemed to be finding ways of relieving my grandmother and aunt from the responsibility of taking care of us while my father and stepmother were absent in Florida and Bermuda in the winter. I was still in the seventh grade in Morris Cove school when the decision was made to send me to a new academy, Loomis, in Windsor, Connecticut. The only drawback was that I would have, somehow, to pass the entrance requirements without benefit of eighth-grade teaching. Fortunately, the seventh and eighth grades occupied the same room at the Morris Cove school, with the capable Miss Jourdain of Branford teaching both classes. We in the seventh grade listened while she ministered to the eighth-grade requirements, and a lot must have passed on to us by a peculiar osmosis when we were supposed to be concentrating on our own class assignments. With a little help from my great aunt Hannah and her good friend Miss Pinney, teachers from way back, I managed to get by the Loomis tests. But to this day I still lack a grade-school diploma, and there are still problems of English grammar that I finesse by instinct rather then by any rote knowledge of the rules.

Loomis, in the years 1916-20, must have been completely unlike any other prep school in America. As a new school it lacked the tradition-encrusted snobbery that was common, as we found out through college contacts at a later date, to Groton, Andover, and Exeter. It welcomed a large contingent of day students from nearby small towns, and where it attracted New Yorkers it was to the sons of some of the better-known dissidents of the day that it made its pitch. James Waterman Wise, the son of Rabbi Wise, Carlton Dennett, whose contentious mother Mary Ware Dennett was a leading birth-control advocate, and Bill Fincke, whose father was shortly to donate Brookwood, the family estate at Katonah, New York, to the labor movement for a college, brought the new "liberalism" into bull sessions. But the bucolic atmosphere predominated. In addition to being a liberal-arts academy it was an agricultural school, complete with barns and henhouses and a hearty rustic character named Joe Goodrich who taught the agricultural courses. I found the school to be an extension of the same sort of open-air freedom that I had known all through my childhood. We had canoes on the Farmington River, one of which I paddled home down the Connecticut to Long Island Sound and New Haven harbor at a term's end. We had a succession of cold winters when the Farmington and the Connecticut rivers froze, allowing us to take skating trips as far away as Windsor Locks. We trapped for muskrats along the Farmington, curing their skins in a malodorous basement room in one of the dormitories. And there was hardly a weekend in the early fall or spring in which a number of us failed to go on camping trips up the Farmington, often with roasting corn ears from the agricultural school bins. This was all extra gravy to an athletic program that let me, as a twelve-year-old, quarterback a midget football team before going on to second-team status as a lightweight upper classman. The headmaster, Nathaniel Horton Batchelder, who also coached football, considered me a "brainy youngster," and he was particularly enraged when I only managed to get a 60 in the college board American history examination. He had taught the course, and taught it well; unfortunately, I had had scarlet fever in the winter of 1920 and missed the whole Civil War period, which I had neglected to make up. At a later date I would never have made Ivy League Yale, but in the teens of the century there was considerably more room for free play at the edges when it came to satisfying entrance requirements. Who knows, maybe it was better that way.

My open-air education at Loomis was helped by World War I. The school turned over its farm acres to some of Herbert Hoover's lieutenants, who proposed to use them for the "food will win the war" program. I enlisted in this program for two summers, though I doubt that anything I did helped to feed a single doughboy in France or a single starving Belgian after the war. One summer was spent nailing shingles to farm buildings; another had us wielding mattocks to get the stumps out of a field which Joe Goodrich wanted for new corn acreage for the school's chickens. No doubt we freed other people to do war work, but the experience left us a bit cynical. And the cynicism was compounded when the school fired Mr. Dane, the German teacher, for the sin of having specialized in the language of the hated Hun. Mr. Dane, who came from rural Vermont, was a good guy, and I had wanted to take his course.

Before he left, for parts unknown, Mr. Dane had told us something about the delights of camping in northern New England. So, with money earned on the farm, a number of us, including Milton Smith who later became quite a mountaineer in the Himalayas, made memorable trips in the White Mountains of New Hampshire, taking little-known routes from below Mount Carrigan to the summit of Mount Washington via the Davis Trail. We slid all over the northern and southern peaks of the Presidential Range, and returned to school much refreshed from the wilderness experience.

I was graduated from Loomis at the age of sixteen, too young, in my father's judgment, to go on to college. But if I weren't going to enter Princeton, my own first choice, or Yale, which would be easier on the family's budget if I could, after winter and summer absences of four years, begin again to live at home, I had necessarily to work. With a friend from Loomis, Collin Stevens, who had decided against college, I grandiloquently named California as my chosen work destination. First, I had to earn the fare to buy a ticket on the old liner *Momus* to New Orleans, from where we proposed to get to Los Angeles as best we could. To get my travel stake I worked on my father's furniture truck with two blacks, Eben Tyler and Cal Stoner, who fortified what I had learned on Park Street about the individualism that must always rise superior to "race." Stoner was what was then called a "rounder"—he had innumerable girls, and he delighted in telling about his parties and his exploits. Tyler was strictly a homebody who loved his wife. He read Richard Harding Davis's stories for diversion, leading me to those marvelous boy's books of adventure, *Captain Macklin*, *Soldiers of Fortune*, and *The White Mice*. In their own separate ways Stoner and Tyler were both happy men.

Getting to California was more adventure of a sort that today would not be judged quite safe. We hitch-hiked across the oyster-shell roads of East Texas, and crawled into a box car one night at Nome to get some sleep. In the middle of the night we heard voices, and decided to get out before they reached us. The next day we realized what had happened: the box car had been loaded in the night with hogs. Dirty and dishevelled, we hiked on to a hotel in Houston. The house detective was wary about letting us in. "Why," he asked, "are you-all beatin' yore way?" We showed him that we had money and a change of clothes in pack sacks, and he passed us. We had had enough of the road for a while, and we used what money we had left to take sit-up coaches by night the rest of the way to California.

Going to the orange-growing region of Pomona, east of Los Angeles under the imposing Sierra Madre crest of "Old Baldy," Collin and I applied to an orchard man, Bill Coon, of the Albany, New York, collar-manu-facturing clan. Bill had been a Yale classmate of my father's who had decided against a business career in the East. He gave us an introduction to the overseer of his orange groves, and we set happily to work picking navels in bright sunshine. (The smog had not yet become southern Califor-nia's nemesis.) Alas, the job lasted only a few days. What killed us as orange pickers was the phenomenon of reverse discrimination: the Mexican boss of the picking crew complained that it was his prerogative to hire for the groves and he preferred his own people. The embarrassed Mr. Coon, faced with a possible strike at the height of the navel season, had to let us go. So we moved over to the town of Claremont, where all races, the *"Cholos"* from Mexico included, were welcome in the orange-packing houses. It was strictly piecework there, the weekly paycheck dependent on how many oranges one could wrap in paper and put in order in boxes in an hour. The fruit came tumbling off a carrier in various graded sizes. One stood at a bin with a rubber finger stall on the left forefinger, plucking a paper from a rack, deftly enclosing it around an orange, and then going on to the next fruit in an endless speed-up. Every one was given a chance at the bigger fruit which took less time to pack. The men at the job were definitely inferior to the women, who seemed to have the defter fingers. But before

Christmas Collin and I were making some $30 a week, which in those days was a decent wage. The only trouble was that it was indoors, and I felt I had been cheated.

But it was not all work in California. We climbed Ontario Peak and moved into the San Bernardino mountains on week-ends, and I went alone for a wonderful week to the Grand Canyon of Arizona. Later I hitchhiked past San Jacinto Mountain to Palm Springs, then, as I remember it, a sleepy desert oasis with only a couple of small inns. After the navel-orange season, we hitchhiked over the mountains from Los Angeles to Bakersfield and on to the San Joaquin valley towns of Porterville and Lindsay, where, as semi-skilled operatives, we got jobs packing Valencia oranges. We lived outdoors in a makeshift tent. And when the Valencia crop had all been picked and packed we tried hiking to the Sequoia and General Grant national parks. The season had not yet started, and we realized we had made a mistake; there was no food to be had at Sequoia. We cadged a big cheese and a sack of raisins from a road crew, living on it for several days. It was not exactly a balanced diet. When we got back to the San Joaquin Valley floor, we robbed a fruit grove near Fresno, getting violent stomach aches. Our hitchhiking took us to Yosemite, still feeling rather rocky. And so we went on to San Francisco. Collin had decided to go to Hawaii; I had had my free year, and had just enough money saved to get back home to go to college.

What impressed me as a teenager on my own in California was the gorgeous freedom of America. The "fruit tramps," so-called, who worked in the packing houses were not an oppressed lot; there were young couples from the apple country of Oregon who had moved south to pack oranges for adventure, and there were girls who had quit telephone exchange jobs. It was a most cosmopolitan work society. In Pomona we lived with a family from Montana; next door was a family from South Africa. One of the Claremont packing-house employees was a British air veteran of World War I. Maybe there was—and probably there still is—oppression in the stoop-crop fields of the Imperial Valley, but I have always taken stories of our depressed migrant workers with a grain or two of salt. The Mexicans who did much of the field work in the California I knew saved money out of their pay checks, and many of them returned home to buy acres of their own.

Returning home in the summer of 1921, traveling by night in reclining-chair coach cars to stretch my savings, and spending days along the way to have a look at such things as the Mormon temple, the Great Salt Lake and Estes Park, I was only dimly aware that the United States was a troubled country. How could unemployment be a problem when two kids coming out from the East had had no difficulty getting jobs in California? Stopping in Denver to visit Ed Baughan, a young man Collin Stevens and I had met on the *Momus* traveling from New York to New Orleans, I heard nothing to make me think the U.S. was a deprived country. Ed had had no trouble getting work in the Texas oil fields. He had gone on to Denver to something more consonant with his college degree. We drove to Estes Park with a young couple who sang the song of the day about there being "nothing surer than the rich get richer and the poor get children, but in the meantime, in between time, ain't we got fun." It was apparent that neither Ed nor his young married friends were suffering from poverty.

But in Chicago, where I met my father at the Illinois Athletic Club (he was in the Midwest on his annual furniture-buying trip), I learned something about the facts of life. The post-war depression had caught up with the furniture business. There wouldn't be enough money to send me to Princeton, whose bright country-club colors had just been celebrated in Scott Fitzgerald's *This Side of Paradise*. I would have to go to Yale, presumably living at home. As one who had been on his own for five years, I didn't relish the prospect. At the last minute I got a reprieve from my grandmother, who scrounged up the money to pay for room and board at the college. So, after spending the month of August reading a textbook on physical geography to take an examination for an easy last-needed point for college entrance, I found myself a full-fledged Yalie, not a day student who would have had to suffer the contempt that would have been accorded me as half a townie. I was still too callow to know what I wanted from college, but I was soon to find out.

Chapter 2

A s a college freshman aspirant, I had totally miscast myself. I had
written for school publications, and, indeed, had been editor-in-chief
of both the Loomis *Log* and a year book called the *Loomiscellany*. I had
had one excellent English teacher, Lewis Clough, who didn't care what his
pupils read as long as they read assiduously. I had been through a whole set
of Kipling and most of Jack London with Mr. Clough's blessing, but had
skimped such staples of the day as Dickens, Scott, and George Eliot. Mr.
Clough didn't care. He did discipline me once for handing in twice the
same theme on Dickens (I had thought mistakenly that he had failed to read
the paper the first time), but mostly he let us write what we pleased on
subjects of our own choice. I deluged him with nature themes, and he didn't
mind in the least.

In spite of a bent toward writing, I had resolved, on entering Yale, to
become a civil engineer who would spend a life on construction problems
in the open air. I wanted to build big dams in the West. So I loaded my
schedule with four math courses—trigonometry, solid geometry, and dif-
ferential and integral calculus. I also took chemistry, which I had avoided in
favor of physics in school. Alas, I soon found that I was over my head. I
flunked chemistry and dropped it at midyear, and I failed the June examination in integral calculus, which meant that I had to take it over again. My
faculty adviser, Professor Richard Newhall, noticing that I had gotten good
marks in English and history, suggested that he might keep me from being
busted if I would promise to change to a linked major and minor in history
and economics, which I promptly did.

I had made another miscalculation as a freshman. My father had been art
editor of the *Yale Record* (he also did covers for Cole Porter songs), and I
fancied myself as a cartoonist who might follow in his footsteps. So I
started submitting drawings accompanied by two-line jokes or bits of verse
in French forms to the *Record*. The drawings never made it, but the jokes
and verse did. Francis Bronson, the *Record* chairman who later became the
editor of the *Yale Alumni Magazine*, had a distinct flair for light verse,
particularly *ballades*, and when it turned out that I had an aptitude for the

same things, he shoved me along. I made the board of editors at the end of freshman year, which enabled me to become chairman as a junior.

What was it that turned college generations in the first quarter of the 20th century to writing *ballades, villanelles, triolets,* and *rondeaux?* It's a great puzzle. The tradition had no sanction in the rather good English courses taught by Bob French, Billy Phelps, and Chauncey Tinker, but there it was, ensconced at Yale as it was at other Ivy League universities. It was part of America's literary immaturity, which was, in the late teens and early '20s, being fought by fledgling critics such as Van Wyck Brooks, Randolph Bourne, Waldo Frank, Lewis Mumford, and Thomas Beer. Despite the fact that Waldo Frank and Thomas Beer had gone to Yale, their names were not known on the campus when I was a freshman in 1921-22. Nor did we realize that poets such as Stephen Benet and Archibald MacLeish had written for the *Yale Literary Magazine*, or that Sinclair Lewis, who had just come out with *Main Street*, had been a most unhappy Yale undergraduate before World War I.

Bob Hutchins said that the most appalling thing that had happened to him as a Yale undergraduate was to go through college without reading a single great book. It wasn't as bad as that in 1921-25, as Karl Young went through every play of Shakespeare and Bob French forced us to master the Middle English of Chaucer's *Canterbury Tales*. William Lyon Phelps jumped around from year to year from Tennyson and Browning to Henrik Ibsen and George Bernard Shaw and the great Russian novelists of the 19th century, and Tinker insisted on solid reading both in the Age of Johnson and in the English poets. But we didn't read Adam Smith or Karl Marx, or even John Stuart Mill, in a rather extensive economics minor, and biology was not taught from the pages of Darwin's *Origin of Species*. I had to read all the economic "greats" from Smith and Ricardo to the Austrians for myself in the '30s and '40s when I really got interested in the subject. And if I hadn't taken an elective in classical civilization, my knowledge of the great Latins and the great Greeks would have been limited to Caesar's *Commentaries*, which I had had to read in my two years of Latin in prep school. Hutchins was all too correct in his general criticism of college curricula, and things were to get worse on the campuses before they were to get better. When we were comparing notes in the '30s, Clifton Fadiman, a graduate of Raymond Weaver's and Mark Van Doren's Columbia University in 1925, observed that we were the last college generation to get a good literary education. Weaver, as the rediscoverer of *Moby Dick*, gave Fadiman the right to talk. But if Fadiman was right so far as it applied to me, it was largely because of a happy accident.

The accident was a young Irishman from Chicago with a Jesuit training, William Troy, whose acquaintance I made as a sophomore and with whom I roomed in junior and senior years. Bill Troy was a revelation. Allen Tate, the Southern agrarian critic and poet who met Bill in the late '20s, described him in 1966 as "among the handful of the best critics of this century." In the early '20s he was already steeped in the literature of the Irish Renascence, from Yeats and Joyce to such minor voices as Liam O'Flaherty and Padraic Colum. To amuse himself he wrote about imaginary improbable encounters, with Oscar Wilde crossing lances with Somerset Maugham, but, as his own most fastidious critic, Bill never got around to publishing his *jeu d'esprit* pieces. The same was true of his excellent verse. He admired James Joyce not only because of Joyce's genius, but because that great Irishman had never repeated himself. From a slim volume of beautiful lyrics (*Chamber Music*) and an Ibsenesque play (*Exiles*) to *Dubliners*, a great book of short stories, and from a novel, *Portrait of the Artist as a Young Man*, to such indeterminate experimental forms as *Ulysses* and *Finnegan's Wake*. Joyce had always been the explorer. But what really impressed Bill was that Joyce had written the "best villanelle ever," which happened to be tucked away in the pages of the *Portrait*. Bill didn't see why college versifiers should write in French forms after reading Joyce's single example. I took the soft impeachment as justified and wrote no more *ballades*.

Coming as he did from Chicago, which had a much livelier contemporary literary tradition in the early '20s than New York, Bill introduced me to Sherwood Anderson, Theodore Dreiser, Ben Hecht, Floyd Dell, Carl Sandburg, Burton Rascoe, and others of the Midwest renascence. Both Chicago and Dublin were a long way from New Haven, but two years of browsing in Bill Troy's personal library and collection of periodicals gave me a dimension that I would not otherwise have had. To cap it all, Bill was as steeped in French literature as he was in Irish or American. Taking off from his example, I read ten French novels through in French during a summer in France, beginning with the simple lucidity of Pierre Loti and Anatole France and going on through Balzac and Flaubert to the first volume of Proust's *A La Recherche du Temps Perdu*, which I staggered through with immense difficulty. Later I had little difficulty translating André Maurois's French letter for the *New York Times Book Review*.

Bill, who taught at Bennington and in several other universities, was a regular reviewer of both books and films for the *Nation* in the '30s. He also wrote extensively for the literary quarterlies. Because of what critic Stanley Edgar Hyman calls his "mad Irish perfectionism," he never got around to collecting his 70-odd essays and reviews. Hyman, who gathered some 20 of the Troy articles for a posthumous book published by the Rutgers University Press in 1966, has made up for some of Bill Troy's neglect of his own talents. The Troy essay on Scott Fitzgerald as the tortured narcissist is the best that has been done on the subject. Hyman says Troy was the finest lecturer on literature he had ever heard. He was already that when I knew him as an undergraduate and roommate at Yale.

One stereotype of the decade of the '20s is that it was a time when apathetic students conformed. Another is that it was a time of wildly alcoholic irresponsibility. Actually, not many of us wanted to be bond salesmen, and Serious Drinking, as Lucius Beebe called it, was, save for an occasional Big Game week-end, limited to a fringe group that was not much admired. Beebe, who later reformed sufficiently to become a competent critic and chronicler of Broadway happenings for the *New York Herald-Tribune* and a reknowned railroad buff, washed himself out of college when he stood up in a box at the Hyperion Theatre to shout "ham, ham" at the actors while he tossed pennies on the stage. This convivial evening ended with Lucius throwing a mail truck through the door to the office of Dean Jones, a particularly thorny disciplinarian. As a columnist in the Franklin P. Adams, or F.P.A., tradition for the *Yale Daily News*, I collected some nostalgic tributes not only to Beebe's poetic talents (he had already published a book of creditable verse) but to his Beau Brummel wardrobe. We were sorry to see him return to his native Boston, where he mustered sufficient influence to get himself accepted by Harvard, which put up with his eccentricities and saw to it that he kept his natural flamboyance under better control.

Politically speaking, I suppose we were an apathetic college generation in the early '20s. But if we were, we didn't know it. The evils of the Versailles Treaty had not yet become apparent to us. Charles Evans Hughes had succeeded in his battleship-limitation program, and new wars seemed incredibly remote. The Palmer Red Scare was behind us, and prosperity had returned after the 1921 shake-out. The 1924 election contest between Calvin Coolidge and John W. Davis, a Wall Street lawyer, excited nobody, and the third-party candidate, "Fighting Bob" La Follette, seemed very much a voice of the pre-World War I past, which was pretty much terra incognita to us anyway. It was rumored that Max Lerner, an upper classman, and Simon Whitney of our own class, were socialists, but if they were, they made few converts. We took them as liberals without defining the term. Lerner went on to have a distinguished career as a social democratic philosopher with an increasingly conservative bias, and Whitney, as soon as he began to digest his chosen subject of economics, ended up as a sturdy supporter of the market system. His two books on *Economic Principles: Macro and Micro* contain a profound critique of everything that became known as Keynesianism, but in the early '20s nobody on the Yale campus had heard of Keynes.

Innocence is a better word than apathy to describe our political state. We could be roused on local issues. As a *News* columnist writing under the *nom de plume* of Ayesha, which I had taken from the cover of a Rider Haggard novel without reading it, I joined the crusade to rid the college of compulsory daily chapel. It was not that I was anti-religious; I was simply disgusted with the hypocrisy of the whole thing. Students would hurry into chapel still wearing pyjamas under coon-skin coats; they would brush up on their daily assignments by concealing their textbooks behind open hymnals. On

Sunday one could choose between Battell Chapel on the campus or one of the local New Haven churches. But giving our word that we would attend the latter did not mean that we had promised to stay for the sermon. Bringing compulsion into religion made it a farce. So, when President James Rowland Angell denounced "Ayesha" from the Battell pulpit one morning as a menace to sound Christian doctrine, I could only feel that he had missed the point. History, in any event, was with us; we got rid of the compulsion. Whether we helped Christianity at Yale is a moot point. Later, when I wrote an introduction to Bill Buckley's first book, *God and Man at Yale*, it did not occur to me that I might have been guilty of helping to establish the secular atmosphere which was one of his targets on the Yale campus. The trouble, as I saw it when Bill asked me to do the introduction and still see it today, is that the prevailing modern "scientism" keeps university faculties from designing a curriculum that will expose the student to the whole heritage of the Graeco-Roman-Christian West.

We had a bias in the early '20s toward freedom. The "compulsion" of chapel offended our instincts. Alas, Yale, in the '20s gave us no grounding in the great classics of freedom. We took British constitutional history with Sidney Mitchel, and he was a good teacher. But we did not read John Locke's treatises on government, which did so much to spark the American Revolution. We took American history, but spent no time on *The Federalist Papers*. John C. Calhoun, to us, was a Southern states' righter, not the author of *Disquisition on Government* who has proved the necessity of a second vetoing body in addition to king or executive if a free system were to endure. We didn't read Hobbes, and it was the esthetics of Aristotle and Plato, not their profound political differences, that were stressed in classical history courses.

Since, in the high noon of Coolidge prosperity, the State seemed to menace nobody in the U.S., it is scant cause for wonder that we jumped at the opportunity to make H.L. Mencken's new magazine, the green-covered *American Mercury*, our anarchistic Bible. Mencken, while preferring Coolidge to Woodrow Wilson, that "tin-pot Paul" who had "bawled from the roof" of the White House in our teens, laughed at all politicians, and that suited us. We might come from Republican families, but we were cynical. My father, I had noticed, contributed to both the Republican and Democratic parties. He did it for practical reasons: as a furniture-store proprietor he had to have truck access on the street to his storage rooms and basement, which meant that his truck drivers had to count on a complaisant interpretation of the parking laws no matter who was mayor. But beyond practical reasons, there was another cause for our cynicism. Our parents were for economic freedom; they were also for the protective tariff. So, like Louis Adamic, one of Mencken's contributors, we "laughed in the jungle." We could not take politics seriously.

In the '30s we were to pay for our ignorance of fundamental political and economic theory by succumbing to collectivist panaceas without realizing that the personal individualism which we prized could not flourish in a planned system. In the early '20s, however, we could be quite oblivious to doctrines of any sort. The class war, as we knew it in our freshman and sophomore years, was limited to fraternity rushing which gave preference to Andover and Exeter athletes and intellectual "Grotties" from Groton. But, after an initial sorting out (as a graduate of Loomis, a "new" prep school, I made the intermediate fraternity of Zeta Psi), the class war gave way to a fairly generalized democratic feeling. In my freshman year a Jew, Mandell Cohen, whose brother Elliot later made *Commentary* into one of our sharpest critical magazines, could be turned down by an anti-Semitic *Record* board despite his obvious talent. But this sort of thing was on its way out as we grew older. We were natural Jeffersonian individualists who believed that careers should be open to talents. My roommate Bill Troy, who disdained Victorian models, could make the *Yale Literary Magazine* along with Frank Ashburn, whose spiritual forebears were Matthew Arnold and Tennyson, and I could join them by writing essayistic attacks on the prose of our economic textbooks.

Thirty years later, in a foreword to a class reunion book, I noticed that the individualists whom I had known as an undergraduate were still doing a lot of different things according to personal bent and idiosyncracy. Ben Spock—or Dr. Benjamin Spock—had shed his crew-man naïvete to emerge as America's greatest authority on the care and feeding of babies, and his book, addressed to puzzled parents in a permissive generation, had become the most fantastic best-seller since the King James Bible. His college roommate, George Dyer, had gone from a career of writing detective stories to subterranean fame as a World War II intelligence agent, and after the war he had founded something called the Dyer Institute for Interdisciplinary Studies, which specialized in matters related to national security. Later, the divergences of Spock and Dyer, which I was to remark upon in a column called "A Tale of Two Roommates," became really pronounced as Ben took to the picket lines along with Jane Fonda and Jerry Rubin protesting the Vietnam War. George Dyer fought back valiantly: his "interdisciplinary studies" became more and more patriotic as he took to staging re-enactments of such events as the colonists' 1775 March on Quebec, which had been led by the then untraitorous Benedict Arnold. Dyer had a supreme contempt for Ben Spock's new values, but he recognized that Ben, like himself, was incorrigibly wedded to doing his own thing.

In my 30th-reunion foreword I noted some of the ironies of change. The individualism which we took for granted in the early '20s had resulted in some utterly unpredictable careers. Louis Sudler, who had been managing editor of the *Record*, waxed great in his native Chicago as a real-estate man, and put a good part of his fortune at the disposal of Chicago opera and the cultivation of his own magnificent singing voice. The Newbold Morris whom I had known as a rather lazy aristocrat had become a liberal politico who barely missed out in his drive to succeed Fiorello La Guardia as New York City's mayor, But along with his politics, Newbold had cultivated a second career as a figure skater, competing with much younger skaters at the New York Skating Club's Iceland Rink. By that time I no longer went along with liberal politics, but as one who had succumbed to the lure of figure skating for myself, I could only bow in envious admiration when I watched Newbold move counter-clockwise over the ice in a spirited *paso doble* with Sheila Muldowney, a national champion, as his partner.

Tom Bergin was another individualist in our class who did remarkable things. Tom, a "townie" who lived at home, could be lured into arguing about the virtues of A.E. Housman's poetry, but for the most part he kept his own quiet counsel. The reason: he was spending 16 hours of the academic day in mastering a dozen foreign languages. He later emerged as a witty public speaker, a fine administrator as Master of Yale's Timothy Dwight College, and the greatest expert since Walter Camp on Yale football. All of this was in addition to his real work as America's foremost Dante scholar.

Our freedom in the early '20s extended to the summers. Luckily for my career as a critic and journalist, I worked in a summer hotel in Maplewood, New Hampshire, next to a friendly secretary who taught me the touch system in typing as I struggled to produce an elaborate card index system for the hotel's proprietor. In a subsequent summer I signed on with several classmates to take a cargo of mules from Portsmouth, Virginia, to Tarragona, Spain. We were joined by Kentuckians and Missourians, one of whom, Buddy Rogers, was later to marry Mary Pickford. The mules were destined for the now-forgotten Riff War in North Africa, and we, as oceanic muleteers, were destined to be paid off in Spain when our freighter, the *Lancastría*, was sold to an Italian firm for delivery in Genoa while we were still in mid-ocean. Under the terms of the La Follette Seamen's Act, we were entitled not only to our pittance as muleteers but to enough additional money to return home in style as passengers. Some of us, taking the unexpected passenger-fare windfall, chose to live on the extra money in Europe for the entire summer. With the inflationary exchanges that favored the American dollar, that could easily be done.

When the time came to return to college, I sold the second-hand bicycle which I had been riding around England to settle a boarding-house bill and applied to the American consul in Southampton for a job on the *Leviathan*. I came back to New York pressing pants in the ship's tailor shop. The following years I repeated the same pattern, this time washing coffee pots in the *Leviathan* pantry. We could do things like that in the early '20s, for the sailors' unions had not yet become organized to the point of eliminating competition from non-union college kids who were bent on seeing the world. I owe what literary proficiency I have in French—and, to a much lesser extent, in Italian and Spanish—to the fact that they had an open shop on the seas in the '20s, which may prejudice me in favor of right-to-work laws for today. I believe in voluntary unions, but the world pays too high a price when organization is pushed to the extremes of compulsion that have become fashionable with the modern liberal.

In the humming world of the mid-'20s, when business was booming, sports records were falling, and the government in Washington seemed utterly superfluous, the question of freedom versus organization (Bertrand Russell's way of putting it) was too abstract to worry our heads. We were ultimately to pay for the failure of our education to teach us the use of abstractions as the key to a necessary grounding in principles. As Billy Phelps handed us our diplomas, our education was still to come. Meanwhile, the immediate thing was to get a job. The best that can be said for a Yale education as of 1921-25 is that it did not kill our curiosity. Nothing was foreclosed, and we would be learning from our mistakes the rest of our lives.

Our bias toward freedom, however, had been unconsciously set, and in the end it would be the dominating factor in saving ourselves—and, so one is permitted to hope, the whole unconscious Western world.

Chapter 3

I n the middle '20s the magic door to a writing career of any sort was journalism. And New York City, which then had 17 newspapers, by an actual count extending to the Bronx and Brooklyn, was the obvious place to look for a job.

One did not need a school of journalism degree in that blessedly unorganized time to get past the door to a city editor—indeed, the few schools of journalism then in existence were in ill-repute in professional circles, and Carl Ackerman had hardly gotten started on making the Columbia postgraduate course in newspaper work respectable. My mistake was not a matter of credentials; it was in running into a well-meaning conspiracy to keep me out of journalism.

My mother, after a World War I career at a desk job in the U.S. Navy and a second misadventure in marriage, was then living in New York. A pretty woman with a bubbling sense of humor, she knew people on Park Row. I thought it would be a cinch to get a reporter's job on the *Morning* or *Evening World* through her good journalistic friends. So I cultivated Vincent Treanor, the *Evening World* sports writer, and Bill Grace and Roger Batson, two reporters who were in Treanor's circle.

They were affable fellows, and they provided me with introductions. But nothing came of it. Treanor and Grace, as I learned later, had protective feelings toward my mother that extended to me. They had a low opinion of the financial rewards of newspaper work, and had resolved to steer me into an advertising agency. So, mysteriously, I found myself with an invitation to become a copy writer for the Thomas F. Logan Company at a prestigious Fifth Avenue address not far from the University Club. (The building has long since been demolished.) The salary was $25 a week, which I suppose was munificent for a beginner. But it seemed little enough as I churned out acceptable copy celebrating the virtues of Schwartzell, Rheem and Hensey First Mortgage notes, (they were safe), Radiograms (they were swift, accurate, and direct), and the New York Central Railroad. Eddie Hamburger, who edited the copy with hardly a change and lectured me on the necessity of learning all about Cheltenham, Bodoni, and

17

other type faces, and Waldemar Kaempffert, the company's scientific expert who passed on the technical aspects of the safety series which I did for the first mortgage notes, were making rather magnificent livings. When I pointed to the discrepancy in rewards between the "creative" and the editing and checking ends, all I got from Bill Lilliecrap, who ran the agency, was a Branch Rickey-type sermon on the virtues of "waiting." Years later I ran into Waldemar Kaempffert, who had become a *New York Times* editorial writer, and recalled our early relationship. "Ah, yes," he said of life in an advertising agency, "filthy business, wasn't it."

I shouldn't be hard on advertising—after all, it is basic to a free business system. But I had to find a way to circumvent my mother's conspirators. Luck intervened. One evening, at a party at the home of another of my mother's old friends, Judge Parker Nevin, I ran into a fabulous character named Sir Frederick Cunliffe-Owen, C.B.E. (for Chevalier of the British Empire). Sir Frederick did a column for the *New York Sun* called "Tales of the Old World," published, as I recall, under the signature of the Marquis de Fontenay. When I told him of my predicament he said, "I'll give you a letter to my old friend Freddie Birchall at the *Times.*" Birchall, an Englishman like Sir Frederick, was the *Times'* Acting Managing Editor— condemned to a "provisional" job because Adolph Ochs, the publisher, had qualms about hiring a "foreigner" to run his paper. "Acting" or not, however, Birchall had supreme control of hiring. The Cunliffe-Owen letter, duly passed down to Osmund Phillips, the *Times'* shy day city editor, got me a job within 24 hours. And so, on January 2, 1926, I found myself the newest cub in the *Times* city room. It had been ridiculously easy.

The '20s, as I had learned when I got jobs on the *Leviathan* without a seaman's union card to get back from Europe, were like that. They did not demand certificates and degrees and long resumes. Yet, mysteriously, people found themselves in jobs they were capable of doing.

The *Times*, in 1926, was, to quote Henry Luce, "the world's greatest unedited newspaper." It had its great front-line reporters—Alvah Johnston (who was later a mainstay of Harold Ross's *New Yorker*), Bruce Rae, Russell Owen, Russell Porter, and Jim Hagerty. They worked on a guarantee-plus-space rates basis, and endless were the tricks they used to string out their stories. Alvah Johnston, who knew shorthand and could be succinct when he wanted to be, entranced us cubs with his explanation of something he called the "wheel technique." This consisted of ignoring the "who, what, when, where" canon of journalism that insists you put it all in the first paragraph. Johnston would construct a story that couldn't be cut anywhere between the beginnng and the end without destroying a sense that depended on the circling of the wheel. He had other tricks: he once concocted a report on the Ringling Brothers-Barnum and Bailey circus that had every word in it, save a few prepositions and articles, beginning with the letter "b." Bruce Rae, who covered the big trial stories such as the

Hall-Mills case, was a master of the "as if" dangler to the descriptive sentence: if someone in a story happened to add up a column of figures, it had to be explained (after a dash) that it was "as if" the man were a grocer's clerk totting up a balance on the back of a paper bag. Thus the *Times'* stories were dragged out to increase the weekly take of some great, if sometimes cynical, journalists.

We of the staff who were cubs could only marvel at the tolerance of prolixity. But we did learn that there could be artistry in length. The space was there to fill—and its existence gave all of us a chance to make extra money out of "when room" stories to be filed away and used "when" something was needed to fill out a first edition. There were amusing and no doubt apochryphal tales of how Edwin L. James, then the *Times'* Paris correspondent, had earned his nickname "Jesse." He had, so the recollection went, specialized in grabbing stuff off the city-news ticker, rewriting it a bit, and putting it into the "when" category as his own to be paid for at so much a column.

The older generation in that *Times* city room of the mid-'20s was set in its ways: the idea of using newspaper work as a jump-off perch into literature or business or public relations was less prevalent among the *Times* staffers than it was five blocks away at Stanley Walker's *Tribune* on West 40th Street, or downtown on the Park Row of the *World.* And the jockeying for the "power and the glory" that was interconnected with ideological politics was still in the future. The legendary Carr Van Anda, who, as Och's managing editor had sold the King Tut story to America, had been officially retired, but he still spent much of his time in an office spot that had been reserved for him.

Van Anda gave the *Times* its institutional flavor, and he had his younger admirers who were ready to be loyal *Times* men for life. Bob Garst and Teddy Bernstein, the lords of the night desk, made copy editing a career, teaching it later in their off hours at the Columbia University Graduate School of Journalism in what was virtually a *Times* training extension. Bernstein carried on a lifelong romance with the Engish sentence, but it always seemed incidental to doing it for the *Times.* Old Jim Hagerty, who had the mind of a computer when it came to handling the predictive element in election night stories, had a son who moved easily into Washington politics as a White House secretary. Jim was proud of his son, but it would have horrified him if it had ever been suggested that he might have left the *Times* to do the same. The rewrite men—Shannon Cormack, Morris Gilbert—seemingly had no aspiration for anything else. Osmund Phillips, the day city editor, wanted to be nothing more than honorable and competent at his job; Raymond McCaw and Neil MacNeill, the night editors, liked what they were doing despite some ribbing as the "Catholic bullpen"; and when Ed Klauber, the night managing editor, who taught me how to broadstroke a lead and many other tricks of diversity, quit his job to go to work for Eddie Bernays in public relations before moving on to the Columbia Broadcasting System as right-hand man to Bill Paley, it caused the same kind of incredulous flutter that had marked Elmer Davis's departure to write novels.

There was more volatility among my own contemporaries in that city room of the '20s. Hanson Baldwin, fresh from the naval academy at Annapolis, was to stick for life to the *Times*, but he would have quit in a minute if he had not been able to function without worrying about 10th-floor editorial policy as a military reporter and commentator. He was always a patriot first and a *Times* man second. My good friend Ferdie Kuhn, who held the English war correspondent Sir Philip Gibbs in proper awe, wanted desperately to get abroad. After the third or fourth turn-down of his application for foreign work, he announced one day that he was going to Europe anyway, and would be happy if he could do free-lance work for the *Times* in France, England, or wherever. Not wanting to lose Ferdie, Birchall found a place for him in the London bureau. Ferdie was to have a long career as a London correspondent, a *Times* editorial writer, an aide to wartime Secretary of the Treasury Henry Morgenthau, a *Washington Post* writer on foreign affairs, and, with his wife Delia, a mainstay of the *National Geographic* magazine. I remember Ferdie best for his gentle sense of humor in describing the great of this world, including some of his revered colleagues. Turner Catledge, the *Times* Washington correspondent who was later to become managing editor, was a great *raconteur* himself, but Ferdie's take-off of Turner's homesickness in London, where he spent his time audibly wondering what Senator Jimmy Byrnes was doing that night in Washington, was as funny as any of Catledge's own mimicry.

I started in as a reporter just about the time a saturnine Columbia University student of Dante became secretary to Acting Managing Editor Birchall. The Dante student, Herbert L. Matthews, and I had a common friend in Dante scholar Tom Bergin of Yale, who thought highly of Matthews' linguistic potential. But though Matthews and I became friendly enough through Bergin's introduction, I never could quite make him out. He had no desire to become a city-side reporter. Instead, he asked to be put on the newly formed cable desk. The whispers went around that Matthews's secret desire was to become, not a mere reporter, but a Lawrence of Arabia, a scholar-adventurer affecting the destiny of nations.

Matthews finally parleyed his cable desk job into what he wanted, an assignment abroad. Unlike Ferdie Kuhn, who had standards of objectivity, he was to become one of the growing breed of active journalists who couldn't resist taking sides. The "Lawrence of Arabia" gag (Lawrence was a partisan of the Arabs) turned out to be more truth than rumor. Matthews wanted to make history as well as to record its making.

He covered the Ethiopian war from the Italian side, which had people back home whispering that he was a Fascist because he thought Mussolini had a "civilizing mission" in Africa. But he was only provisionally a Mussolini admirer. In Spain, where he was assigned to cover the war from the Republican side of the lines, he had what he himself described as a "political and moral conversion." It was no great journalistic sin, given the temper of the times, to favor the anti-Franco cause in Spain, and the Matthews "conversion" did not keep him from out-scooping William P. Carney, who reported the war for the *Times* from the Franco side. Matthews pulled a brilliant coup when he authenticated for the first time the presence on a Spanish battlefield of an Italian expeditionary force. The *Times* had refused to believe the Italians were actively implicated in the war, and Matthews blamed this blindness on the so-called Catholic bullpen in the *Times* city room. In this particular instance Matthews was right and the "bullpen" was wrong. But the Matthews partisanship caused him to overlook the growing Stalinist atrocities against the Spanish anarcho-syndicalists and even against liberal Spanish social democrats who opposed Franco. A friend of Ernest Hemingway, Matthews said nothing about Hemingway's quarrel with John Dos Passos over a particularly revolting Stalinist murder of one of Dos Passos's friends that surely deserved reporting.

Matthews was really a tremendously enterprising journalist, but he suffered from being seduced by his own scoops. His penetration of the Sierra Maestra in Cuba, where he found Fidel Castro alive, was something worthy of a Stanley meeting up with Livingston. But instead of taking it on the level of a scoop, he felt compelled to make political capital of his exploit. Castro had to be a "democrat" and the savior of Cuba. Matthews had simply neglected to read background material which had been made available by an enterprising Alice-Leone Moats' article in Bill Buckley's *National Review* which detailed information from Mexico police sources to prove that Castro was a Communist well before holing up in the Sierra Maestra.

I kept running into Matthews when he was lecturing college audiences about the inevitability of "communism or another form of collectivism as the only road to modernization" in Third World countries. I felt queasy about arguing with him when he came to Tom Bergin's Timothy Dwight College at Yale as a Chubb Fellow, for I had been pro-Republican in the early days of the Spanish Civil War myself. But I had had my own "political and moral conversion" after Dos Passos's return from Spain with the indisputable evidence that Stalinism was the inevitable concomitant of communism, and that any form of collectivism must involve the suppression of human freedom. Matthews had become far more famous than his 1926 colleague Ferdie Kuhn as a *Times* foreign correspondent, but Kuhn was the better man—and journalist—for all that.

The tendency of the younger *Times* reporters such as Lewis Nichols, later a dramatic critic, and myself was to measure ourselves against the more style-conscious types who worked for Herbert Bayard Swope's *Morning World* and Stanley Walker's *Trib*. We of the *Times* younger generation were all tremendously envious of the *World* "op. ed." page, which featured F.P.A.'s "Conning Tower" (I had tried to imitate it in college with my *Daily News* column signed "Ayesha"), Lawrence Stallings' book reviews, Heywood Broun's column, Frank Sullivan's humorous pieces, and Alexander Woollcott's dramatic criticism. And everybody admired the *World* editorials of Walter Lippmann and Charles Merz, both of them veterans of the liberal *New Republic*. The *World* star reporters, Dudley Nichols and Oliver H.P. Garrett, gave a literary finish to their front-page stories that could not be matched in the more prolix *Times*. And some of the *World's* younger reporters—St. Clair MacKelway, later a *New Yorker* writer, was one—stood ready to take over for their elders. They were rudely interrupted when the *World*, unaccountably as it seemed to us, failed. The loss of the *World* was not total—Walter Lippmann moved uptown to the *Tribune*, and Charles Merz and Arthur Krock caught on at the *Times*, where Krock ultimately lost out to Merz as editor-in-chief. It was as a consolation that Arthur was sent back to his old haunts in Washington, an assignment he did not relish at the time. He eventually became reconciled to the "banishment" when depression and war made Washington the center of the American news world. With a column that was made memorable by scoops obtained from friends of New York days such as Joe Kennedy, Krock became far more famous than Charlie Merz, whose talent for Menckenian broadstroking (see his *The Great American Bandwagon*) could find no scope on the *Times* editorial page.

Competition with the *World* taught us all while it lasted. I distinctly recall a lesson in good newspaper writing which I got from St. Clair MacKelway. We had been sent by our respective city editors to cover a fire on the New York East Side. I stuck around to get all the details I could from firemen and police. But MacKelway, who always hated routines, quit early. His story, when it appeared, was far more vivid than my own prosaic "who, what, when, where" account. Details were not lacking in the MacKelway piece, but they were wholly subordinated to the flavor. When I asked him how he did it, he said he had first returned home to his Greenwich Village apartment to soak himself in a Maxim Gorki short story. Then he had gone to the office to pick up the city-news ticker account of the fire. Putting Maxim Gorki together with a few facts, he had something that was accurate enough but altogether far more readable than anything I could have written at the time.

Uptown, at the *Trib*, Stanley Walker specialized in paying low salaries to talented individuals who were destined, like Nunnally Johnson, to write for Hollywood, or, like John O'Hara, to become novelists. Joel Sayre, soon to become famous for *Rackety Rax* and other raffish productions, was a *Trib* discovery. Walker's idea was to make use of young talents who regarded the city room as a way station before passing on to book or magazine triumphs. It made for a readable paper, though the *Trib* obviously could not match the *Times* as a definitive "journal of record." In the long run it was the Adolph Ochs idea of journalism that lasted. But New York City has never recovered from the loss of the *Morning World* and the *Herald Tribune*. Years later, when I did a weekly book review for the fledgling tabloid-size paper called, succinctly, *The Trib* (which also ran my King Features editorial-page column), I had a sense of returning to a remote past. It was great until *The Trib*, edited by an old *Herald Tribune* veteran John Denson, ran out of money in just three months time. New York, to its shame, had simply lost the taste for good newspaper variety. Denson, incidentally, was a genius at presentation. Where he erred was in caring more for the looks of a paper than for questions of hitting the streets.

My ability to do "light" stories, such as the appearance of Uldine Utley, a 14-year-old evangelist, in the fundamentalist pulpit of the Reverend John Roach Straton, or the annual city room apparition of Dexter Fellows, the press agent for the Ringling Brothers-Barnum Bailey circus, as spring's most certain harbinger, saved me from a lot of dreary work as a police reporter. And, since I was not out on a beat covering police blotters, my presence in the city room in early afternoon hours guaranteed my availability for an occasional hurry-call major assignment. The race to be the first flyer to cross the Atlantic from a Long Island flying field was on in earnest in 1927. Russell Owen and Lauren, or Deke, Lyman had first call on promising aviation stories, but more than two men were needed to watch developments as Admiral Byrd, Bert Acosta, Clarence Chamberlin, and others jockeyed for the chance to be first off the ground in the Paris sweepstakes. Simply because Owen and Lyman were tied up I got the assignment to cover the flight of Clarence Chamberlin and Charles Levine, his sponsor and passenger, to Germany. Charles Lindbergh, of course, had beaten Chamberlin, Admiral Byrd, and all the others to it, but a trans-Atlantic flight to Germany was a bit further than one to Le Bourget field in France, and it got me a front-page spread.

I was all alone in the city room when news came to the desk that Charles J.V. Murphy, the *New York World* aviation reporter, would be coming through New York from Canada with Baron von Huenefeld, Captain Koehl, and Colonel Fitzmaurice, the first flyers to cross the Atlantic from east to west. The three had landed on an ice floe in the St. Lawrence, and Murphy, with the agreed-upon rights to von Huenefeld's and Koehl's personal stories, had gone north from New York to intercept the flyers and shepherd them to Washington. The *Times*, with pre-arranged rights to Fitzmaurice's story, had not seen fit to challenge the *New York World* in being first to greet the flyers. But when city editor Osmund Phillips received the flash that Charles Murphy and his charges would be passing through the Pennsylvania Station in Manhattan en route to Washington, he had to react in order to get something from Fitzmaurice that would not be scooped by von Huenefeld and Koehl in the *World*.

So, as the only ready reporter, I was told to get aboard the Washington train and make swift contact with Fitzmaurice. This was easier said than done. Murphy was taking no chances; he simply refused to let me see the flyers in the special compartment he had arranged for them. As the train moved on through New Jersey, I was at my wit's end. But I finally got a message through to Murphy that convinced him Fitzmaurice, who had headed an Irish air force that had no planes, was legitimate *Times* property. After some hemming and hawing, Charlie Murphy finally agreed to let Fitzmaurice meet me on neutral ground in the baggage car, where I took notes for a first-person Fitzmaurice account for the *Times*. In Baltimore I jumped off the train and ran for Western Union. The story reached New York in time to hit the streets at the same hour that Murphy's ghost-written accounts from the other flyers appeared in the *World*.

Strangely enough, my encounter with Charlie Murphy, a great reporter who far outdid me in chutzpah, led to a firm friendship. We met later on other stories. And we were both to go to work for *Fortune Magazine* in 1936.

Reporting, in the '20s, entitled one to a ringside seat at the movable feast that Westbrook Pegler has immortalized as the *Era of Wonderful Nonsense*. Though everybody around us seemed to be making money, buying stocks on margin, money was not our object. There were ways of eking out the low pay (I was still getting $40 a week after a year of marriage). Practically every day brought a luncheon or dinner assignment, with accompanying free-loading opportunities. Acting Managing Editor Birchall, trusting his reporters to take care of their own integrity, encouraged junkets; indeed, he used them to reward reporters for good work on difficult assignments. I drew a choice one in the form of a week spent with my wife at the Chateau Frontenac in Quebec, where I was sent to cover a folksong festival sponsored by the Canadian Pacific Railroad. An old Loomis school friend, Hollister Noble, was among the junketeers. He happened to be the managing editor of *Musical America*, and I was grateful for his help in steering me through an unfamiliar field. If there was any "corruption" involved, it consisted of taking Holly Noble's musical judgments on trust. I am sure the *Times* benefited from it.

The whole uproar about junkets that surfaced in the '70s seemed to me to be utterly ridiculous; Freddie Birchall was right in trusting his staff to be properly skeptical of anything set forth in a press kit that might be designed to trap the unwary. Many years after leaving the *Times*, I went on a junket to Panama. It was probably arranged by the Torrijos government, though I never knew for sure. The obvious aim was to win our favor for relinquishing the Canal. I returned home convinced that we should keep the Canal forever, and said so in columns. Irene Kuhn, who had also been on the junket, supported the same conclusion. The truth about junkets is that the organization issuing an invitation takes its chances. Everybody knows this, and if there is any corruption involved, it is the fault of the newspaper in picking a dishonest reporter in the first place. Such characters don't last very long in journalism no matter what the prevailing philosophy regarding junkets may be. Junkets, I am sure, never bought anybody on the *Times* in the '20s.

The favorite indoor sport of the intellectuals of that decade was debunking, a word coined by historian W.E. Woodward to describe a not exactly new practise of knocking the halos off the heads of established rulers. It was the age of the F. Scott Fitzgerald look, with the flappers more in evidence than the philosophers. The common remembrance of the '20s is that they "roared," whatever that may mean. There was, admittedly, a lot of defiant drinking of bathtub gin and "Jersey lightning," the New York City word for applejack. Speakeasies abounded. I knew plenty of reporters who had trouble handling their liquor—John O'Hara was one of them; and Forrest Davis, then of the *Herald-Tribune* and the *Daily News*, loved an occasional spree. I recall my mixed feelings about a particularly hilarious evening when Joel Sayre and St. Clair MacKelway, welcoming their foreign-correspondent friend Vincent Sheean back from some of his wanderings, practically wrecked my apartment at 85 Barrow Street. The Artists and Writers Club, conveniently located just under the *Herald-Tribune* offices on West 40th Street, was always a home away from home for a reporter who needed one last drink. But my memory of the *Times* city room does not recall a single souse on the whole *Times* staff. Ben Hecht's and Charles MacArthur's raucous play, *The Front Page*, may have constituted an accurate picture of life in a Chicago city room, and it may have been applicable to journalism as practiced on the *New York Graphic*. But the stereotype did not fit the *Times* in any way.

We took the sillier aspects of the '20s as amusing spectacle; marathon dancing and flagpole sitting were aberrational expressions of a basically laudable hunger to join the record makers. In his sprightly *Only Yesterday*, Frederick Lewis Allen has popularized the view that Lindbergh, with his boyish grin and unassuming daring, somehow rescued the American people from the depths of cynicism. But the real truth is that Lindbergh, whom a sympathetic "Deke" Lyman almost succeeded in turning into *Times* property, was very much of the '20s himself, a hero in an age that, skeptical though it was, actually worshipped heroes with the sole proviso that they should be non-political. (It was the politico—Dr. Woodrow Wilson, the "tin-pot Paul," and the "mean man" Theodore Roosevelt—that Mencken caught repeatedly in his cross-hairs.) The '20s were, as has been said repeatedly, the age of the sports hero, Bobby Jones in golf, Big Bill Tilden and Little Bill Johnston in tennis, Jack Dempsey in boxing, Babe Ruth and Lou Gehrig and the rest of Murderers' Row at Yankee Stadium, and Red

Grange of Illinois who was once carried two miles on the backs of admiring students for his exploits in football. Our heroes had to be men of action; Doug Fairbanks, who married America's sweetheart Mary Pickford, owed his transcendent screen popularity to an athleticism that was as remarkable in its way as anything exhibited by the Four Horsemen of the Apocalypse (Stuldreher, Layden, Crowley, and Miller) who rode down the gridiron opposition for Notre Dame.

The worship of athletes was not mere dumb-jock appeal; it was part of a wider admiration for skills. The '20s had this admiration as no decade has had it since. The writers who dominated the latter part of the period—Fitzgerald, Hemingway, Glenway Wescott, Elizabeth Madox Roberts, Edna Millay, e.e. cummings, T.S. Eliot—were above all style-conscious craftsmen. In industry, the decade brought the intricacies of mass production to their perfection as Henry Ford, Bill Knudsen, and "Boss" Kettering extended the skills provided by Frederick Winslow Taylor, the time-motion genius who thought the value of a tool was best measured by the exact cutting speed at which it was completely ruined at the end of 20 minutes.

The *Times*, in its idolatry of heroes, sent practically the whole New York staff to Washington to cover Lindbergh's homecoming. My introduction to Washington reporting consisted of mingling with the crowds to catch popular commentary. During the whole of Lindbergh's stay at the temporary White House on Dupont Circle, I stood on the curb listening to policemen who had been born in Georgia talk about segregation. I saw Lindbergh only at a distance, though I came to know him at the end of the '30s when *Fortune* magazine, knowing that we thought alike on the subject of America's entry into World War II, used me as the go-between when submitting manuscripts involving aviation and even geopolitics to him for his opinion. When the rest of the world was going crazy over "Lucky Lindy, the flying fool," Deke Lyman of the *Times* accurately spotted him as the very embodiment of the concept of the calculated risk. Actually, Clarence Chamberlin and Admiral Byrd were the "flying fools." Chamberlin, who was my pigeon in covering Long Island in the spring of 1927, took his chances on a forced landing in Germany, and Byrd was lucky to wade ashore after ditching his ship in the sea off the French coast. But Lindbergh had the skill to hit Le Bourget field outside of Paris squarely on the nose. That made him one with Babe Ruth, who was popularly credited with the ability to call his home run shots before making them.

Courtly Dick Oulahan, the head of the *Times* Washington bureau, took me to lunch during the Lindburgh week. He was that kind of man, concerned with encouraging the young in the newspaper work which he himself loved. During short-handed periods he welcomed me as a temporary addition to his bureau. Lou Stark, who covered labor for the *Times* in a most admirably even-handed fashion (he refused to join the Newspaper

Guild because he wanted to retain his objectivity), was too tied up to do sustained Washington work, so I drew an assignment to cover an investigation into the troubles that were then coming to a head in West Virginia's Logan County. Watching the young leader of the United Mine Workers, John L. Lewis, take on Senator Warren Gooding of Idaho and steel man Charlie Schwab in a Capitol Hill committee room, brought me face to face with the sort of problem that the *Era of Wonderful Nonsense* preferred to forget. John L. Lewis was not the kind of hero the '20s welcomed. But even he fitted the criteria of the decade. He took his own calculated risks, and he was never fool enough to try to stop the mechanization of the coal mines. He had seen what the anti-mechanization spirit had done to hurt industry— and the workers—in the Wales of his ancestors, and he wanted none of this for America. He was willing to see fewer miners in the day of modern cutting machinery and loaders as long as they were highly compensated and provided the owners contributed to a fund to take care of the aged disemployed.

Reporting on things political for the *Times* in the '20s was hardly a preparation for what was to come after the market crash. It was only an occasional assignment, such as the one to cover Union Square crowd reaction to the execution of Sacco and Vanzetti, that disturbed the pattern of a decade that was defiantly apolitical. I'll never forget the low moan that ran through Union Square when the news was flashed that the "anarchistic bastards" (Judge Webster Thayer's quoted description of the men he had doomed) had finally been put to death. I was quite willing to take it on trust that Sacco and Vanzetti were innocent (Francis Russell's sifting of the ballistic evidence to prove the contrary, at least in the case of Sacco, was still in the womb of the future). But the miscarriage of justice in Judge Thayer's Massachusetts, as John Dos Passos, Edna Millay, and Heywood Broun of the *World* portrayed it, seemed like a bad dream left over from a post-war Red Scare that the '20s had repudiated. Nobody in the late '20s was disturbing the Menckenian form of anarchism that gave us *carte blanche* to laugh at politics.

We covered political investigations as spectacles that were not really intended to produce any reform. I recall getting up at dawn for days on end to commute to Trenton, New Jersey, when the Case investigation into the affairs of Hudson County was holding its hearings. It was perhaps useful to know that the Mayor of Hoboken could explain his personal fortune by telling about lucky bets at the race track, but the investigation changed little in national politics. Mayor Frank ("I am the law") Hague of Jersey City hung on to become part of the Roosevelt coalition. The Al Smith Democratic presidential campaign of 1928, with its challenge to the 18th Amendment, was exciting, but covering it in Hudson Valley towns revealed little about the depths of religious prejudice that doomed the Smith candidacy in what was then the anti-Catholic South. With his rasping voice, and his "Let's look at the record," Al Smith seemed momentarily important. But Al's career ended in a lugubrious irony: it was he who gave Franklin D. Roosevelt the opportunity to shine as his supporter and his successor as Governor of New York. F.D.R., ever the opportunist, was to carry the Democratic Party a long way away from the Smith principles. With his friendship with John H. Raskob, who built the Empire State Building, Smith was no enemy of capitalism. Ultimately his sense of honor made him take a walk from his party.

The politics of the '20s, a sideshow, could hardly compete for fun and games with such assignments as the one handed to me to cover heavy-weight champion Gene Tunney's lecture on Shakespeare to Billy Phelp's English class at Yale. Gene brought down the house with his observation that Ajax, in *Troilus and Cressida*, was just a big bum "like Jack Sharkey." But it was wrong to laugh at Tunney's cultural aspirations. He was an intelligent man, quicker than most of us to grasp the nature of the Soviet menace in the '30s. When Bill Buckley, with his *National Review*, eventually hove into sight, Gene was one of Bill's earliest supporters. It must have caused Gene great anguish when his son John, as a United States Senator, turned out to be just another typical Teddy Kennedy liberal.

By the time the '20s were about to move off stage I had had my fill of city-room work. Keeping the phone open at Ossining for Alvah Johnston on the night of the executions of Judd Gray and Ruth Snyder, who had revoltingly murdered Mrs. Snyder's unoffending husband, was an experience that should have made me an unequivocal advocate of capital punishment. But it did no such thing. The circus aspects of the electrocutions seemed to degrade all life. I remember Gene Fowler, the Hearst star reporter, jumping up from his typewriter after writing a most harrowing account of the executions. "Let me bust you one, Maisie," said Gene ebulliently as he bumped into Maisie Clemens, a woman reporter who was well endowed frontally. No doubt this was Gene's way of blowing off steam. He could be a most amusing writer, as his racy books on harum-scarum newspaper characters and his biography of John Barrymore show. But it was somehow disconcerting to me to be part of the crocodile-tear circus of reporting the deaths of two loathesome characters who might have been punished more adequately by jailing them for life. Of course, life imprisonment for premediated murder should not be subject to commutation if it is to remain a deterrent to crime. The permanent deprivation of freedom has always seemed to me to be the most horrifying of punishments. The courts should be inexorable about enforcing life sentences. If they are not, then capital punishment can be justified as a deterrent that must be accepted as second best.

In the *Times* city room of the late '20s, two individuals seem in retrospect to have had a particular prophetic flair. One of these individuals was Joe Shaplen, an old-line socialist who, in his experience as a Berlin correspondent during and after the inflation, had sensed the coming doom of the Weimar Republic. Joe wore his socialism on his sleeve, and it was labeled, as he often announced in a characteristic growl, as "extremely right wing." Joe's economics were, of course, faulty, but he knew that the defection of the German Communists from the social democracy of Eduard Bernstein, who had proved statistically that capitalist development had actually improved the position of the working classes, would fatally split the German Left, making it easy for the triumph of a Hitler. In addition to his prophetic qualifications, Joe was the capable teacher-father of Robert Shaplen, who was to become one of our truly knowledgeable reporters on Southeast Asia.

The other man of foresight in the *Times* city room was a young Montanan named Clarence Streit, who had been a correspondent in Geneva. Clarence, when I first knew him, was doing a stint on the *Times* cable desk as an interlude in his career of European correspondent. With a French wife, and with his own memories of World War I, Clarence was even then convinced that the League of Nations wouldn't be enough to forestall a repetition of the 1914-1918 bloodletting. As a cub who went along with Clarence to help cover the landing of the *Graf* Zeppelin at Lakehurst, New Jersey, I could only admire the Streit deftness at interviewing Europeans. His certainty that Western civilization was all of a piece was something that I resisted at the time. But if there could have been a federal union of the Atlantic democracies, as Clarence came to advocate in the '30s, there would have been no World War II. The Streit formula, as communicated to Jean Monnet, has produced whatever unity Western Europe may have as the Soviets build their tank strength in Poland and East Germany. A federal union of the democracies might still save the world by extending the NATO defenses to the oil regions of the Middle East. But Clarence Streit is still a prophet without honor in his own country.

At the end of 1928, after covering local New York and New Jersey aspects of the Al Smith campaign, I got stuck with the so-called lobster trick that every young city-side reporter on the *Times* had to endure. The lobster trick consisted of doing night rewrite from eight in the evening until four in the morning and then going home along Eighth Avenue to the rattle of the milk trucks. Ordinarily, this entailed sitting around after midnight on the unlikely off-chance that a late story of particular importance might force the revision of the front-page make-up. In several months of such waiting, I don't remember ever having to hit a typewriter after one A.M. The boredom was overpowering until I had made the acquaintance of J. Donald Adams, the editor of the *Sunday Times Book Review*. Adams was willing to let me review some detective stories, which gave me something to do after midnight. After a brief novitiate with the detective stories, I was handed a Gilbert Chesterton novel, *The Return of Don Quixote*. Adams didn't contemplate a long review, but I gave him one anyway. It carried a by-line, and it turned out to be an introduction to a new life as a critic, which was something I had always had at the back of my mind ever since I had roomed with Billy Troy at Yale.

Chapter 4

I n taking assignments from the *Times* Sunday book section, I had met Adam's assistant, John Franklin Carter. I had heard Wilbur Finley Fawley, the *Times* society editor, refer to Carter as a "bleak young man." The description didn't quite fit, but John Carter had an abrupt way of speaking his mind. He was tired of literary desk work, and he had had an offer to go to Washington for the State Department. At the time, he was a staunch defender of the Kellogg-Briand Pact and Republican foreign policy. His insistence that "peace" was U.S. policy did not quite square with his book, a hard-fisted tract called *Man Is War*, nor with his prediction that someday the Anglo-Saxons would begin to move down the *cordilleras* of Latin America to fulfill an interrupted manifest destiny.

Carter's Republicanism and somewhat incongruous imperialism didn't last very long once he caught the post-1929 drift in Washington. Under the pen name of Jay Franklin, he became one of the first of the New Dealers, writing provocative articles and books that led him, ultimately, to offer a Tugwellian manifesto called *1940*, in which he advocated a planned order that would have been fascist for all of its "progressive" label. Toward the end of his life he made another philosophical switch, which led to a job with Tom Dewey. It was Carter's job-jumping, not his philosophy-jumping, that interested me as I wrestled in 1929 with some of the better books which Don Adams was letting me handle. Carter tipped me off that his job would be vacant, and told Adams that I would like to take his place. Adams, not wanting to be a raider, said I'd have to take it up with Birchall, who agreed to let me go after delivering a little lecture about newspapermen's wives who had spoiled many a journalistic career because they couldn't put up with irregular hours. Birchall knew I had been on the deadly 8:00 P.M. to 4:00 A.M. lobster trick, and he had drawn his inferences.

It was a wrench to leave the city room, with its special cameraderie. It meant giving up the horseback rides organized by assistant city editor Walter Fenton for Thursdays (my day off in the six-day-work-week pattern) in Brooklyn's Prospect Park. It meant an end to reading at random on long subway rides to Brooklyn and Bronx assignments (I had gone through

The Forsyte Saga and *Green Mansions* on the way to cover happenings in
Flatbush or on the Grand Concourse). It meant no more reminiscing with
Tom Chubb, a Yale poet who was supporting his literary aspirations by
working for Skipper Williams's ship-news department. It meant no more
discussions with Hal Denny, the foreign correspondent who had come
home from Europe to cover the American trip of Queen Marie of Rumania
and was waiting around for his assignment to Moscow. Denny was a
strange character who functioned best when far away from a home office.
He considered it demeaning to be sent to the Bronx. His morning avocation
was to spend hours in the bathroom trying to pinpoint the exact historical
moment when Christianity began to go wrong, and he liked to talk about it.
I did keep some friends in the shuffle between jobs—Jim Kieran, the
brother of sports writer and ornithologist John Kieran, was a Greenwich
Village neighbor; and my wife Peggy and I continued to see Ed Klauber
and his wife Gladys on week-ends after Ed had left the newspaper business. But mostly life in the tenth-floor book department was far removed
from the third-floor clamor of the city room. I was eventually to return to a
third-floor cubbyhole to do a daily review for the *Times*, and it was like
going home. But that was still four years away.

Don Adams, a reserved man, was difficult to know. He had been
brought to the *Times*, after a background of editorial writing for Frank
Munsey's *Herald*, by J. Brooks Atkinson, who edited the *Sunday Book
Review* before he began his long and illustrious career as a dramatic critic.
When I became Adams' assistant a big argument was raging about his
literary tastes. He had an Aristotelian view of literature, preferring heroes
"of a certain magnitude." This left him out of sympathy with much of the
experimental writing of the '20s. Greenwich Village didn't like him. He had
a Russian wife, Alya, who had understandable prejudices against the Bolsheviks, and a charming daughter Mary. In 1929 the New York literary
world had not yet gone over to its various accommodations with the Left,
but it was not considered "liberal" to be friendly with Russian "white
guards." Adams came in for a lot of criticism because he used a Russian
expatriate, Alexander Nazaroff, to review books on Russian history.
Adams stuck by reviewers such as Nazaroff to the intense displeasure of
Lester Markel, the *Times* Sunday editor, who kept annoying Adams by
trying to absorb the book review section into his own empire. (Eventually
the absorption was consummated, but only after years of infighting).

Visiting the Adamses at their summer place in Woodstock, New York, as
my wife and I did frequently, was for the most part pleasurable. On one
occasion we met two young Yale radicals, William Harlan Hale and Selden
Rodman, publishers of an obstreperous campus magazine called *The Hark-
ness Hoot*. Adams had no objections to native campus rebels, but the air
became overheated when the subject of Russia came up. To Don Adams,
Lenin and Trotsky were simply "monsters." I tried to defend them as

"better than the Romanoffs" only to invite a torrent of reproof from Alya Adams. She, of course, knew what she was talking about. She could appreciate Max Nomad's essay, "The Kaiser and Czar Were Liberals," from her own personal experience.

For all his reserved exterior, I found Don Adams to be an extremely good friend under his crustiness. He had been a student of Vernon Parrington, whose three-volume history of American literature he revered and often praised. Parrington was, of course, completely Jeffersonian in his politics. A Jeffersonian himself, Adams was willing to tolerate political dissent in reviews even when it went against his deepest instincts. He let me review favorably John Strachey's Communist *The Coming Struggler for Power*, and in picking some young reviewers—Liveright editor Louis Kronenberger, Knopf editor Harold Strauss, poet Eda Lou Walton, free-lance critics Herbert Gorman and John Crawford—he made no effort to inquire into their politics provided they stuck to the Mencken-Spingarn theory that it was a reviewer's first business to ascertain what an artist had tried to do and then tell the reader how well he had done it.

The *Times*, in those days, had not gone over to the policy of searching out academic specialists to do its reviewing. Adams had on call a number of trusted people to provide him with weekly copy. Percy Hutchison, who dabbled in the stock market, did the poetry. I had to rewrite most of Percy's tangled leads, but the body of a Hutchison review was always clear and sympathetic. Simeon Strunsky, an ex-socialist who had quit his party because, as he said, it was entirely unsociable, did a specialty page each week "about books more or less" that was more essay than review. P.W. Wilson, a Britisher who was a member of the Plymouth Brethren, handled subjects involving European and British history and politics. William MacDonald and Charles Willis Thompson covered American history. Thompson, a former *Times* Washington correspondent, had a rat-trap mind that was death on authors who were careless about facts. T.R. Ybarra, half Venezuelan and half Bostonian, wrote colorfully and flamboyantly on Latin topics. And Robert L. Duffus, a veteran editorial writer and novelist with a supreme gift for clarity, jumped all over the lot, handling two reviews a week in addition to his work in the editorial department.

Such were the "regulars." Their lease on space did not preclude going "outside" for reviews. John Crawford was among the first to do justice to Hemingway's "lean, hard, athletic narrative prose." Louis Kronenberger had a sure touch with European literature. I had plenty of scope as a reviewer for myself, and a certain latitutde in picking books that seemed particularly interesting, the sole proviso being that copy editing, headline writing, translating André Maurois' French letter, and doing make-up in the composing room, had first call on my time.

The virtue of depending for the most part on the same performers week after week is that one came to know their tastes and could accordingly make personal judgments about books. The drawback of using occasional specialists is that they often have axes to grind that one is in no position to know about.

The proof of the pudding is in the eating: American literature of the 20th century grew and prospered in the day of the newspaper critic. With the exception of Professor Billy Phelps at Yale, academia, in the early 1900s, was mired in the Genteel Tradition. It took a Mencken on the *Baltimore Sun* to discover the virtues of Theodore Dreiser. It was James Huneker, the Steeplejack of the *Seven Arts*, who "brokered" modern European literature to an American public in Philadelphia and New York papers. The newspaper critics in Chicago—Francis Hackett, Floyd Dell, Burton Rascoe, and Harry Hansen—were the trumpet voices that brought novelists such as Sherwood Anderson and poets such as Carl Sandburg to the attention of New York publishers. Rascoe, both single-handedly and single-mindedly, made James Branch Cabell's *Jurgen* a popular book. And it was Rascoe's long quarrel with Professor Stuart Sherman over the latter's "Puritanism" that finally resulted in Sherman's conversion to a more "modern" point of view. By that time Rascoe had gone from Chicago to New York to run the *Herald-Tribune* Sunday book section, where his *Bookman's Day Book* diary carried a running weekly commentary on all the new writing schools. It was a supreme irony—and to my mind a dirty trick—when Stuart Sherman ousted Rascoe at the *Trib* only to carry on with a point of view that Rascoe had himself made popular.

To his credit, Sherman gave an assistant editor's job to the gracious Irita Van Doren, a Southern lady who had married critic Carl Van Doren. People today have no idea of how the Van Dorens dominated the New York literary scene before World War II. Irita was a member by marriage of a family that included Professor Mark Van Doren of Columbia and Mark's son Charles, who was credited with being a fount of all knowledge until he was caught stacking the deck on a rigged TV question-and-answer show, the "$64,000 Question." Dorothy Parker may or may not have been the first to say she put herself to sleep by counting Van Dorens. They were all over the place.

The Van Dorens connoted power. Irita had her ways of being influential beyond her job as editor of the *Trib* book section after Sherman's untimely death. Wendell Willkie was fascinated by her vivacity, and she did more than a little to convince him that he would make a most able President. After I had left the *Times* in the middle '30s, Irita paid me the compliment of letting me do some of her first-page reviews, singling me out for Hemingway's *For Whom the Bell Tolls*, Ayn Rand's *Atlas Shrugged* and a volume of e.e. cummings' poetry. Criticism of poetry was not my special forte, but Irita had heard me recite several of cummings's sonnets from memory at a rather hilarious party given by publisher Curtice Hitchcock at his apartment on Gramercy Park. I told her I liked cummings because, behind the typographical curlicues, he was an old-fashioned romantic, not a modern metaphysical poet, but she said she'd take her chances with whatever I wanted to say. With her gracious live-and-let-live attitude, she did nothing to disturb Isabel Paterson, a sub-editor and the conductor of the weekly department called "Turns With a Bookworm." Isabel disagreed with Irita about practically everything under the sun. She was as acidulous as Irita was sunny. I shared Irita's opinion about Isabel's opinions, which led to some caustic interchanges that got into Isabel's bookworm chatter. But arguing with Isabel had a way of clarifying issues. Her *God of the Machine*, which was to take her far afield from literary gossip to political economy, struck me all of a heap when I read it during the war. But that was a still distant story in the '30s, when we were trading polite insults. Isabel had me tabbed as a sad dupe of the Communists.

Moving into a desk job at the *Times* Sunday book review was not, in 1929, a desertion of the so-called real world for a seat in an ivory tower. Literary New York, in the '20s, was seething with ideas at a time when Washington, D.C., was a somnolent Southern town and Wall Street, even with its margin gambling and boastful customers' men, qualified as little more than a repetitive bore. Economics and politics, which are group manifestations, had not yet taken over the front pages; the individual experience, which is the stuff of literature, was still important. And New York publishing was thriving as never before or since as the literary revival that had begun in the teen decade of the century moved toward maturity.

Week after week the publishers poured their books, many of them excellent, into the *Sunday Times Book Review* hopper. The new firms of the teens and '20s—Alfred Knopf, Liveright, Harcourt Brace, Covici Friede, Viking (with B.W. Huebsch), Reynal and Hitchcock, Brewer and Warren, Simon and Schuster, A. and C. Boni—the names suggest a Ph.D. dissertation on the stimulation of creativity that cried aloud to be written but never was. The older publishing companies, forced to a new competition, gave free play to new editors such as Maxwell Perkins (Scribner's), Jim Putnam (Macmillan), Florence Bowers (Dutton) and Ed Aswell (Harper's). When a good man, such as Pascal Covici, the true discoverer of Steinbeck, ran into money troubles, he would be taken on by a more solid firm such as Harold Guinzburg's Viking. Advances were easy, though they were generally small—the era of the big Hollywood supplement had not yet arrived to distort values and to cause authors to look beyond the basic claims of the good English sentence.

Looking back on the period for a *Life Magazine* article in 1947, I wrote that the United States had already achieved the pre-condition for an Elizabethan revival before World War I. Where Sir Francis Drake and the other nautical pirates and merchant adventurers of Queen Bess had made England wealthy enough to support great playwrights, the Americans who were scoffed at as robber barons had accumulated the riches to endow universities and support the fledgling literary careers of many an aspiring poet or novelist. An Elizabethan sense of wonder was in the American air as Harvard nurtured cummings, Dos Passos, Robert Hillyer,and others in the group that Malcolm Cowley called the Dandies. Waking to the mechanical wonders of the automobile, the Mazda bulb, and the telephone, Americans looked up from their material blessings to wonder if that was all. The children, living on the old man's suddenly-acquired money, said no. A generational war was on. Babbitt, as I said in my *Life* article, was the war's first victim. He received no thanks for having made a renaissance financially possible.

The New York publishers of the '20s had had the ground plowed for them by the little magazines of the teens. *The Masses* came in 1911, shepherded by Max Eastman with help from Floyd Dell and, at a later date, by John Reed. The *Little Review*, more radical in form and less radical in politics, followed in 1914, and the *Seven Arts* (a bit more "sociological" than the *Little Review*) in 1916. Harriet Monroe's *Poetry*, hospitable to all the new verse, whether rhymed and metrical (as in Vachel Lindsay and Robert Frost), or free and imagistic (as in H.D.), was published in Chicago in 1912. Coteries were born. Some of them stayed home (the Southern Agrarians in Nashville). Others moved, like iron filings drawn by a magnet, to Greenwich Village in New York, where the rents were cheap, or to the summer annex of the Village in Provincetown on Cape Cod, where George Cram Cook gave Eugene O'Neill his first theatre. The Harvard Dandies had their counterparts at Yale (Sinclair Lewis, Waldo Frank, Thomas Beer, Archibald MacLeish, Stephen Vincent Benet, Thornton Wilder), and at Princeton (Edmund Wilson, Scott Fitzgerald). It was the age of the "quest" novel, written in native fashion by the Floyd Dell of *Mooncalf* or by Steve Benet and Scott Fitzgerald in flagrant imitation of the Englishman Compton MacKenzie's *Sinister Street*.

Guiding the renaissance were the prophets I had adopted as my own. Van Wyck Brooks, Randolph Bourne, Lewis Mumford, and Waldo Frank. Quite consciously this loosely-joined foursome had set out, in the late teens, to go back of the Genteel Tradition of the academics to recover for their contemporaries a "usable past." Brooks was preoccupied with the idea that America had had few "sustained careers" in the arts. And when he found a "sustained career," as in Mark Twain and Henry James, he lamented the troubles they encountered. Waldo Frank, in his stirringly written *Our America*, was more affirmative than Brooks. He concentrated on the high points represented by the "multitudes in Whitman." Lewis Mumford went back to the "golden day" of Emerson, Thoreau, and Herman Melville, writing off the late 19th century as the "brown decades." And Bourne looked to England for inspiration in the clean spirit of Bernard Shaw (he didn't like the "thick and gluttonous" Chesterton). It was Bourne who gave us that searing observation, "War is the Health of the State." Frank Chodorov, a later libertarian, could not have said it better.

My four prophets had their shortcomings, and I was eventually to break with their basic socialism. I also had to break with their solemnity. I recall Simeon Strunsky shaking his head at Brooks's idea that America had repressed Mark Twain. "That's not my Mark Twain," said Strunsky, who enjoyed laughter for its own sake. Max Eastman, with his *Enjoyment of Humor*, concurred. It was part of the fun of reviewing for the *Times* to deal with Bernard DeVoto's *Mark Twain's America* and Constance Rourke's *American Humor*, books that explored the vital effect that the tradition of frontier humor—the "tall story"—and harum-scarum realism had on *Huckleberry Finn*. If it hadn't been for a humor in the American past that Brooks and Mumford tended to overlook, the American rhythms that Fitzgerald and Hemingway exemplified at a later date would have sputtered and died.

DeVoto and Rourke, for all their differences with Brooks and Mumford, were actually in their debt. What the Brooks-Mumford preoccupation with the need for a usable past did was to provide a focus. Along with Bill Troy, Brooks and Mumford gave me a sense that America was rich in possibilities and that "sustained careers" in fiction could become something more than exceptions to a disheartening rule. As I dug into my job on the *Times Book Review*, hoping for a long career as a critic, I felt that I was a living part of a "usable present" that had grown directly out of the Brooks-Mumford-Frank concern for a usable past.

At the end of the '20s we were very much preoccupied with the idea of the quality of life as something that could exist quite apart from questions of economics and politics. The big quarrel over Humanism—sometimes called the New Humanism—that enlivened one New York winter at the decade's close, posed a lot of questions for critics who were troubled by the disparity between life "as it was" (see Dreiser, Sinclair Lewis, and the Dos Passos of *Three Soldiers* and *Manhattan Transfer*), and life as it might and should be. The literature of the '20s, satirical at bottom, abounded more frequently than not in Waste-Land images that seemingly denied the possibility of qualitative redemption. There was T.S. Eliot's Apeneck Sweeney. The cruel fighter of Ring Lardner's *Champion* began his career by assaulting his mother and his crippled brother. Ben Hecht's *Eric Dorn* dealt with a character who couldn't attach value to anything. Dreiser's Clyde Griffiths was foreordained to be a murderer. Faulkner's and Erskine Caldwell's Southern ensembles abounded in monsters, and when Hemingway sang a dirge to impotence in *The Sun Also Rises*, Gertrude Stein made her observation that "you are all a lost generation."

The Humanists, led by Paul Elmer More and Irving Babbitt, who believed in something called the Inner Check, didn't like all this. Life, they said, was something more than an "explosion in a sewer." The Humanists blamed the artists for insisting on a negative report. But what if the scene did not produce individuals of heroic dimension, neither wholly good nor wholly bad but of a certain magnitude? The artist had to have living models—if he were to create heroes out of whole cloth, he would be denying the truth.

I got into the argument by contributing an essay, "Drift and Mastery in Our Novelists," to C. Hartley Grattan's 1930 symposium, "The Critique of Humanism." My point was that the New Humanists, in their laudable concern for the quality of life, were trying to force artists who must remain close to "what is" to take on a didactic role that is unsuited to the imaginative writer. The business of the novelist, I said, was not to create values but to put them into circulation if they were to be observed in the living model. It was the business of the social critic to set forth the aims that might improve society, and the novelist should be content to take it from there as the social critic makes his converts.

Paul Elmer More's attack on John Dos Passos particularly annoyed me. Professor More had peremptorily dismissed "Dos" for writing *Manhattan Transfer*, a novel which had been built around a number of characters who did not live by the ethical laws approved by the New Humanists. It seemed to me that if Dos Passos had suppressed the evidence of his senses in favor of producing a tract, he would have been guilty of depriving the social critic of evidence needed in any campaign to change things.

To note that we had had a literature of "drift" in the '20s did not preclude the desirability of "mastery." But if the "drift" was there, it had to be recorded in fiction. The fact that there wasn't much volition in Dreiser's women, or that F. Scott Fitzgerald's Amory Blaine treated ideas as playthings, or that Jim Farrell's Studs Lonigan submitted to the peer pressure of moral monsters, was a datum. If Hemingway's heroes were impotent, or given to making separate peaces, why, that was the way that Hemingway saw them in the aftermath of a futile war. The New Humanist moralist, taking over from this point, would be justified in crusading for a different and purposeful order in which wars might be avoided. But the novelist or the poet might properly be excused from the New Humanist's crusade on the ground that artists have their own work to do.

Anyway, even granting the Humanists had something of a case against novelists of the early '20s who had a taste for the gutter, the phenomenon of volition as an attribute of the human organism was observable in such novelists of the late '20s as Edmund Wilson, Thomas Wolfe, Glenway Wescott, and Elizabeth Madox Roberts. I left it there in my "Critique of Humanism" essay.

Years later, in the article on American writers which I did for *Life Magazine*, I had some second thoughts about "drift and mastery" as they had been exhibited in the '20s. "The big novels of the Twenties," I wrote on mature reflection in 1947, "were all based on a feeling for the type of person who tries to make a career, to follow a gleam, to create a style, to do something or to be something. The hero of *Babbitt* may have been a naïve boor but at least he had a fumbling concern for his city of Zenith. Doc Kennicott tried to hold fast to the ideal of simple village friendliness in *Main Street*; Martin Arrowsmith pursued the ideal of disinterested scientific research through a hundred vicissitudes; the automobile manufacturer in Lewis's *Dodsworth* had a craftsman's feeling for the cars he made. The bootlegger protagonist of Scott Fitzgerald's *The Great Gatsby* was no fit candidate for the role of Aristotelian hero . . . but at least he chased the green light that led him to a Long Island lawn in pursuit of the delectable Daisy. As for Willa Cather's *A Lost Lady*, she held fast to an ideal of style even though she had no idea of a proper morality."

All of Willa Cather's work, in fact, exalted the purposeful human being. She came from "Old West" Nebraska at, to quote her own phrase, "the very end of the road-making West." The one thing that unites her pioneer women and her more complex railroad builders, artists, singers, professors, and archbishops is a romantic fighting quality of persistence in pursuit of a dream. As a reviewer I never had the opportunity to encounter the dogged singer Thea Kronborg (*The Song of the Lark*) or Claude Wheeler, the Nebraska farm boy who made the Allies' cause his own in World War I (*One of Ours*), but memories of their personal qualities tinged my attitude to the anti-heroes that took over the novel in the late '30s. Somehow good characters make for good prose; the feeling for form, integration, and style in human personality spilled over into the craftsmanship of the '20s.

In the days before the Crash, we were really too close to see that we were living in a grandly creative age. It definitely wasn't materialistic. In 1974, writing in Bob Tyrrell's hospitable *The Alternative: An American Spectator*, I could stand off from the period even more effectively than I had in my *Life* article of 1947. The crime news of the '20s, in default of stories of economic and political misery, had taken over many a headline, thus giving substance to the Ben Hecht-Charles MacArthur stereotype of *The Front Page*. But I recalled for Bob Tyrrell's readers that the inner spirit of '20s' journalism was better explained by the character studies of news-room types that Henry Justin Smith, the managing editor of the *Chicago Daily News*, had put together in his *Deadlines*. The '20s were the time of journalistic *jeu d'esprit*; archy, the lower case cockroach, and his girlfriend Mehitabel, the cat, dispensed a columnistic wisdom that puts our modern op. ed. commentators to the blush. And if the city room of the '20s had been totally filled by *Front Page* types, there would have been no Dorothy Thompsons, no Edgar Ansell Mowrers, no Vincent Sheeans to report the coming of Hitler.

The '20s were, of course, the age of the automobile, a quite utilitarian conveyance. But in addition to being the transportation medium for a free people, the automobile of the '20s took America out of mourning clothes. Where Henry Ford had once said his customers could have any color car "just so long as it is black," the cities blossomed in the '20s with blues, yellows, and reds. The Naderites can legitimately complain about smog, but if it had not been for the internal combustion engine we would have had no decentralization, and millions would now be piled on top of millions in a dozen American versions of India's Calcutta.

As in Westbrook Pegler's *Era of Wonderful Nonsense*, the '20s had their wild parties. Literary New York was no exception. But there was method in some of the madness. Tommy Smith of Liveright used parties to sign up authors. The talk at a Liveright party was by no means all frivolous. At one particular party—I remember that Louis Kronenberger, Isidore Schneider, Leane Zugsmith, Saxe Comins, and Tommy Smith, all Liveright editors, were there—the discussion turned to Will Durant's popular *Story of Philosophy*. I had been reading George Henry Lewes' *Biographical History of Philosophy*, written in Victorian times, and mentioned that it was a superior work. Tommy Smith was interested; he knew that Lewes, who had been George Eliot's consort, was a Goethe specialist, and he wondered why he was not better known in the United States. Before the evening was over I had agreed to sign a contract with Tommy Smith to do a book on George Henry Lewes for Liveright. The advance, as I recall, was $400.

I set about in all earnestness to learn something about the literary scene in Victorian England, which led me to my first real acquaintance with John Stuart Mill. Meanwhile, the stock market crashed. In the suddenly changed atmosphere, Mill on economics seemed more interesting than Lewes on philosophy, but I plunged on with my assigned subject. In the spring of 1930 I cadged a leave of absence from Don Adams and, with my wife, sailed on one of the comfortable smaller White Star liners—I think it was the *Baltic*—for Liverpool. I planned to spend time on Lewes in the British Museum.

A month in London convinced me it wouldn't work. The trip itself was thoroughly enjoyable as I renewed contact with Ferdie Kuhn, who found us an apartment in Chelsea and took us to visit Sir Philip Gibbs in the country. We rode horses on Hampstead Heath, and went for a couple of long week-ends in Paris. But the more I tried to concentrate on Victorian themes in the British Museum, the more I found myself thinking of what was happening at home.

Suddenly it struck me that I ought to be writing a book to clarify for myself the strange fact that a depression could happen in America. We in the '20s had ignored politics. The hard times of the 1890s the *Sturm und Drang* of the pre-World War I Progressive Movement, even the short, sharp downturn of 1920-21, were hazy in our minds. I remember closing a book on logical positivism in the British Museum with a resolve to earn that $400 advance from Liveright by writing something that was not mentioned in the Lewes contract. The book that was already taking shape in my mind would be about the United States.

Two years later I turned the manuscript of *Farewell to Reform: The Rise, Life and Decay of the Progressive Mind in America* in to Tommy Smith without comment. He blinked when he saw that it was not about George Henry Lewes. Then he smiled. The year was 1932, and there were plenty of troubles afoot. A book on an obscure Victorian man of letters could have been a terrible dud. A book on America's political past would assuredly do better.

Chapter 5

The break from one set of convictions to another is always a ragged process. My interest in radical economics and politics was stirred, faintly enough at first, by the troubles of my father, who was having a hard time keeping the family retail furniture business afloat when people stopped buying in 1930. On a visit to New Haven, my father asked me innumerable questions about a man named Howard Scott, the originator of technocracy. The questions didn't mean much to me, but I had seen Howard Scott in Lee Chumley's off Barrow Street in the Village. He was an habitue of the place, and one evening I found myself talking with Scott and a young economics teacher from Princeton named Leon Henderson.

I listened with amazement as Scott and Henderson cooked up a plot to go downtown and "scare hell out of the bankers." The Technocrat proposed putting a soviet of engineers in charge of the whole North American continent, Canada included, and running it from a central conning tower as one huge business. It was straight out of Thorstein Veblen, as I discovered when I started rummaging through Veblen's *The Engineers and the Price System* for myself. Later Leon Henderson was to desert Scott to go to work as a Franklin Roosevelt brain truster. His economics took on greater subtlety as he turned back to Brandeisean trust busting in Roosevelt's second term, when he was put in charge of the TNEC (Temporary National Economic Committee). John Strachey, on his visit to America in the middle '30s, credited Henderson with rescuing him from the dogmatic Marxism of his *The Coming Struggle for Power*. As for Henderson, he was rescued from dogmatism himself by his discovery that government spending could be used to shift market forces. But in 1930, listening to the babble of the Technocrats at Scott's table in the Village, the adaptation of John Maynard Keynes to American politics was still a far-off thing.

The *Times Sunday Book Review* kept its sheltered literary character through the early months of the depression, but I began to notice a difference in the young people who came in to ask for reviewing assignments. One brash visitor was Eliot Janeway, who came down from

42

Cornell with a letter from the English political philosopher George Catlin. Eliot wanted to take on books about Hegel and William James, but had to be satisfied with a Western story. He was soon off to other things, including a marriage to an Ohio banker's daughter and an interval with Communism, neither of which lasted very long. He found it boring to distribute Marxist pamphlets in Harlem, but it was the boring quality of the pamphlets themselves that turned him away from orthodox radicalism.

Eliot was the first economic journalist of the early '30s to discover that Washington politics was important to Wall Street market research. With his second wife, Elizabeth (Babs), to stabilize him, Eliot became a grounded as well as a coruscating character. I was to see a lot of the Janeways in the '30s and early '40s when, as a literary scout for Doubleday, I recommended Babs' first novel, *The Walsh Girls*, to editor Ken McCormick. Eliot's view of economics was that of a physician faced with the problem of patching up an ailing organism to keep it going. Unlike a lot of his Democratic Party colleagues, he believed in the market. But he never cavilled at legislating the use of a crutch here, or a tourniquet there, or even a major blood transfusion. He made money as an analyst by communing with his Washington friends, Bill Douglas, Abe Fortas, and Jerome Frank, as well as with his corporate informers. He had an engineer-brother with Chrysler who kept him up to date on industrial technology. Occasionally known as Calamity Janeway, he thrived in falling markets. But he was never a professional pessimist—and he sometimes called a good upward turn. He made the business-news department of *Time Magazine* something to be reckoned with simply because he spent more time in Washington than in New York.

Another visitor at the *Sunday Book Review* was Bob Cantwell, a young novelist from the Pacific Northwest who wanted desperately to believe the working classes were, as he said, the salt of the earth. Bob was the author of *Laugh and Lie Down*, which was too sensitive to be categorized as a proletarian novel. Bob's curiosity about Marxism led him in one direction; his interest in good writing pulled him in another. Jim Farrell, the author of the *Studs Lonigan* trilogy to which I had contributed an introduction based on my own friendship with the New Haven Irish, spoke of Bob as "Robert Cantwritewell," but that was the envious reaction of a writer of raw power to the writer who depended on finesse. Jim, as a Trotskyite, could have been contemptuous of Bob Cantwell for his more orthodox radicalism.

Bob was to follow me later to *Fortune Magazine*, where he wrote on steel labor and kindred topics. His wife Betsy distrusted the Communists, but Bob, caught up in a growing movement, became implicated with them in ways that made him uncomfortable even though he considered it his duty to be a revolutionist. He accepted a grant, arranged for by Lincoln Steffens as I recall, to go to San Francisco to write a novel that was tentatively titled *City of Anger*, about Harry Bridges and the radical West Coast maritime unions. Bob bought a car with his grant money and set out for California across a country whose place names he always loved, and which he celebrated in non-*Timese* prose in a later period when he was one of Harry Luce's favorite front-of-the-book *Time* writers.

Once in San Francisco, Bob dug into the union problem. It was a devastating experience; all the Marxist labor "pluses" with which he began his research kept turning to minuses as he got deeper into his novel. He felt shattered to find his heroes becoming villains. Eventually he gave it up. Back in New York, I heard him say to himself in a Rockefeller Center elevator, "Robert Cantwell, your name is Schmelka Ginsburg." He was obviously referring to the Soviet defector, General Krivitsky, whose name was Schmuel Ginsburg. That told me more about Bob Cantwell's experience in and out of the Communist movement than any list of dates and and facts.

When he finally emerged from his period of mental and emotional turmoil, Bob Cantwell settled down to become a fine weekly journalist, winding up as a sports-story writer for *Sports Illustrated*. He did sterling work in anything that he touched, but it was a great loss to serious literature that Bob had to settle for one of those deflected careers that were characteristic of the period.

Jim Farrell, Bob Cantwell's severest critic, would never have made a journalist. But it was not his Trotskyism that kept him from pushing his curiosity into new fields. He had an obsession for a narrow Chicago slum scene that persisted through 50 books. Jim's partisanship for Chicago extended even to baseball—Jim could quote the averages of Big Ed Walsh of the White Sox or Hack Wilson of the Cubs where he was quite oblivious to the exploits of other heroes. To do him justice, he was more of a humanist than is immediately apparent in his *Studs Lonigan* trilogy. Unfortunately, he lost readers when he wrote a tetralogy about a young character modeled on himself. He could never make virtue as appealing as vice. Jim's Trotskyism didn't last—he ended his life as a good social democrat, an admirer of Hubert Humphrey. But the Trotskyite interlude (Trotsky himself had written perceptively about literature) sharpened his senses about the anti-cultural aspects of the official Communist movement. He remained a sensible critic at a time when the Mike Golds of the Stalinist machine were spitting on Thornton Wilder for choosing universal themes instead of depicting a crudely conceived class struggle.

The younger publishers' representatives of the early '30s were all in their various ways moving toward an ill-defined Left. Bernard Smith of Knopf, who wrote a stimulating if doctrinaire book on American literary criticism, had at some point become an out-and-out Marxist. Henry Hart at Scribner's and Cap Pearce at Harcourt, Brace were tending that way. Louis Kronenberger at Liveright never became immersed in politics, but he sympathized with Izzy Schneider and Leane Zugsmith, Liveright colleagues who really became embattled. Our luncheons at the Hotel Woodstock on West 43rd St., just off Times Square, became more animated, but they were not yet acrimonious.

Even before I had dropped the George Henry Lewes project for the book that became *Farewell to Reform*, I had been lured into seeking some extracurricular work for publications that were more political than the *Times* Sunday book section. Seward Collins, not yet a partisan of corporate state ideas, let me write a long essay for his *Bookman* on "The Negro as Writer." My curiosity about black writers had been spurred by Claude McKay's poetry, and as I dipped back in time to the 19th-century novels of Charles Chesnutt I came up with something that was, in its way, a trailblazing bit of critical writing. I was less concerned than Carl Van Vechten, author of *Nigger Heaven*, with making Harlem a fashionable slumming point for downtown whites, although we all enjoyed going to the Cotton Club. The black writer (we did not then use the adjective *black*, for *Negro* was still the accepted word) had considerably more than fashion to recommend him, as Langston Hughes, Countee Cullen, and Claude McKay were busy proving. Claude McKay's novel, *Home to Harlem*, seemed to me excellent.

Seward Collins was not really interested in ethnic writing, nor even in imaginative literature. He let me review *Look Homeward Angel*, a novel by an unknown Southerner named Thomas Wolfe who was teaching at New York University with my college roommate Bill Troy. But I couldn't go much further with Collins, who was about to shuffle off *The Bookman* in favor of publishing a Rightist political magazine.

Through pretty Helen Gude, a New York University colleague of Tom Wolfe and Bill Troy, my wife Peggy and I met Betty Huling, who did editing and make-up for the *New Republic*. We all had in common a growing passion for tennis, but there was the lesser game of deck tennis that was played in the backyard of the *New Republic's* building in Chelsea on West 21st Street. This literally opened a back door to the office of the exalted Edmund, or Bunny, Wilson, who rather condescendingly (as I thought at the time) let me do some short book pieces for him. I later discovered that Wilson had a diffident streak that could have been simple shyness. Whatever it was, I did better with Malcolm Cowley, who succeeded Wilson as the *New Republic* literary editor.

Cowley had just returned from the Paris which he lovingly celebrated in his *Exile's Return*. Odd as it must seem in retrospect to those who later accused him of putting the *New Republic* book section on the Party line, he went "political" at a slower rate than the rest of us. I remember his advising me to "give up politics." He had a passion for good sentences, and he had at me for not bothering to put my ideas in *Sunday Times* reviews into cleaner, sharper prose. I know I benefited from the criticism: years later Professor Hudson Strode of Alabama commended me for my sentences, and Ed

Roberts of the *National Observer* said I never wrote a sloppy one. One could not know Cowley for long without encountering his supportive friends, Matthew Josephson and Kenneth Burke. The talents of this lively trio were entirely different, but like the three musketeers they were all for one and one for all.

Burke was a profound student of the arts of rhetoric, which he explained in psychological terms. One of his typical *tours de force* was to present Mark Antony's subtle eulogy of Julius Caesar with a running interior monologue that showed Mark Antony's awareness of just what he was doing to subvert his audience. When I let him read one of the advertisements I had written for the New York Central Railroad when I worked at Thomas Logan's, Kenneth remarked on its similarity to a sonnet in its tight construction and summary conclusion.

Burke lived on Bank Street in the Village when he was not "dug in" on his farm at Andover, New Jersey. It was a curious *ménage*. His wife Lily and her sister Libby competed for his affection, with Lily taking the bitter crust of a companionship that was limited to periods of weeding the garden in common and joining to keep a firm control of some lively daughters. Matty Josephson was full of admiration for Lily's ability to keep the whole family going on the "iron rations" that were commensurate with Burke's limited income. Instead of being a Victorian tragedy, the *ménage à trois* somehow worked out without animosities. Kenneth was in love with Libby, whom he married in 1933, but he respected Lily. And the sisters were united in supporting Kenneth's obvious talents as he jumped from literature to curious economic proposals, such as the one he made for bond money. Burke's ingenuity came legitimately from his father, who invented a sugar-cube wrapper that opened at a light touch.

Josephson and Cowley had been more immersed in experimental literature than Kenneth Burke, but they were coming out of it when I first knew them. Matty had marked out a special career for himself, alternating between big biographies of French men of letters and bold accounts of 19th-century American tycoons and their political agents. Although he was extremely gifted in managing a small patrimony that gave him the leisure to write on a farm in Gaylordsville, Connecticut, where he lived with his helpful wife Hannah, he was thoroughly anti-capitalist in his approach to businessmen. His *The Robber Barons* set the tone for practically all the writing about industrialists in the '30s. He gave a smooth literary gloss to the stories of skulduggery that Gustavus Myers had dug up in his history of the great American fortunes. Yet I think Matty secretly admired the Rockefellers and Vanderbilts who pioneered the industrial system, and he certainly had a soft spot for such of their 20th-century successors as Pan American's Juan Terry Trippe and Robert R. Young, the railroad man who was called the Populist of Wall Street. Before I went to work for *Fortune Magazine* I shared Matty Josephson's opinions about business. Later, after exposure to the workings of the market system, I came to disagree with the whole idea that "robbers" had built industrial America. Matty and Hannah wondered audibly about what had gotten into me, but they were always pleasant about our widening differences.

At the height of the Humanist controversy, when I joined with Burke, Josephson, and Cowley in signing a letter calling on the Humanists to point out a single work of literature they had written, we were all moving Leftward at different paces. But Cowley in particular still resisted the politicization of literature. His beautifully sensitive poetry, collected in *Blue Juniata*, drew the stern approval of my editorial boss, J. Donald Adams. It was at this point that, despite Cowley's mild warning, I began my own adventure in politicization, dipping back into the '80s and '90s to get a running start for *Farewell to Reform*.

My adventure in coming to terms with the pre-World War I Progressive Movement was played out in a time of increasing depression that struck home when the *Times* sliced all wages and salaries by 10 percent. In addition, I had to cut down on extracurricular journalism in order to find time for a huge reading program for the new book, and this caused a financial stringency that gave a personal point to my feeling that the capitalists couldn't manage their own society. I came to believe that any reforms pitched to making the competitive system workable would shatter on capitalist stupidity and political venality. I began to see things in terms of sharp antitheses, and came, at least momentarily, to admire qualities of intransigeance. I saw Teddy Roosevelt as a trimmer, and Woodrow Wilson as a renegade who had, for reasons of personal emotional aggrandizement, lost contact with the idea expressed in Randolph Bourne's *War is the Health of the State*. Among the practical politicians only Bob La Follette, the elder, retained my admiration. But he, too, seemed vulnerable in his quest to establish a "return" politics that would recapture the lost world of Thomas Jefferson.

I look back on *Farewell to Reform* with mixed feelings. The chapters that sought to assess the impact of the economic and political novels and the muckraking journalism of the late 19th and early 20th centuries will, whatever their deficiencies, stand up as a pioneering attempt at a sort of social criticism that was to sweep the boards in the '30s. Arthur Schlesinger, Jr., has told me that these chapters made a big impression on him in college. The section on Theodore Roosevelt, which grandly dismissed that good man as a "villain," missed the whole value of Teddy's role as an exemplary moral teacher. The final chapter, which vigorously criticized such "planners" as Charles Beard, Stuart Chase, and George Soule for their failure to see that a society controlled from the top would eventuate in a tyranny, still retains a certain cogency. But the tone was—and is—brash and unconstructive. I was made to feel quite contrite when George Soule, a *New Republic* editor, asked me to do a series on "blocked roads" to freedom for

his magazine. And the sense of contrition was deepened when Beard—
"Uncle Charlie"—exhibited no rancor. We became fast friends, particularly
after the war clouds began rolling up in the mid-'30s, and I responded to his
thesis that America had its own special destination.

On more than one occasion, including a visit which I made with *Fortune*
editor Bill Furth and Yale Law School teacher Fred Rodell to the Beard
farmhouse above New Milford, Connecticut, Uncle Charlie patiently
explained to me that his economic interpretation of history derived from
James Madison, not Karl Marx. And he insisted that the economic
interpretation of the Constitution for which he had become famous was
only one interpretation. As Beard made plain in a book on the structuring of
the republic that Harry Luce asked to serialize in *Life*, the Founding
Fathers had virtues that transcended their economic appetites. They were
interested in creating mechanisms that would let freedom reside in the
interstices of a check-and-balance system. Beard resented being classed as
a materialist. Though he twitted me for accepting the theory that natural
rights are decrees from nature's God, he nevertheless held tenaciously to
the 18th century's idea that some things must be accepted as inalienable. He
had an overview of society that caused Eugene Davidson, his Yale
University Press publisher, to symbolize him in a poem as "great eagle,
knower of the skies." He was all of that, and the curious thing was that, in
physiognomy, he really did resemble the American bald eagle.

The reviewers of *Farewell to Reform* were extraordinarily kind. The
socialists among them passed over my negativism, which accepted
socialism with the notation that it was only a belly creed. They might have
foreseen that I would desert socialism if I ever managed to recover from a
failure of nerve, but they missed the opportunity for prophecy by their
willingness to overlook the tonal aspects of my last chapter. As for the
Progressive critics, they were just as kind as the socialists. William Allen
White of the *Emporia Gazette* foregave me much, for I had, as he said,
made the movement quite vivid in which he had spent his life. During a
visit to New York with his wife, he invited me to join them at the Players'
Club in Gramercy Park for tea. We had a great talk, not about my book, but
about William Jennings Bryan. I remember Mrs. White breaking in at some
point of criticism to expostulate, "But Will, he was like a flame." She said it
over and over again. Progressive politics lived in the hearts of its exemplars
even though I had tried to kill it—and it would shortly revive under a
second Roosevelt.

Another direct result of the book's publication was a call from Lincoln
Steffens, who asked me to drop in on him at the Hotel Commodore. Since
he, the pioneer muckraker, had pronounced his own farewell to reform, we
had a most amicable meeting. Later he was to chide me, in a kindly way, for
doubting that the "future," which he had said he had seen working in Soviet
Russia, would be all that rosy.

With its attack on Chase-Soule-Beard top-down planning, *Farewell to Reform* prefigured radical opposition to the New Deal first term, with its price fixing and its Blue Eagle marching insignia. When General Hugh ("Iron Pants") Johnson moved in to regiment business under the terms of power granted by the National Recovery Act, it seemed to validate my expressed feeling that congealment was to be the fate of capitalism.

Ironically, however, the popular feeling that workable reforms were destined to come after Herbert Hoover had been bounced out of the White House caused some avid readers to overlook the tone of my last chapter. It was enough that I had written a book that revived memories of the Progressive era, when Washington was counted on to provide New Freedoms, New Nationalisms, and a Square Deal. In early 1933 I got a bid from Noble Cathcart, who was anything but an anti-reformer and anti-capitalist, to come and talk with him about the prospects of the *Saturday Review of Literature*, which he, as its publisher, proposed to expand with a promised subsidy from Tom Lamont. Noble was satisfied with the general direction of the *Saturday Review* under Henry Seidel Canby and a veteran board of editors that included Christopher Morley, Amy Loveman, and William Rose Benet. But he wanted some younger journalistic blood to cope with the revival that he saw coming once the banks had stopped closing and fear itself had been banished.

After a most convivial evening Noble and his gracious wife Anne exacted a promise that I would join with George Stevens, later famous as a book publisher, on an expanded *Saturday Review* board. The idea was to give a coverage of books on public affairs that Henry Canby and Chris Morley were inclined to overlook in their zeal for pure literature.

I did not really want to quit the *Times*, and I had no wish to let Don Adams down. But the *Saturday Review* job promised more scope and, incidentally, more money. Adams saw my point of view. During a two-week vacation period in Bermuda, my wife Peggy and I were invited to tea by none other than Mr. and Mrs. Tom Lamont. I thought it ironical that writing *Farewell to Reform*, which was anything but sympathetic to the House of Morgan, had come to this. But it was soon evident that Mrs. Lamont, at least, liked radicals, and Tom himself wanted, for his own adaptive reasons, to know about them. Possibly he wished to keep contact with his son Corliss, then a budding revolutionary.

A good part of the tea-time session was given over to Tom Lamont's laments for what had been happening to his liberal friends in Japan. "They are killing them," he said morosely. The afternoon ended with his statement, unsolicited, that there were no strings attached to any decision Noble Cathcart might make for the *Saturday Review*. I tested him later with some contributions that might have raised his hackles, particularly with a piece (written after I had left the *Review*) commending the Leftist League of American Writers for staging their first writers' conference with

Communist blessings. As a father to Corliss, Tom had no doubt had to cultivate tolerance. But there was some slyness involved; with Wall Street fighting off various scandals, and with the *New Republic's* John T. Flynn leading a successful charge that was to eventuate in the Security Exchange Commission, it was good for the House of Morgan to project a liberal image. Tom Lamont's spirit, like that of his co-partner Dwight Morrow who had left Morgan's to become Coolidge's Ambassador to Mexico, could have been expressed as "if you can't beat them, co-opt them." It was a technique that was brilliantly used at a much later date by Yale President Kingman Brewster, whose momentary co-opting of rebellious campus youth in 1970 saved Yale's buildings from threatened arson and bombings.

The four months I spent on the *Saturday Review* were among the pleasantest of my life. It soon developed that editing the *Review* meant working with Amy Loveman. Henry Canby, engaged wth his books on American literature, took responsibility for the editorials and for presiding at luncheons that paid off in good contributions. But he left the book assignments mostly to others. Chris Morley, with his Three-Hours-for-Lunch Club, had an elaborate schedule as a literary man. William Rose Benet had his department and his function of passing on poetry. But it was the unappreciated Amy Loveman who had done the dog-work in getting out the paper.

Amy had absolutely no trace of jealousy, and she welcomed working with George Stevens and me in bringing a newsier flavor into the *Review*. Amy mothered us, and, with her infinite sagacity, kept us from going off on unprofitable tangents. She took care of an aged father, who sat silently by at some of Amy's "evenings" when she would bring historian Allan Nevins or some other notable to meet with George Stevens and me for discussions. Without the Amy Lovemans of this world, nothing would persist.

I left the *Saturday Review* in September of 1933 because of a great temptation. I was reading Laurence Sterne's *Tristram Shandy* in a hammock on the farm of my good friends Caroline and Larry Wilkinson in East Haddam, Connecticut, when I got a call from Don Adams in New York. I put down *Tristram Shandy* without realizing that it was the last book I would read for pure pleasure for many years.

The New York Times, so Adams told me over the phone, had decided to run a daily book column. It would be a five-times-a-week job. I could have it if I could prove to publisher Arthur Sulzberger that I could stand the pace. Beginning right away I was to do five experimental reviews of new books, turning them in one at a time for a week by five o'clock in the afternoon. If all went well—and it did—I was to have a permanent lease on some of the most valued book space in America.

Amy Loveman said, "Don't think twice about it." She sent me off with her blessing. Noble Cathcart was a bit miffed, for I could give him no margin before I left. But he, too, agreed that I couldn't turn the offer down.

So I was off to a new career. It was to coincide with the radicalization of the New York literary scene and with that early phase of the New Deal when everything important that Roosevelt touched (the National Recovery Act, the Triple-A experiment in limiting agricultural acreage) seemed to end in a Constitutional crisis.

The new books, reflecting a turbulent scene, involved me in turbulent decisions. Often it was a crisis a day. There were periods of fun (I enjoyed parodying Ogden Nash and writing a rhymed review of the seed catalogues), but there was always the daily discipline. I couldn't have had a better training for anything in journalism that was to come.

Chapter 6

E ugene Lyons, with special reference to New York City and Hollywood, has called the '30s the "Red decade." Purists may contest this—and it is probably quite true that the Communist Party in America, even at the crest, never had more than 75,000 members, with only a lone infiltrator or two sitting at an important editor's desk. But, as Communist leader Gus Hall put it, there must have been ten "state-of-mind Communists" for every Party card holder in the '30s. I was quickly made aware, as I began doing the *Times* book column, of atmospheric realities that escaped statistical tabulation. The Communists did not "control" New York publishing. But there were rings within rings of influence as the technique of organizing innocent clubs and setting up transmission belts developed. It was the periphery that accounted for the trendiness.

The pressures on me were quite intangible. No one told me what books to review, or how to review them. My copy went directly to the office of Managing Editor Edwin James, where Isabel Sloane, his pleasant secretary, ordinarily waved it in front of her boss's nose to get the usual acceptance. Only once in three years did I have any censorship trouble. It was with a review of Radcliffe Hall's novel about Lesbianism, *The Well of Loneliness*. Somehow Arthur Sulzberger caught sight of the review in proof. He questioned James about the propriety of discussing such a topic in the *Times*, and James, agreeing that a review might be "unnecessary," asked me to substitute something else at the last minute. I found a pamphlet-length book that I ripped through in half-an-hour, and managed to hit the deadline.

But just as no one seemed to care that I had written a radical critique of Progressive history in *Farewell to Reform*, no one ever criticized me for an often Leftish review of a book on history or economics. Occasionally Rollo Ogden, Adolph Ochs's old-fashioned liberal editor-in-chief, would make some remark in the elevator about that "young man" on the book page, but that was all. Simeon Strunsky, who wrote the sprightly column "Topics of the Times," regarded me with amused tolerance. After all, he had been a socialist himself.

The idea of Communism was sufficiently in the air to cause the Communist Party to make a special drive for a "Foster and Ford" intellectual political committee in the presidential contest in 1932. I had attended a couple of organizing meetings in Greenwich Village, but, largely because of the skepticism expressed by Herbert Solow, who was attracted to Trotsky, I had remained aloof. I joined Henry Hazlitt and Elmer Davis in supporting the socialist Norman Thomas for President. Among some of my Leftward-going friends—Granville Hicks, Edward Dahlberg— that was considered a cop-out, if not a downright bit of pusillanimity.

I was invited nonetheless to attend a seminar at Smith College, where Granville Hicks, Newton Arvin, and Corliss Lamont, among other critics and professors, held forth on the inevitability of Communism. Predicting blood in the streets, Granville Hicks said, "It will be perfect hell." Facing up to his fears, he saw no alternative to a violent "final conflict."

I was never quite convinced that "history" could be predicted within a given time span with any accuracy. My friend Pascal Covici, a Chicago publisher who had transferred his office to New York as Covici, Friede, agreed with me. Pat was as liberal as they come, and he had a young author named John Steinbeck in tow who was radical without being orthodox about any Marxist strategy or tactics.

Steinbeck had written a novel called *In Dubious Battle* about labor warfare in the California country, and Pat wanted me to read it and give him an opinion. I thought the manuscript eminently publishable, but was puzzled that Pat Covici needed any corroborating verdict. It turned out that one of Pat's sub-editors, Harry Bloch, was a convinced Leninist and objected to the Steinbeck novel because it did not endorse the prevailing Communist strike tactics. Harry, in Pat's momentary absence, had tried to forestall acceptance of the Steinbeck work, and Pat had to move quickly to mend a rather shaky fence. He wanted an "independent" opinion to show the rest of his office.

Harry Bloch was in many ways a capable editor, but thought himself entitled to his view of radical truth. He was married to the Mexican Malou Cabrera, the daughter of Carranza's finance minister Luis Cabrera, and was part of a circle that included Lewis Gannett, the daily book critic of the *Herald-Tribune*. Gannett himself was a liberal with sympathy for Communism, and subjected to the same sort of pressures that I felt in conducting my own column. He would have agreed with me about Steinbeck, but saw no objection to the general pervasiveness that allowed Leninists to function freely on publishers' payrolls.

Later, in the period leading to the Nazi-Communist pact, Harry Bloch did lose his footing in New York. He went to Mexico City, where his wife, who looked like an Aztec princess, had entree to government circles. Harry wound up with a contract to print the Mexico City telephone book, and became a wealthy man. I visited him in Mexico, and instead of denouncing me as a bourgeois renegade he seemed quite content with what had happened to the Mexican Revolution. Pointing out of the window, he said, "You see, it has been a great success." But it still had, he said, to solve the land problem. We did not mention the Steinbeck incident. Maybe he had forgotten about it. But it always seemed representative to me of what went on in the New York of the '30s.

Some of the publishers' representatives who had swallowed the Marxist line were subtle about presenting their lists. Bernard Smith of Knopf never actively sabotaged a book by Max Eastman; he simply failed to press its claims. Similarly it was a matter of comparative eloquence with Henry Hart of Scribner's and Cap Pearce of Harcourt, Brace. If they liked a book on their lists, they went all out for it. If they disapproved, they said little or nothing.

The trick, of course, worked both ways. E.P. Dutton was represented by Florence Bowers, an old-time socialist who had no use for either Lenin or Stalin. Her assistant was George Novack, an early Trotskyite schismatic. If they had had Eastman on their lists, he would have fared well. Florence was quite honest about her preferences. She had an earthy American streak and was a great baseball fan. She approved of me because, sometimes with Jim Farrell, I would carry a novel with me to the Polo Grounds or Ebbetts Field in Brooklyn, reading it on the subway and even between innings in order to combine pleasure with meeting the *Times* daily deadline. It was through Florence's influence that I became a judge of Irving Marsh's annual collection of the best sports stories, a job that I enjoyed for more than 30 years.

In an indirect way Florence Bowers was the cause of my early break with the Communists. One day she brought a book into my cubbyhole-office on the *Times* third floor with her face all glowing. It was *Escape from the Soviets*, by a woman named Tatiana Tchernavina who had with great hardship managed to get out of Stalin's paradise through Finland. I must review it.

If it had been a few months earlier I probably would have put the book to one side on the specious theory that the Russian Revolution, while admittedly imperfect, needed time to work itself out without being hectored by dissenters. But I had heard something from the *Times's* own Moscow correspondent, Walter Duranty, that was really disquieting. To a group in the *Times* elevator Duranty had almost casually mentioned that three million people had died in Russia in what amounted to a man-made famine. Duranty, who had floated the theory that revolutions were beyond moral judgment ("You can't make an omelette without breaking eggs"), did not condemn Stalin for the bloody elimination of the kulaks that had deprived the Russian countryside of necessary sustaining expertise. He simply let the three-million figure go at that.

What struck me at the time was the double iniquity of Duranty's performance. He was not only heartless about the famine, he had betrayed his calling as a journalist by failing to report it.

So, in talking of the Tchernavina book, I made mention of the millions of starved peasants. When the *New Masses* challenged me I attributed the information to Walter Duranty. The result was a grand denunciation of me by the Communists. Duranty, with his Russian visa hanging fire, denied ever having said anything. That put me on the spot with Arthur Sulzberger, who would surely have fired me for prevarication. Luckily for my scalp, Simeon Strunsky came to my rescue. He had heard Duranty tell about the murdered peasants, too. The whole truth about the famine came out, of course, when William Henry Chamberlin and others, with less concern about their visas, broke the grand silence.

The Duranty episode marked me as a dissident radical, but it did not put an end to my willingness to cooperate with American Communists. In his *Writers on the Left*, Daniel Aaron quotes me as praising the First Writers' Congress for ending the so-called RAPP (a Soviet writers organization) period in American literary Communism. The threat of reaction, I said, had forced a broad front among anti-Fascist writers. I gave credit to Henry Hart, Matthew Josephson, and Malcolm Cowley, among other fellow-travelers, for provoking a right-about-face in the Communist ranks and bringing an end to the RAPP terrorist spirit.

If only for tactical reasons, the Communists were lenient with Kenneth Burke for his heresey in substituting the word "people" for "worker." And I was accepted by the League of American Writers, an obvious Communist affiliate, in spite of my wondering out loud why a "united front" could not be expanded to include people like Max Eastman, Louis Adamic, Charles Beard, Clifton Fadiman, Edmund Wilson, Louis Hacker, and Ben Stolberg, all of whom were demonstrably anti-Fascist. These were all my friends, and I knew them to be sincere critics of capitalist shortcomings. Max Eastman, interested in the motive patterns of those who were attracted to socialism, made what seemed to me a valid distinction between collectivist idealists like Scott Nearing and power-hungry Leftist mobsters. Louis Adamic, a Mencken discovery, wrote warmly about the generation of immigrants whose Plymouth Rock happened to be Ellis Island. Clifton Fadiman, with whom I traded "profiles" (he wrote one of me for the *Saturday Review*, and I did a piece called "Fadiman for the Millions" in the *Saturday Evening Post*), was a great champion of books like Ed Dahlberg's *Bottom Dogs*. Louis Hacker was getting a leg up on his life work of applying Charles Beard's economic interpretation to the America of Andy Carnegie. Edmund Wilson, somewhat naïve in his hopes of "taking communism away from the Communists," was nonetheless one of the more honest of our reporters of what he called the "American jitters."

As for Ben Stolberg, he was, in addition to being a most perceptive journalist, one of our great wits. A favorite of the garment workers' leader

David Dubinsky, Ben had written a most stylish history called *Tailors'*
Progress. Ben disliked pretense—to him the "Young Plan" for solving our
international payments troubles had been "born dead," and he refused to
temper his words just to get them into the *Herald-Tribune*. Of Woodrow
Wilson, the Messiah, Ben said, "Fillmore and Buchanan were better men."
Ben wrote me amusing letters which he signed, "Nicholas Murray, butler to
Mr. Stolberg," and he really meant it as praise when he said, "Bob Taft is so
honest that even tact annoys him." Ben was so tactless himself that Sue La
Follette proposed *Alone at Last* for a title of his unwritten autobiography.

It wasn't long before the word was passed that I was an unreliable
because of my friends. Alec Gumberg, a pro-Communist business advisor,
asked me if I intended to name my daughter "Leona" after Leon Trotsky. I
was not a Trotskyite, but the truth is that I found the ex-Communist
dissidents—Max Eastman, Leon Dennen, Isaac Don Levine, V.F. Calverton, and Ben Stolberg—far more convincing than the intellectuals who
persisted in their attempts to reconcile a personal independence with the
Communists' selective interpretation of popular-front tactics. The year
1934 was a watershed year; the word had gone out from Moscow that a new
line—"Communism is 20th-century Americanism"—was to be adopted.
Joe Gould's quatrain

> From Russia, Earl Browder
>   Is getting divorscht,
> He prefers clam chowder
>   To noodles and borscht

sticks in my mind. But the Communists, while they were willing to tolerate
"deviations" if it were a question of welcoming a new big name for a
manifesto or a call for a congress, remained unrelenting about older devia-
tors. Ben Stolberg—"pejorative Ben," as Malcolm Cowley called him—
would never be welcomed to a popular-front gathering; he had, quite
unforgiveably, accused the Communists in the '20s of diverting Sacco-
Vanzetti funds to their own uses. Leon Dennen was "out" because he had
protested the dissolution of the John Reed clubs without a vote of the
membership. Don Levine, unfairly tabbed as an anarchist, remained persona non grata because of his insistence on bringing up the Bolshevik
murder of the Kronstadt sailors. Eastman had mortally offended with his
Artists in Uniform and his criticism of the totalitarian potential in basic
Marxist theory. And V.F. Calverton, an incurable eclectic, continued to be
hated for his *Modern Monthly*, a publication that remained hospitable to
writers of all shades of Leftist opinion.

Just before the "Communism is 20th-century Americanism" line went
into effect, the Communists tried to take over a meeting at Madison Square
Garden that had been called by the Socialists to honor the Viennese socialist
workers who had been killed by Austrian Chancellor Dollfuss's soldiers.

Scheduled speakers were shouted down by Communist goons, and a number of innocent people were hurt by flying chairs. A short time later John MacDonald, who was subsequently to become one of *Fortune* magazine's most valued writers, shoved an open letter into my hands protesting the Communist disruption of an anti-Fascist meeting. Ed Dahlberg, who had turned MacDonald down, yelled at me as I was about to sign—"Don't do it," he said, "it's a Trotskyist plot." Nevertheless I signed. So did John Dos Passos. He thought the Communist-provoked rioting at the Madison Square Garden meeting was "unintelligent fanaticism." His statement lent a sardonic point to his greeting of Malcolm Cowley and Izzy Schneider in a restaurant, "Writers of the World, Unite, you have nothing to lose but your brains."

The exile and the attempted muzzling of Leon Trotsky was the next source of contention that made mock of a united front. As I remember it, a Committee for Asylum of Leon Trotsky preceded the creation of the American Committee for the Defense of Leon Trotsky, less formally known as the Dewey Committee. There were Trotskyites on the Dewey Committee, but John Dewey's interest in holding hearings in Mexico was not ideological in the least. Dewey was animated by a simple preference for justice. Other members of the committee—Suzanne La Follette, Ben Stolberg, Professor Edward Alsworth Ross, Carlo Tresca, John F. Finerty, and I—were not Trotskyites. Nor was Carleton Beals, an original member of the committee who quit in Mexico for reasons that are still unknown to me, even though I tried to draw him out years later when I saw something of him in Connecticut, where he was busy doing a book on "Our Yankee Heritage."

I did not go to Mexico, but I was one who subsequently voted to accept Suzanne La Follette's summary of the Dewey Committee's findings. Neither our work, nor the supporting journalism of those with a real Trotskyite affiliation such as Jim Farrell and Dwight MacDonald, helped save Trotsky, who was ultimately to be pickaxed to death by a Stalinist assassin in his inadequately guarded retreat in Cuernavaca. Defending Trotsky's right to asylum was enough to tab me, along with Mary McCarthy, Edmund Wilson, Calverton, MacDonald, and Charles Yale Harrison, as a "renegade" who was unfit to appear at the second conference of the League of American Writers. I don't remember ever formally resigning from the League. I was simply dropped.

The Moscow Trials, which coincided with the united-front period of the mid-'30s, competed with the Trotsky business as a prime disrupter of anti-Fascist harmony. Leon Dennen, who had once worked for the legendary Borodin on the *Moscow Daily News*, found the trials too much to take. And even Waldo Frank, who could find it believable that the mystical Slavic soul could revel in the self-abasement of confession, brought himself to question the Communist sense of public relations in staging the trials at a time when amity among Western anti-Fascist intellectuals was important. For his failure to keep silent about his doubts, Waldo Frank was eased out of his position as chairman of the League of American Writers.

As for Leon Dennen, who later became a most sympathetic colleague of mine in writing daily newspaper columns, he found a haven on Sol Levitas's anti-Stalinist *New Leader*. Sol, a philosopher who had escaped from Russia by moving east (he functioned briefly, as I remember, as the anti-Leninist mayor of Vladivostok), paid little or nothing for contributions, but his publication served as a life-giving way station for writers who found their markets circumscribed because of Communist disapproval. William Henry Chamberlin and Willi Schlamm were both welcomed as columnists for the *New Leader* before finding larger publics in writing for the *Wall Street Journal* and the Luce publications. Sol was no American Progressive, but he let me write about young Bob and Phil La Follette for his pages. I had become fast friends with all the La Follette clan—Fola and her husband George Middleton, Governor Phil, and Senator Bob—because of my section on old Fighting Bob in *Farewell to Reform*. So, in one more eclectic step, I did columns for the *Progressive* in Madison, Wisconsin, where Morris Rubin, the editor, ran his Midwestern version of the *Nation* and the *New Republic*.

One of Sol Levitas's endearing facets was distributing fish to his unpaid contributors at Martha's Vineyard in July and August. During the 12 summers I went to Martha's Vineyard when my daughters were growing up, I benefited greatly from Sol's largesse. We had many a good talk on the Menemsha breakwater as Sol hauled in fish he never ate himself. What he taught me about the ins and outs of Soviet policy in between baiting his hook has been invaluable. Years later I paid him back in some degree by carrying to him a generous contribution in Time, Inc., common stock which Henry Luce wanted him to have to help keep the *New Leader* going.

Spain, at the close of the popular-front period, was the only thing that held the fragmenting New York intellectual Left together. One could attend fund-raising meetings designed, I suppose, to pay for the boat passage of Abraham Lincoln Brigade volunteers, with a warm feeling that it was important to keep the Spanish Civil War from becoming a rehearsal for greater anti-Fascist collapses to come. Alas, even Spain was fated to become a source of intense disillusion before Franco's victory killed what John Dos Passos had called the "republic of honest men."

It was Dos Passos' own story that brought word to New York that the Stalinist united front in Spain was a cheat. With all the goodwill in the world Dos Passos had tried to cooperate with Archibald MacLeish and others in funding and making a film on the "Spanish earth." But in Spain Dos Passos discovered that the Stalinists were more interested in fighting Trotskyists and anarcho-syndicalists than they were in helping Republicans to oppose Fascists.

Dos was particularly revolted by the Communist murder of one of his good anarchist friends. His decision to return to New York and tell what was happening to betray the cause of the Spanish Loyalists led to his famous break with Ernest Hemingway. As Bill White, the son of William Allen White of the *Emporia Gazette*, recalled hearing the story from Dos Passos, Hemingway warned Dos that the "critics in New York" would kill him if he tried to expose the gangster strategy of the Stalinists. Whereupon Katy Dos Passos, Dos's anti-Stalinist first wife, said in her breathless way, "Ernest, that's the most opportunist thing I've heard in all my life."

Curiously, during all the Leftist fratricidal struggles, I managed to maintain friendly relations with Malcolm Cowley, Hamilton Basso, Betty Huling, and others in a *New Republic* orbit suspected of Stalinist proclivities. Later, on my leave of absence from *Fortune* to write *The American Stakes*, Malcolm took a weekly review from me for the *New Republic*. Maybe he was not such a Party liner after all. His wife Muriel expressed her own skepticism by saying, "There's too much killing going on in Russia."

The problem of maintaining old friendships became acute for me when the question of Communism in the American Civil Liberties Union arose. I had joined the ACLU at Roger Baldwin's invitation. The ACLU fought many good fights, but it was hard to reconcile its professed principles with Harry Ward, a Soviet sympathizer, presiding over its deliberations; and the presence at board meetings of Elizabeth Gurley Flynn, a Communist Party member, was always disconcerting. Roger Baldwin's own attitude was a bit mystifying, for he admired Lenin and made "exceptionalist" excuses for the Russians. In time I felt called upon to resign from the Union.

But I never could break with Roger Baldwin as a person. Our oldest daughters were born in the same hospital at the same hour in April of 1938, and Roger and I suffered the same uncomfortable mixture of anticipation and worry as we waited outside the delivery room for news. Roger was always the most generous of friends; he and his wife Evelyn gave us the freedom of their marvelous stretch of south shore beach at Mememsha in Martha's Vineyard, and the Baldwin tennis court, situated out of the wind under a bluff, was ours at almost any hour of the day.

What made Roger Baldwin a particularly delightful companion was his ability to forget politics. He was a born naturalist who actually preferred canoeing on the upper Hackensack and Passaic rivers in New Jersey to spending time at his Martha's Vineyard summer home. Fresh water wildness and the bigger variety of birds appealed to him more than salt water gulls and terns. He had a still unblighted chestnut tree on the walk to his beach which he carefully pointed out to visitors. I'll never forget the note of horror in his voice when he said, "Norman Thomas talks about politics even in the woods." It was as if Norman Thomas had excommunicated himself from the human race.

Living in Greenwich Village and consorting with editors, writers, and publishers' representatives who were all touched in varying degrees by the felt need to go Left might have led me into serious distortions in my conduct of the *Times* daily book column. I think I guarded against this by limiting polemic writing largely to the *New Republic*, to Calverton's *Modern Monthly*, and to *Common Sense*, the new liberal magazine edited by Alfred Bingham and Selden Rodman. Looking back on the period, I find it remarkable how little the First New Deal in Washington touched the Manhattan intellectuals. At V.F. Calverton's and Charlie Studin's parties in the Village it was taken for granted that F.D.R. would fail and more revolutionary days would come. We could see the Washington failures as the "sick-chicken case" dealt a Supreme Court death to top-down planning. But the writers did not regard the New Deal "for real" until, with the continuing deepening of depression, Washington began to come through with writers' projects that gave employment to hungry wordsmiths who could demonstrate a facility to write guide books.

For the book column I tried to maintain a balance. There were controversies that had little to do with the running controversy about Communism. When the mail man dumped a four-volume translation of Vilfredo Pareto on my desk I knew I was in for taking part in an exciting fight. Bernard De Voto had been sticking his neck out for Pareto and was being shot down for it. A quartet attributed to Alexander Laing was circulating at publishers' cocktail parties. It went:

> Bernard De Voto
> A fellow of noto,
> Went down to defeato
> Because of Pareto.

I tried to do my duty in presenting Pareto for what he was despite the manifest impossibility of reading all four volumes in a given week. It was easier dealing with a book by Albert Jay Nock on Henry George. I always loved Nock's shapely sentences, but I found it cause for comment that it was only Thomas Jefferson who rated a deferential "Mr." in front of his name in a Nock book. My comment drew a one-line letter from Nock. It read: "Young man, know your betters."

My willingness to try to give a quarterly-review depth to the column whenever a really serious work came along did just as much to excite young college intellectuals as my hospitality to an occasionally good proletarian novel. Alfred Kazin, who became one of our better literary critics, wrote to me to tell me what my columns meant to young students riding the subway. He dropped in on me one day and, impressed with his intensity, I gave him an introduction to Malcolm Cowley at the *New Republic*.

In his book, *Starting Out in the Thirties*, Kazin gave me some credit for launching him on a career. He tempered his praise by saying that I disappointed him in subsequent years by my inability to talk about girls and music with him.

I can only say that I have always been puzzled by talk about music as opposed to listening to it. I do much of my writing at home in a room that is just ten steps away from the studio in which my wife conducts her modern-dance classes in the Doris Humphrey method. When her students are performing to Vivaldi, Corelli, or Bach, I find it very easy to write. When my son comes home and puts on the rock music, hard or otherwise, I find it disconcerting. I love Vivaldi, and I never tire of watching any company stage my wife's reconstruction of Doris Humphrey's dance to Bach's *Air of the G-string*. It is a lovely spiritual dance to equally lovely spiritual music. But talk about the music by a non-technical listener degenerates inevitably into adjectivitis. If Alfred Kazin had tried me, I think I could have kept him going for an evening repeating words to Cole Porter that, unfortunately, I haven't the voice to sing. As for talk about girls, New Englanders don't wear their hearts on their sleeves. I once watched Alfred Kazin as he stared entrancedly at a spirited *Time* researcher named Felice Swados. All I can say is that I approved his taste.

Another visitor who was stimulated by my reviews was a ghost from the past named Harold Stearns. As a young intellectual of the Wilsonian period, Stearns had written a discerning book called *Liberalism in America* and had edited a thunder-clap symposium, the famous—or notorious—*Civilization in the United States*. Unlike Mencken, whose views about the zoo-like quality of life in America were similar to Stearns's own, Harold Stearns chose to do his laughing at a distance in Paris. He was the first exile to depart and the last to return. Paris meant drinking and horse races, but the depression had made these too expensive. Anyway, the action had moved away from Montparnasse. Stearns had become bored.

He came into my cubbyhole one day looking like a burned-out planet. But the planet still had some flash. Knowing a look of hunger, I offered Stearns some eating money as one newspaper man to another. He took it gratefully, saying he was waiting to be paid for a couple of reviews he had written for the *Herald-Tribune*. Then he launched into his story. He wanted to signal his return from exile by editing a new symposium on America Now. He had printed Van Wyck Brooks's famous lament that a sustained literary career was impossible in the America of the teens. What he wanted from me was an essay pointing out that sustained careers had become possible in the America of the '30s. Hemingway, Fitzgerald, Edmund Wilson, and Van Wyck Brooks himself had proved the error of Brooks's original thesis. I agreed to help Stearns with his project, and did the essay. Though his health was precarious due to his decade of dissipation in Paris, Harold Stearns carried through with his new symposium idea. He also wrote an interesting and appealing autobiography before he died, *The Street I Know*.

A second burned-out planet followed Stearns into my office, drawn by some remark I had made about the muckrakers of the early century. I was amazed to discover that I was talking to S.S. McClure, who can legitimately be called the father of American investigative journalism. Alas, what he had to offer was hardly acceptable to the young radicals of the '30s whom he hoped to move. He wanted to sell Mussolini.

Though a dollar was a dollar in the 1933-36 period, it was impossible to save any money on my book-column pay, which never exceeded $100 a week until I got a $25 raise in 1936. Wanting desperately to have a *pied-a-terre* in the country where it would be possible to raise children with some access to greenery and sunlight, I took on a supplementary $100-a-month task of summarizing the books of the month for *Current History* magazine. What I received for an extra job that was tough enough when piled on top of my five daily deadlines per week went into the savings bank. In time it became enough for a down payment on a Cape Cod house in Cheshire, Connecticut, which came cheaply because of the depression and the distance from New York City. I remember the strange denuded feeling of finding myself with less than $10 in cash after clearing the legal expenses that went with buying a house and the car that was necessary to get to it. But my wife and I made out.

Doing some of my work in the country took me away from the radical Greenwich-Village atmosphere. I missed the arguments that I had had with Kenneth Burke, who lived just a few doors away from me on Bank Street. But I found more time to apply a Burke theory that novelists and dramatists must not suddenly reverse the "arrows of expectancy" when midstream in a story or play. The Burke theory explained the exasperation which some readers felt with Scott Fitzgerald's *Tender is the Night*. I loved that book in spite of its technical failure, and, with Burke's inadvertent help, I think I did a top-notch review of it. Years later, in 1971, Professor Matthew Bruccoli, biographer of John O'Hara and James Gould Cozzens, and editor of the Fitzgerald-Hemingway Annual, paid me the compliment of referring to my "two splendid reviews of *Tender is the Night* in 1934." "Your follow-up review," he wrote to me, "is one of the high points of American reviewing." I would like to think I did other reviews as discerning as those I wrote, with Burke at my elbow, of Scott Fitzgerald. Some great novels appeared in the early '30s as Thomas Wolfe, Hemingway, Dos Passos, James Cozzens, and John O'Hara were producing in stride. And Katherine Anne Porter wrote some first-rate short stories. I had the opportunity to write about them all. But I haven't found a Bruccoli to boast of me across the board. And Kenneth Burke did not have a theory to cover every type of novel.

Living part-time in the country and getting my hands into the soil of a garden had an undoubted calming effect. When I made the acquaintance of Katherine Gauss Jackson, the daughter of Princeton's Dean Gauss, at Scribner's, where she helped Fritz Dashiell edit *Scribner's Magazine*, I picked up a strand of the '30s' revolt that looked to agrarian decentralization rather than big-labor hegemony as the cure for our troubles.

Kay Jackson was, in her quiet way, a doer. With her good friends Herbert and Eleanor Chilton Agar, she helped start a magazine called *Free America*, which brought a much-needed note of self-help into a dialogue that had been dominated by the statists.

Agar was a curious eclectic: he believed passionately in Jeffersonian goals for America, yet he held that a class system was best for Britain. (Years later, after divorcing Eleanor Chilton, who was quite an aristocratic-looking girl herself, he married into the British aristocracy.) His statement that the Tennessee Valley, with its TVA, had become the "great hopeful region of America," did not jibe with his feeling that people must stop looking to government for their salvation. But the *Free America* group, who had their connections with the Tennessee Agrarians who clustered around Allen Tate and Robert Penn Warren, were not ideologues. They were quite willing to accept public support for big dams and power installations as long as the electricity generated by government money ran milking machines on small family farms.

The *Free America* program seemed quite consistent with a book by Marquis Childs, *Sweden, the Middle Way*, which Eugene Davidson and Norman Donaldson of the Yale University Press brought into my office one day. During the period of my transit from socialism to a revived trust in a non-statist voluntarism tempered with trust-busting, I found a compatible half-way house in Mark Childs' Scandinavian Utopia. But eventually that, too, seemed to involve too much government interference for a good libertarian's taste.

When I quit the *Times* book-page job in 1936, Kay Jackson prevailed upon me to do a monthly round-up of books for *Scribner's Magazine*. I followed her later to *Harper's Magazine*, where I continued to do a monthly book section with her assistance. Kay's infinite patience enabled me to keep functioning as a reviewer on the side during ten years of non-book work for Harry Luce. She kept *Free America* going through the war years, and when I couldn't get a critique welcoming Hayek's *The Road to Serfdom* into *Life* magazine she took it for *Free America* publication. Publicist John McClaughry, who ran a Foundation for Liberty and Community in Vermont before moving into the Reagan White House, traces something of his own development to *Free America's* pioneering. Kay Jackson would have been thrilled to know that her influence, at one remove, had become part of a McClaughry-inspired 1980 Republican platform plank that stressed the need for the sort of decentralized neighborliness ("family and community") that *Free America* espoused.

The Rooseveltian reforms of the First New Deal, which depended on centralized control, never panned out. But we had not reckoned with F.D.R.'s plasticity—he, as the quarterback, was always willing to gamble on a new play. In 1936 the stage was set for the Brandeisians who, with

Tommy Corcoran and Ben Cohen pulling the strings, proposed a return to a trust-busting policy that would be congenial to the decentralizers. Tired of the New York City literary atmosphere, tired of Granville Hicks' taunts that I had never done anything for Marxian labor, I was ready for something that would bring me close to Second New Deal action. It was all a bit nebulous in my mind, but when Archibald MacLeish suggested that I might like to work for *Fortune* magazine, I was ready to listen.

Old Charlie Lincoln, the Pulitzer editor who had come to the *Times* as an advisor after the failure of the *New York World*, thought it quite marvelous that I would be willing to give up a daily by-line for *Fortune* anonymity. He told me to go. The irony of it was that I managed to keep my own identity, including the by-line, alive through a long association with Henry Luce in ways that neither Charlie Lincoln nor I could foresee.

Chapter 7

B ill Troy's library at Yale was my first Alma Mater; *Fortune* Magazine was my second. When I finally succumbed to the invitation offered by Archibald MacLeish to join its staff in February of 1936, I was still a New York literary liberal. I was not quite a fellow traveler of the Communists, for I had those run-ins with Walter Duranty and the *New Masses*; nor was I quite a socialist, for I had equivocal feelings about the State. But I still believed that big business was a conspiracy against the anti-trust acts, and I still thought that unions were sacrosanct. In the fall, I would vote for Roosevelt, not out of any conviction that the New Deal had logical consistency but simply because no "liberal" of the mid-'30s could conceivably be Republican. I was still willing to be a watchful waiter about the "Russian experiment."

The stress of working for *Fortune* tore me loose from all my preconceptions. First of all, there were the intermittent contacts with Hary Luce. Unlike Ochs of the *Times*, who seldom visited his city room, Luce was very much the working journalist; when Wilder Hobson, the first President of the Time, Inc., Newspaper Guild chapter, waited on him to inform him that *Time* and *Fortune* were to be unionized, Luce's immediate—and quite characteristic—response was a question, "Why can't I join, too?" The class war, which was then Topic A with any New York intellectual who pretended to be "in," always bored Luce. He had never had much use for economics, and the idea of a fixed "wages fund" would have thoroughly mystified him. His idea of a guild—and Heywood Broun's new union of newspaper workers was calling itself just that—was one that would be interested primarily in craft matters. Good pay would naturally flow out of competence. So, naïve though it appeared in the savage mid-'30s, Luce saw no reason for excluding people on the hiring end of journalism from a guild organization. As I knew from what had happened to my paycheck after quitting the *Times* for Time, Inc., Luce had proved his good faith toward the working journalist by doubling the salary ranges then prevalent in New York. He, more than Heywood Broun and the Guild, was responsible for putting editorial employees on a par with the men who scurried up the advertising for the press.

Luce's idea of play was to mix it with work and to make it part of a competitive scheme of life. Max Ways has called Luce the most "attentive" man of his time, and a party was always an excuse with Harry to pump someone, or to listen for journalistic leads in casual conversation. At the week-end parties at his Greenwich, Connecticut, home, he was interested on the tennis court in "Pres" (Senator Prescott) Bush's big serve, but even in walking around the net to change sides he couldn't resist asking political questions of a politically knowledgeable opponent. At tennis Luce, who made up in competitiveness what he lacked in form, bored in just as he did in talking. Once, when we were playing on the same side, we fell behind 0-4. Luce' annoyance, though held in leash, was obvious in the increased forward thrust of his head. I didn't dare miss a shot, and we finally won a long match. It may have been the Luce seriousness that provoked John Lodge,a sometime tennis guest, to swear picturesquely in Italian. John Lodge didn't care whether he won or lost as long as he could play with panache.

I can't say that I was ever one of Luce's intimates (it is doubtful that he had real intimates), but he could be confiding when he sensed that you were willing to go his way. He had absolute integrity when it came to questions of ultimate philosophy, but his view of tactics as opposed to strategy was flexible in the extreme. Though he thought in terms of considered game plans, he was a thorough improviser when it came to matters of weekly presentation. He was a stutterer, not because of any speech defect, but simply because his mind continually raced ahead of his ability to finish a sentence. Sometimes he had changed his mind before the sentence could be completed. His eyebrows, beetling in the manner of labor leader John L. Lewis, presided over inquisitorially sharp blue eyes, but the smile beneath a definitely positive nose was kindly enough. All of this made him a paradox in many eyes, confusing those among us who thought we were going his way only to discover that he was about to take one step backward after going two steps forward. He was a Christian who was wrapped up in questions of theology, but he was also a Promethean—and Prometheus, of course, was the mortal who had defied the gods. Luce was too good a journalist to think that there would be much peace in the 20th century, but his temperamental optimism kept betraying his keener judgment at critical moments. A Calvinist and Presbyterian by upbringing, he still was no predestinarian. Temperamentally he could not believe in any fixed "elect." "Emergent evolution" appealed to him, and he often fell into the so-called Gnostic heresy of thinking that Heaven would some day be found on earth. His spiritual compass vibrated between the pessimistic metaphysics of Reinhold Niebuhr and the scientific hopefulness of Teilhard de Chardin and Lecomte du Noüy who thought of man in "breakthrough" terms that made humanity a creative accomplice of the Deity and put little if any limitations on our earthly future.

Luce's failure to see Communism for what it is, the cow that birthed the calf of Facism, was somehow bound up with his gnostic hopefulness. Never soft on Hitler as he had been on Mussolini for "unwopping the Wops" (despite his complete lack of race prejudice, he was wryly amused by the phrase used by *Time's* foreign editor Laird Shields Goldsborough for what in the '20s seemed to have been Mussolini's achievement), he was so contemptuous of Communist economic theory that he utterly slighted the perverted evangelical appeal of Marxism. He could say on one day that "Communism is cancer" (meaning that once it "got hold" of a country the disease would prove irreversible). But on another day he could write, as he did in December of 1965, that "Communism becomes every day more irrelevant to the future of the world, both because of its economic incompetence and its absurd philosophy. . . ." He told me that he had felt in his bones that if the West failed to topple Hitler it would have been "finis" for Christian civilization. This was prelude to a further statement that he didn't feel the same way about the Communists; although Russia, with the atom, was a danger, it could be wangled.

So the backing and filling about Communism was always reflected in Harry Luce's editorial treatment of the Cold War. Luce kept two sets of editors at work on the problems raised by our forced alliance with Joe Stalin during and after World War II. One set, headed by Willi Schlamm, his close adviser on foreign affairs for the war and immediate post-war period, and by Whittaker Chambers on *Time* magazine, dealt with Communism as an implacable menace. In the counter camp, Teddy White, *Time's* Chungking correspondent, and John Osborne in the *Time* home office, were no such die-hards on the subject of possible eternal cooperation between an increasingly social democratic West and the Communists of both Russia and China. There was consternation at the time of Yalta in several Time, Inc., cubicles when Whit Chambers got his famous "Ghosts on the Roof" fable into the "book" at *Time.* The fable, which told about the landing of Czar Nicholas on the Yalta roofs with the announcement that he had become a Marxist because the Bolsheviks were achieving Imperial Russia's immemorial aims in foreign policy, caused a lot of laughter, but it didn't seem at all funny to the fellow travelers. The fight between the two forces for space in *Time* veered this way and that, and Luce, who knew the value of good journalistic theatre, let it rip.

The tension sometimes produced exciting journalism, but it did little to promote any sound long-term assessment of Marxism in the *Time* high command. Some of Luce's most trusted lieutenants were only secondarily concerned with ideology or intellectual direction anyway. Editorial director John Billings, though temperamentally a conservative, once lightly proclaimed that he had to hire Lefties for technical reasons in order to "get out the paper," and Dan Longwell, Luce's "favorite Middle Westerner" who ran *Life* for years, was more wrapped up in cultural trends than in geopolitical questions. (It was Longwell who said of some political zealots on *Life* that "If they don't like it here let 'em work for the *Survey Graphic*.") Luce deferred to his lieutenants in the smaller decisions, and he did not disturb personnel if everything seemed to be functioning. It was pretty clear that Harry Luce liked to keep such anti-Communists as Whit Chambers, Calvin Fixx, Bob Cantwell, Willi Schlamm, Charley Murphy, John Davenport, and young Henry Grunwald (then Whit Chambers' protégé) on tap, but he wasn't letting them get on top.

Luce quarreled with Teddy White, but not irremediably; he let the separate "foreign" and the "international" departments of *Time* contradict each other on Russia in bewildering ways. Willi Schlamm tried to warn Luce that supporting the U.N. at San Francisco would lead to unforseen woes (Willi predicted the Soviet use of the veto), but was told that no journal that wished to keep its influence could afford to go against "world organization" and an approach to "world law" (always a passion with Luce), no matter how futile it promised to be. As an ironic commentary on this whole period, Roy Alexander, *Time's* managing editor, laughingly noted a switchover on the part of John Osborne in the late '40s. "John," he said at lunch one day to an Osborne who had come to admire James Forrestal, "you sound just like Whit Chambers."

By this time Harry Luce was sounding less and less like Whit Chambers. Luce protected Whit up to a point, but he was not taking the Cold War as a fighting matter. He was more concerned with the arithmetical distortions of Joe McCarthy than he was with the possibility that somewhere, behind the Wisconsin Senator's inability to handle figures, grammar, and nice gradations, there was the genuine problem of Communist infiltration in Washington. Well before the "McCarthy period," I did a piece for *Life* that took the form of an open letter to Robert Morss Lovett, who had just gone to Washington as an assistant Secretary of State. Ray Murphy, the so-called "cop of the State Department," had told me about the softness of many State Department key people on China and Russia, and Loy Henderson had corroborated some of the details. The piece, as it developed, was more Ray Murphy's than my own. Years later Vic Lasky laughingly accused me of "starting McCarthyism" with the open letter, but Lovett himself, after he had returned to Wall Street, said he had found me quite accurate. Luce himself passed it at the time, but the burden of it did not stick with him.

I was always close to Whit Chambers and Willi Schlamm and to *Fortune* writer Charlie Murphy, and they spoke freely to me of their struggles with Harry Luce's hesitancies. Assigned to do a close-up of the Devil for *Life* magazine, to which he also contributed his marvelous articles on the history of civilization, Whit Chambers remarked one day that "sometimes I find the Devil is Harry Luce." Whit meant it only facetiously, for he had both reverence and gratitude for his employer, but he was subsequently shaken when, after the Hiss case had hit the headlines, Time Inc., for reasons of its public relations, officially put a good deal of open water between its corporate self and its troubled and embattled ex-editor. Though Chambers was always the most charitable of people, he felt Luce had let him down. After his vindication by the court decision that Alger Hiss had committed perjury, Whit couldn't resist a feeling of admittedly malicious satisfaction that it was the *Saturday Evening Post* rather than *Life* that got the magazine rights to his *Witness*. As for Harry Luce, he had been miffed by one thing in particular: Whit Chambers had never told him he had been an underground Communist courier.

For his own part, Charlie Murphy never did get over Luce's concurrence in *Life's* decision to kill the four-part series on Chiang Kai-shek which he, as a favored Luce writer, had done as part of a Far Eastern assignment in the immediate post-war period. Chiang was then the bete noire of all the Western "liberals," and, after the failure of the Marshall mission to China to bring the Kuomintang and the Communists together, he was being beaten from pillar to post in his effort to hold the mainland against the Soviet-armed troops of Mao Tse-tung. John Billings, as the Time, Inc., editorial superviser, had passed the word along from Luce's advisory board that it was "time to get off the hook of Chiang." Though Harry Luce never turned on Chiang personally, he decided at this point to take one of his tactical backward steps. The Murphy articles never appeared.

Later, when I was doing the editorials for *Life* under Luce's intermittent supervision, I had occasion to know how Charlie Murphy felt. I had been told on a Tuesday that the week's editorial was to deal with General George Marshall's blindness in the China situation. I worked hard of a Wednesday to give ordered and factually supported editorial expression to Luce's feelings about Marshall's inability to see that Chiang needed American help to counter the Maoist possession of the arms which the Soviets had taken from the Japanese in Manchuria. General Albert Wedemeyer, whom Marshall called "too big for his britches," had made known his opinion about the necessity of stopping the Communists on the Asian mainland. On Thursday, when the deadline for closing the editorial page was approaching, Harry Luce had sudden tactical qualms. Yes, he said, the editorial was what he had wanted. But, if it were to be printed, would it do any good? Wouldn't it put George Marshall's back up? After much debate with himself, Harry came through with a new order on Friday; I was to "recast" the editorial, giving most of the space to fulsome praise for what Marshall had done to put war-riddled Western Europe on its feet. Then, in a final paragraph, I was to lament that Marshall had failed to do for China what he had done for Europe. Luce hadn't changed his mind; he had simply changed his tactics. I couldn't quarrel with his decision, for the *Life* page belonged to him. It was the one acknowledged pulpit he had in all of his magazines. But working for a person who could pull tactical switches at the eleventh hour was not particularly comfortable.

Tactics, in time, gave way to something else: a real conviction that the Cold War had not really been too serious. In 1966 Luce was to write, "The Cold War, we now hope, is thawing—may even be an outmoded expression." And, in a "pre-Czechoslovakia" jaunt through Eastern Europe in the same year of 1966 with some U.S. businessmen, Luce surmised that Communism was dying in the captive nations as an ideology, and that "bridge-building" might be the way to wean the satellites back to the West. Whether, after the Soviet tanks had moved into Prague to kill the hopes for a new Czech "springtime," Luce would have allowed *Time* to proclaim Willy Brandt as the 1970 Man of the Year for his Ostpolitik policy of seeking accommodation with Moscow is a nice question. But the basis for such a choice can be found in Harry Luce's own temporizing on the subject of the Cold War.

One can easily forgive Harry Luce his tactical zigs and zags, his blowing hot and cold on the issue of getting along with Communists, simply because he was so much better both as a human being and as an editor than practically any other big publisher in America. The opportunity he gave me to study the American business sytem close up as a *Fortune* writer saved me from going into middle age as just another New York liberal, and I will remain forever grateful to him for putting me on a personal Road to Damascus. After he wrote his "American Century" editorial in 1941, I, in an uncharacteristic moment of brashness as one of his hired hands, insisted that he let me answer him. With characteristic courtesy and willingness to listen, he let me go ahead—and did me the honor to include my objections in the book which publisher John Farrar made out of the Luce editorial and several commentaries thereon by Dorothy Thompson, Robert Sherwood, and others.

When I read my own words over again in the days of our retreat from Southeast Asia, I marveled at my own prophetic statement that we would never have an "American Century" for the simple reason that "Uncle Sam would someday desert his trusting friends." Uncle Sam would "desert them," I said, "the moment that his internal troubles became *more* important to *more* Americans than the world situation." (My italics in the original.) Does this sound like 1972 or even the four years of Jimmy Carter? If it does, I take no joy in it. I wish with all my heart that Harry Luce had been right about the American Century, and my only lament is that he helped undermine his own position by his failure to see that Communism and Nazism are fundamentally one and the same thing.

Knowing him for the intuitive man that he was, I feel that he would have come around to feel in his bones as he had felt about Nazism, that if Soviet Russia ever gets the atomic jump on us it will be finis to Christian civilization. I couldn't prove that this would be Luce's attitude, but he could, on occasion, be a most daring man. And now, with the Soviets threatening to get a first-strike jump on us, is surely the time for a response that will save us from the coming of the Russian Century. The Luce prophecy of an American Century needs some subtle reworking, but who is there to do it? Echo answers, "Who?"

Working closely with Luce was always exciting. His feeling for the form of a story was unmatched. Every so often he would step in and edit an entire issue of one of the magazines; the result was always electric. In between his big editing sprees he kept watch on the stories that interested him. He liked abrupt, sometimes jagged, transitions and would occasionally advise roughing up a smoothly articulated story just to jolt the reader awake. Once, after I had turned in an extremely long *Fortune* article on the Kelly-Nash political machine of Chicago, Eric Hodgins, the *Fortune* Managing Editor, told me to cut some of the detail. But Luce, with his almost Henry Jamesian sense of the relation between form and content, sent down an order to preserve the detail on the ground that successful ward politics is built out of the strict attention of district politics to very small things. Jack Jessup, *Life's* editorial writer for many years, says that Harry Luce's esthetic sense had blind spots. As a profound student of what Eliot Janeway liked to call "the Luce vibrations," Jessup could have been right about his boss's failure to appreciate ballet and abstract painting. Nevertheless, when it came to understanding how to present a story, Luce had a novelist's sensitivity to the importance of the seeing eye. I recall my wrestling with a long article on "The War at Sea." The first half of it had gone off very well; the second part straggled out. Luce read the first draft, accurately noted that I had told the first part of the story from the point of view of the British Admiralty, and then picked me up for my failure to identify myself with any seeing eye for the second part. "Tell the second part from the point of view of the Germans looking out past Heligoland to the oceans," he said. After that the rewriting came easy.

When I went to *Fortune* at the end of Franklin Roosevelt's first term, I thought I was to concentrate entirely on political and sociological stories. Arch MacLeish, who was trying to clear the decks for a trip to Japan, had been told that he could get away for three months if he could find a substitute for himself to do a story of the Nine Old Men of the anti-Rooseveltian Supreme Court. I was acceptable to Hodgins, the Managing Editor, and to Ralph McAllister Ingersoll, the *Fortune* publisher, probably because they knew me as a liberal who would presumably favor the Stone-Brandeis wing of the court over the McReynolds strict constructionists. Everything went smoothly as MacLeish's great friend, Professor Felix Frankfurter of the Harvard Law School, gave me off-the-record briefings at his home in Cambridge on the Court membership. ("Felix" was very much behind everything in 1936.) I had a particularly warm two hours with Justice Harlan Stone, a distant cousin of mine through my Grandmother Elizabeth Stone Davis's side of the family. The article came off well with Hodgins, although he complained that I hadn't shown much sweat in writing it. (How could I after the discipline of writing five book columns a week for the *Times*?) But when the article went up to Luce he quibbled about my adulation of Brandeis. "Yes," he said sarcastically, "I understand Brandeis is a great man among the myrmidons." The article ran as written, though it was not all to Luce's taste. It was a long time before I came to accept the Luce point of view that the law should be the law, not a branch of free-wheeling sociology. Despite my blindness, Luce apparently saw more in me than a conventional liberal. MacLeish, as a poet, could get away with refusing to do corporation stories for *Fortune*. But Luce, subtly, had other designs on me. He didn't mind my substituting for MacLeish periodically in covering the New Deal beat for *Fortune* in Washington, but he wanted me to "do the corps," as he put it. He had liked my book column in the *Times*, as I knew from a story about me in *Time*, written by Joe Thorndike (later the publisher of *American Heritage*) under the heading of "He Gets a Box from Mr. Ochs." My anti-business radicalism was something else again. Luce wanted me to understand business as I had certainly shown no competence in doing as a critic of books about the American scene in the first business-baiting days of the New Deal. So it was that, after writing about such things as Youth in College, the Co-operative Movement, and the U.S. Lighthouse Service in MacLeish's absence, I was thrown headfirst into the world of American industry at the very time when Franklin D. Roosevelt, prodded by Tommy Corcoran, Ben Cohen, and Harry Hopkins, was in full cry against the "economic royalists." It was to be a strange and invigorating experience, and I was to come out of it a different person.

The "corporation story" was *Fortune's* distinct contribution to the literature of business. It was Harry Luce's idea, and Luce's alone, to offer a magazine that would present business to itself without fear or favor, differing from the muckraking magazines of the earlier century on the one hand and the puff-sheet approach of the 1920s as exemplified by *The American Magazine* on the other. Britten Hadden's notions of style, derived from Homer ("the wine-dark sea"), had colored *Time* magazine; *Fortune* was to be something different, although the concept of the writer-researcher team was to be carried over from one magazine to the other.

The *Fortune* style was to be far less mannered than *Time* style; it would not deal in the insulting adjectival characterization. New York City's Mayor LaGuardia could have taken justifiable exception to *Time's* "fat, rancid, garlic-smelling Fiorello LaGuardia," and Bernard Baruch always disliked *Time* for calling him "speculator Baruch." But neither LaGuardia nor Baruch had any objection to collaborating with *Fortune* editors, for they knew they would get courteous treatment even when it was critical, as it very often was.

For *Fortune* researchers, Luce wanted young women who preferably had had some experience in business. Elida Griffin, for example, had worked in a bank, which fortunately had not destroyed her merry attitude. The prevalence of graduates from Ivy League institutions caused Eliot Janeway, in a ribald moment, to say that we were dominated by a "dictatorship of the Vassar girls"—and so we were up to a point. But there were girls who weren't "Vassar," such as Nika Standen, a Junoesque character who had been schooled in many languages in Geneva. I will never forget the shocked silence when Nika started off an interview with Mayor Kelly of Chicago by asking him how he had made his money. Nika specialized in calling attention to the fact that the king had no clothes. Today, in a second career, Nika—as Nika Hazleton—writes an entrancing delectations page for Bill Buckley's *National Review*.

No one, not even a league of Vassar girls, could dominate the crew that Luce had assembled to use novelistic techniques and poetical images to describe the world of business. John Davenport, Russell's younger brother, joined the staff after a year off from journalism to study economics at Yale, which gave him the special knowledge that made his writings on Lord Keynes so definitive. But John, like his brother, had been a poet before he had become journalist and economist. Charlie Murphy, one of the great unsung journalists of his time, came on after a year spent in Antarctica with Admiral Byrd. Charlie had great skill as a ghost; he had done Admiral Byrd's book, and, at a later date, he produced a most royal "autobiography" for the abdicated Duke of Windsor.

Dwight MacDonald, a Yale graduate who was destined to pass through every radical ideology on the books, wrote so disrespectfully about the steel industry for *Fortune* that he had the House of Morgan on Luce's neck for it. But the poetical quality of Dwight's steel article got high honors from poet Arch MacLeish. I had known Dwight in college; indeed, I had been a member of the Yale Lit. board that had accepted Dwight's first story about a school master who was a petty tyrant of boys. When I first encountered him in the *Fortune* offices in the Chrysler Building, he was hard at work at his desk in the so-called Ralph McAllister Ingersoll Memorial Wing doing some complicated arithmetic. When I asked him what he was up to, he said he was trying to figure whether the income from his investments would support him if he were to quit *Fortune* and go to freelancing. Dwight admired me for a brief period because I served on the Committee for Asylum for Leon Trotsky; and I admired him during the period when he was editing his own magazine called *Politics*, in which he satirized the liberals who "spoke Wallese, a debased provincial dialect," after the manner of Henry Wallace. Since then Dwight has relapsed into his own form of Wallese, and I, from his point of view, have degenerated into an apologist for the bourgeois order. In the mid-'30s, however, we could function in friendly comradeship as part of a unique *Fortune* team that included a canny esthete and critic (Louis Kronenberger), a temporary refugee from the Yale Law School (Fred Rodell), several novelists (James

Gould Cozzens, Robert Cantwell, Charlie Wertenbaker, and Green Peyton), a strange poet-naturalist (Edmund Gilligan), a student of jazz music (Wilder Hobson), awards-winning poets (James Agee, Arch MacLeish), an ex-advertising writer (Jack Jessup), and unclassifiable originals like Bill White, the son of *Emporia* editor William Allen White. Jessup impressed Managing Editor Hodgins with his "very deceptive slow ball," and ultimately went on from his brilliant corporation-story narratives to become Luce's favored mouthpiece as a *Life* editorialist. Bill White could never take a *Fortune* assignment seriously; he hammed up an article on birth control ("The Accident of Birth") by presenting a little scene in which lawyer Morris Ernst sent out to a drug store for a pessary to convince a judge that nobody need lack for practical information about preventing a conception. This offended Russell, or Mitch, Davenport's sense of gravity, and Bill wasn't long for *Fortune*. He went on to fashion a great career as a *Reader's Digest* writer, a war reporter, and as the author of such first-rate books as *Journey for Margaret* and *Queens Die Proudly*. He surely forgave Mitch Davenport for forcing him to discover his true aptitudes both as a writer and as editor of his father's *Emporia Gazette*, the small-town newspaper with a world orientation.

Fortune would also employ special people for special jobs. John Gunther came in to help with political stories involving Europe, and all he wanted in payment was a few of the fat red pencils that were favored by the Time, Inc., proof readers. Eliot Janeway, then a brash unknown, did some leg work for me on a Westinghouse Electric story. Sometime later, after he had achieved a reputation, he told the *Fortune* management that they might as well hire him on a permanent basis "now—because it will cost you twice as much a year later." A year later he was hired at his own figure to do business news for *Time*.

The photographers were another individualistic crew. Maggie Bourke-White brought her butterfly collection to the office in the Chrysler Building, and Bill Vandivert, doing photographs for my Kelly-Nash Political Machine story, snapped pictues of bookie joints with a camera concealed in his pants, the lens peering from his fly. If it hadn't been for *Fortune's* pioneering with pictures, *Life* would never have managed the great start that made it an overnight success. The irony was that *Fortune* was to make its debut in the period of the Great Depression, when the Rooseveltian view of business ("economic royalists") was ascendant. It prospered in an unlikely period by giving in-depth analytical treatment to labor and the Washington scene as well as to business. And, as I was to discover during the 1940 presidential campaign, it was read just as carefully in the White House as in Wall Street.

I came to *Fortune* sharing Franklin Roosevelt's antipathies toward the business community. As a child of the '20s I had the cynical view: the businessmen preached free competition and fought for the Smoot-Hawley tariff; they said they believed in free association, yet they turned their coal and iron police in Pennsylvania on union organizers. No doubt the hypocrisy was there. But in failing to perceive the deeper reality—that the very size of the continental market forced U.S. business to be competitive—I shared the short-sightedness of my intellectual friends.

It was with a terrific shock, then, to discover that none of the fashionable liberal stereotypes covered the world of business. To begin, the characters involved in the corporate world were far more varied and complex than the characters who formed the lunch groups and went to the cocktail parties in New York literary society. There were Babbitts in business, but they thinned out remarkably in the higher corporate reaches. Every corporation story I did involved me in memorable meetings with vigorous and exciting personalities. I went to Toledo, Ohio, for a look at the Electric Autolite Company with Harold Talbott, a Long Island polo-playing man of wealth who was later to become involved in a purchasing scandal as Secretary for Air in President Eisenhower's Department of Defense. He may have gotten a bum rap for minor indiscretions in dealing with a contractor. Talbott was reputed to be the "Chrysler Corporation man" in Electric Autolite, and he was something of a braggart about his connections and his past. He boasted that he had made his own fortune, which wasn't quite true, but he also resented any imputation that he wasn't to the manor born. He knew his native Ohio backward and forward (he had been president of the Dayton-Wright Company, airplane manufacturers in World War I), and he quite forgot his aristocratic pretensions in telling the local lore as we flew in a small company plane over Ohio and Michigan. He was less perturbed than I was when we narrowly missed a stump in landing in a field at Port Huron, Michigan, and I ended up with considerable respect for his intelligence and charm.

Royce Martin, the Autolite president, was an absolute contrast to Talbott; he disdained the social life of Long Island and even the suburban-Toledo society of Clement Miniger, the chairman of the Autolite board, preferring to return to a home in Lexington, Kentucky, for his week-ends. Martin had had a curious preparation for the motor-accessories business; as a young man he had been Pancho Villa's fiscal agent and had seen to it that the profits of the Juarez gambling establishments (across the Rio Grande from El Paso) went to the "bandit" (which the Woodrow Wilson government considered Villa to be). Martin exuded a frontier air in his Toledo office. Together, the swank Talbott and the hard-boiled Martin ran a tight company, sweating pennies out of the cost of making all the little things that composed the electric nervous system of an automobile. Adam Smith, I thought, would have approved of their company, for it exhibited all the classical virtues claimed for capitalism. It cut costs without sacrificing quality, and it constantly passed on its money savings to the consumer. It did this not because it wanted to, but because it had to in order to keep its market; after all, Chrysler could have ditched it by making its own automotive electrical systems. But regardless of Autolite's motives, competition was working.

The revelation, to me, in the Westinghouse Electric Company, another of my early corporation-story assignments, was Frank Conrad, an inventor with more than 200 patents on his record. Conrad was an anomaly among the engineering-school graduates who worked for Westinghouse; he had never gone beyond the seventh grade. It was said of him that he could intuitively predict the performance of an electrical device before working out the underlying mathematical problem. Self-taught in physics and math, he had invented the pantograph trolley, and it was his radio-receiving set that made Pittsburg's famous KDKA, the first licensed commercial broadcasting company in the U.S., a practical possibility. The man who showed me around the Westinghouse "empire" was a bearded individual named G. Edward Pendray, an ex-*New York Herald-Tribune* science writer who spent his free time in promoting a rocket society that was dedicated to the idea that man was someday destined to go to the moon. His friends considered this a mildly lunatic aberration in an otherwise solid character.

Another vivid personality was Frank Barbour, the chicle expert of the Beechnut Packing Company. He had been the quarterback on that most famous of Yale football teams, the one captained in the '90s by Pudge Heffelfinger ("Hold the ball, McClung is coming, Barbour signals still, Heffelfinger's in the center, win we must and will," as the old song had it). After graduation Barbour had gone to Belize in British Honduras to learn the secrets of good chicle production. It was Barbour's ability to compete with Wrigley in gum that enabled Beechnut to get through the three bad depression years of 1932, 1933, and 1934. People went without eating Beechnut's Mohawk Valley-cured hams and bacon during the depression, but they continued to masticate its gum. Barbour, who thought the New Deal was spoiling the American character, spun some interesting theories about gum, patience, and the will to endure. They contrasted violently with Leon Trotsky's writing about gum chewing as a sign of the vacant capitalist-society mind.

The turning point in my intellectual attitude toward business came during a trip to Michigan to write about the merger of the Kelvinator Corporation, makers of refrigerators, with the Nash Motor Company. I remember staying awake until three o'clock in the morning in an upper berth scribbling a review of a Steinbeck novel for *Scribner's Magazine*, and wondering if Steinbeck's jaundiced opinion of the American economic system was justified. At the end of a morning of interviews at the Kelvinator Plymouth Road plant in Detroit, I had swung back to Steinbeck. Some official of the company who was in charge of relations with the National Electrical Manufacturers Association took my researcher, Emmeline Nollen, and me into his confidence with his boasts about price-fixing. The

15 companies in NEMA, he said, practised a "clean business," meaning that they respected each others' turf and did not chisel on the quoted prices. Emmy Nollen, the daughter of an Iowa college president, looked at me quizzically when our trade-association man turned his back. Here was the evidence for what our skeptical generation just had to believe, that big business practiced universal monopoly.

A couple of days later, however, a production man in the Kelvinator Grand Rapids refrigerator cabinet assembly plant grew confidential about the number of "boxes" that his company made for cut-rate sales by a big mail-order house. This, too, was standard practice in the trade. It was suddenly borne home to me that business was a great tissue of cross-purposes. As General Hugh ("Iron Pants") Johnson said, business was "savage poetry." Instead of giving lip-service to competition and practicing monopoly, the company that belonged to a big trade association really gave lip service to monopoly and practiced competition. Thinking it over, you could see it working all down the line. The retailer had his white sales, the auto dealer shaded the price on the new car by going beyond the book on the turn-in. The "market," in its own halting way, worked.

The high command in Nash-Kelvinator (predecessor of American Motors) was another study in personality differences. The President, George W. Mason, was a fat, indolent-looking man whom one would have sworn was a chronic glutton. Actually, he was a most abstemious eater and incredibly quick in his reflexes. A Dakota farm boy with a passion for machinery, he had owned 23 motorcycles in 46 years and had raced many of them on half-mile tracks. Long before he went to the University of Michigan engineering school, he could take a car apart and put it together again. He had worked for Studebaker and Dodge before going to Chrysler in 1921, where he supervised the sea change of the creaky Maxwell car into the snazzy Chrysler roadster of the early '20s. Although he was a rough outdoorsman in every sense, boasting about his ability as a dry-fly fisherman, Mason had his practical esthetic side. He had a dance choreographer's sense of space, and could spot backtracking on an assembly line at a moment's glance. Whenever he had authority for factory lay-out he changed it. He liked clean lines in all of his products. Once, when shown a new refrigerator model, he said, "Take this cabinet away; it looks like an outhouse." George Romney, who was Mason's protégé when Nash-Kelvinator was in the process of becoming American Motors, gives his old boss much of the credit for killing the Detroit "jello form" shape in automobiles and bringing in the European styling of the Ramblers.

Mason's trouble-shooter, Harold Perkins, was bland, the perfect buffer. I found him hard to deal with in pursuing angles that might have opened up the secret competition that the members of the electrical manufacturing trade association practiced. He employed Eddie Bernays, whom I had known socially in New York, as the Nash-Kelvinator public-relations man, and there was some embarrassment about arguing with an old friend when it came to "negotiating" some details on the final draft of my story. Mason, as it turned out, didn't share his buffer employees' worries. Probably, like Henry Ford and even Henry Ford II, he didn't think writers were worth bothering about.

The more I thought about business in the late years of the '30s, the more remarkable I considered the character of the men whom Harry Luce called "the tycoonery." When New York literary society was almost universally convinced that capitalism had no regenerative powers, the Rockefellers, for instance, decided to go ahead with Rockefeller Center. (Young Nelson was already bitten by his "edifice complex.") I was assigned to do one of the early stories on Rockefeller Center (to which Time, Inc., eventually moved from quarters in the Chrysler Building), and after listening to Todd, Robertson, and Todd, the managers who were in charge of renting three million square feet of carpet space at a time when the competing Empire State Building was only 42 percent occupied, I got a new faith in the business-tycoon's faith. I didn't approve of the fact that the Rockefellers had censored the anti-capitalist frescoes which Diego Rivera, the Mexican Trotskyist painter, had tried to make a permanent feature of a trusting capitalist project, but, as E.B. White of the *New Yorker* was to write, Nelson "owed something to God and Grandpa." Later I could see that it was Rivera, not Nelson Rockefeller, who had been the graceless man.

Some 20 years after doing corporation stories for *Fortune*, I returned to the magazine to write the history of American business that was later published in book form as *The Enterprising Americans*. Depressed by the orthodoxy that explains the 1930s in terms of pump-priming and general political intervention, I thought back to my trips to Pittsburgh and Cleveland, Toledo and Detroit. The headlines of the '30s had been made by such alphabetical combinations as NRA, AAA, SEC, WPA, and TNEC. I had written at great length about the agencies behind these initials. But the New Deal, after all, had failed to put the hordes of unemployed to work; it wasn't until the coming of the war that America began to pick up industrially. What came clear to me after the war was that the business enterprisers of the depressed '30s, placing their faith and their bets on a host of struggling new technologies, had really saved the day for us in war and established the basis for the huge post-war expansion. As I was to write in *The Enterprising Americans*, the '30s witnessed the proliferation of the airlines, the building of the mult-au-matic turret lathe, the discovery of new alloys, the spread of the continuous wide-strip steel mill, the transformation of the chemical industry, the development of synthetic fabrics, the use of computers, and the deepening of the art of pre-testing the market. "The pay-off of all this development," I said, "came in 1941, when it was quickly discovered that our supposedly 'mature' economy, far from 'evenly rotating' in the manner of a textbook model, had been spinning off new things all along . . . it is this all-but-forgotten aspect of the so-called gloomy decade that constitutes the main line of business history, and it is largely virgin territory." If I hadn't broken out of the tight little world of literary New York and gone to work for Harry Luce, I would never have seen what still eludes our Arthur Schlesingers and the others who write what passes for our "history."

The evolution of a point of view is never straightforward. I had gone to *Fortune* magazine as a skeptic of the American businessman's ability to manage his own system. But I was also disillusioned about government power in any manifestation, whether the power rayed out from Communist Moscow, imperialist (as I thought it) London, Fascist Berlin, or New Deal Washington. The corporation story versus the New Deal political story sent one type of dialogue-between-the-two-selves racing through my mind. The barbarities of Nazism versus the balance-of-power conniving of Britain to keep Europe in a state of fragmentation kept another interior dialogue going. Emotionally, as Hitler moved against the Jews and his own German middle-class, I was an interventionist in foreign policy; rationally, and by identification with my own post-World War I generation, I continued to be an isolationist. And then there was the question of Communism and literary New York. I had been turned against the Communists by my experience as a *New York Times* daily book critic, but I was far from clear about my attitude toward socialism when I went to work for Luce. What moved me to take certain stands against the Communists in the mid-'30s was my civil libertarian bias, which had caused me to be outraged by Walter Duranty's casual dismissal of Stalin's "planned famine" which resulted in the liquidation of the kulaks. The storm raised by Stalin's exile of Leon Trotsky, a libertarian matter involving the right of asylum, followed me to Time, Inc., as I was cajoled into joining a Committee for the Defense of Leon Trotsky. Altogether, I was in a state of perpetual ferment as I skipped about from corporation stories in Pittsburgh and Detroit, colloquies with Tommy Corcoran, Jerome Frank, Ben Cohen, and Leon Henderson in Washington, and bruising arguments in New York that were inseparable from mixing with the fellow travelers who believed in the necessity of getting along with Soviet Russia in a united front.

I had not found a reason for voting for Franklin D. Roosevelt until 1936. I was too laggard in clarifying myself to myself to desert Roosevelt for Wendell Willkie in 1940, which I should logically have done.

In 1939, troubled by the swirl of contradictions in my head, I took a short leave of absence from *Fortune* to finish a book, *The American Stakes*. It was a transitional book in many ways, and it didn't take me out of my muddle about all those internal dialogues I had been having. But some things were coming a little clearer. I had lost the pessimism of *Farewell to Reform*, a book in which I had backed into socialism largely because I doubted the ability of businessmen to run their own system. I had had a recovery of nerve, and the either-or attitude to events had disappeared. I saw the democratic state not as the agent of a ruling class, but as something fluid and ragged, the result of a constant tug of forces. (As some reviewer said, I had come to glorify the pressure groups as the guarantors of democracy; Jim Farrell accused me of thinking of democracy as a bargain counter.) I had discovered, thanks to Albert Jay Nock, the concept of social power as something antecedent to political power, though I was not yet too clear about ways and means of spreading the social power and limiting the political power. I had canvassed certain philosophies—anarchism, guild socialism—and rejected them as "blocked roads to freedom" along with the ideas of Soviet gosplanning. I had listened to Leon Henderson and taken him seriously when he said that he wanted to use the Temporary National Economic Committee to work back to an Adam Smith world of fluid prices. Leon's idea was that some compulsory way—say a tax on corporation size—must be found to break up the big oligopolies whose prices were "sticky." The Henderson hint of compulsion was so muffled that I couldn't see it as a contradiction when I went on to praise voluntarism, as represented by the Belloc-Chesterton philosophy of distributism, the consumer cooperative movement, and Ralph Borsodi's experiments in creating subsistence homesteads. I saw the emerging world of the future as consisting of five overlapping economic systems, the small proprietor, the big corporation, the public utility, the government collectivism (the Post Office and TVA), and the cooperative (or private collectivism). I made the observation that "freedom dwells in the interstices of the five economic systems," and was gratified in subsequent years to hear this observation quoted many times.

Of the five books I have written (one was co-authored), *The American Stakes* had the worst sale and is the only one that has been steadily out of print. But every so often someone comes upon it with a sense of personal discovery. My friend John McClaughry, who tried to work up a bill for Senator Percy to spread home ownership and is indefatigably busy prodding politicians to do something effective about enlarging the base of private property, writes that

> frankly, you could delete the parts about foreign policy and the Democratic Party of 1940, revise the remainder, and publish it again. You hit upon the crucial question when you ask how a Jeffersonian state can be re-created in a time of capital-intensive technology and external-war threat . . . unless we find some way to distribute ownership of "social power" (i.e., property) more evenly, we can only come to a situation when political demands force the State to control corporate capitalism, and we slide into "encroaching control"—not by the Guilds, but by the bureaucrats of the State. This is not a way station to the Soviet system; this *is* the Soviet system. I wish to God

this Administration would run through some of the thinking in your book instead of maundering around with questions of how the State can best hand out the fruits of taxation (i.e., robbery) to supplicants—through incomes or services.

One reason for the failure of *The American Stakes* to have at least some impact on its time was the war (the book came out just before the fall of France). As a child of the interwar generation, I was still an isolationist and had made my blueprint for saving the American system for an enlargement of the individual's social power dependent on staying aloof from Europe's quarrels. Physically, it was arguable that we could have kept to an isolationist course in 1940; the intercontinental jet bomber had not yet been made, and the atom bomb and rocket-fired intercontinental missile were still secrets of the laboratory. A split occurred in the middle and late '30s between writers such as Arch MacLeish, who had been of military age during World War I, and those of us who had only experienced as mature individuals the disillusioning aftermath of the war. The MacLeishes quickly lost their pacifism when confronted with the spectacle of Hitler, who revived all the fears that had once been felt about the militarism of the Hohenzollerns. But those of us who had been too young to worry about Kaiser Bill could only remember that Versailles had been a tragic blunder. We saw war only as a repetition of folly and were horrified when Walter Millis, who had fixed our mood with his *The Road to War* and *The Martial Spirit*, threw in with the pro-war forces. But after all, he, too, was of MacLeish's age. We had lost the MacLeishes and the Millises, but we had younger allies, notably Kingman Brewster, a future president of Yale. An admirer of Charles A. Beard, Brewster had visited me at my home in Cheshire, where we sat on a rooftree and talked about the possibility of the "open door at home" and strictly hemispheric defense.

I had taken a leave within my book-writing leave, and had visited the four cities of Cincinnati, Portland (Oregon), Dallas, and St. Louis to moderate a series of "youth on the war" seminars for *McCall's Magazine*. This was in October and November of 1939, at the height of the "phony war," or so-called *sitzkrieg*. The young people of 1939 were virtually of one mind in saying, "Stay out of war." Upon my return to New York I wrote a piece about the young mood for the *New Republic*. I did this at the prodding of Bruce Bliven, the editor, who was then as anti-war as anybody. Three or four months later, Bliven and the rest of the *New Republic* group had become supporters of intervention with the exception of their long-time confrere Edmund Wilson and their economic columnist John T. Flynn. Flynn, an old-fashioned libertarian who combined an effervescent wit with a low-boiling point when his ideals were outraged, used to say that "the *New Republic* is my soap-box; *Collier's* is my banker." He gave up both without a qualm to help found the America First Committee.

After getting my foredoomed book in shape, I went back to *Fortune*
with an eagerness to get on with the business of exploring the world of
business. But *Fortune*, along with the rest of the Luce publications, had
undertaken a new commitment, that of understanding and publicizing the
new world of military preparation and engagement. What followed for me
was a thoroughly schizophrenic year and more in which the journalist in me
quarreled with the isolationist. I had already found myself with no ready
answer when Max Ascoli, who later became the publisher of *The Reporter*,
asked me how I could have done such a sympathetic article on Czechoslovakia and still maintain that the fate of Eastern Europe was primarily a
European concern. I had not gone to Czechoslovakia (the *Fortune* system
was to let researchers do on-the-spot work abroad and feed the material
back to writers in Rockefeller Plaza), but the notes provided by Marcia
Davenport, the extremely talented novelist wife of managing editor Russell
Davenport, were enough to make one fall in love with the country. Marcia,
who later became the special friend of Jan Masaryk, the son of the founder
of the Czechoslovak nation, had a special empathy for her subject, and it
swept me up. When the Sudeten and Munich crises came, I hoped fervently
that the anti-Nazi front in Europe would be able to save the East European
system. But, intellectually, I still felt that it was up to the British, the French,
and the Soviets to do something about their own continent.

The *Fortune* habit of letting the researcher do the foreign traveling was
nicely pitched to getting a maximum amount of work out of the staff
writers. Florence Horn, an engaging Yankee girl from Connecticut who
combined an intense love of gardening (my own diversion since I had
bought what had once been a farm) with a fundamental anti-militarism,
was sent to the Philippines and Hawaii to feed me notes on both places.
Since I had no desire to get into a Pacific war, I let her attitude toward the
military seep through into the first drafts of my stories. Florence had
interviewed General Douglas MacArthur in the Philippines; she thought he
was a grand show-off, and presumably something of a phony. We sent the
first draft of the Philippine article to Captain Bonner Fellers at West Point
for his commentary. Bonner, who was to become a steadfast friend, hurried down to New York, all expostulation about the outrage that had been
done to his hero. The result was some modified prose, but not entirely what
Bonner Fellers had sought. Later, when I had had more opportunity to
study MacArthur's career, I came to see that Bonner was right. Florence
Horn's notes on Hawaii became the basis of a story titled "Hawaii: The
Sugar-Coated Fort." It annoyed important people in Honolulu because of
its Populist attitude toward the Big Five who dominated business in the
islands, and it particularly bothered Harry Luce, who vigorously protested
"Miss Horn's Tugwellian yawp" in a memo to me. But, as was often the
case, Luce let the manuscript stand. I don't know how he explained the
article to his many friends in Hawaii. Since I had never been there I couldn't

very well argue the case one way or another. Tugwellian yawp or not, Florence Horn was a thoroughly trained researcher. Her biases were those of the liberalism of the time, a liberalism which I had only begun to outgrow. Actually, she was not as "Left" as other *Fortune* researchers, coming somewhere between conservative Milly Schwarz and the implacable Elizabeth Sloane, who did the dog work for Ed Kennedy, *Fortune's* crack corporation writer. The paradox was that Miss Sloane, although a convinced Leftist hard-liner, was perfectly trustworthy when it came to checking Ed Kennedy's thoroughly objective articles. She was also something of a skilled psychiatrist, pulling Ed Kennedy out of his occasional bouts of depression which often ended in alcoholic binges. For one who was so able, it was another paradox that Ed Kennedy should so doubt himself. Helen Walker, who researched an article for me on the "labor governors" (George Earle of Pennsylvania and Frank Murphy of Michigan), was another convinced Leftist, but she let her attitudes run off into an amusing whimsy. Governor Earle had contracted mumps, which postponed our trip to Harrisburg to interview him. So, in the research handed to me by Helen Walker, I came across a poem, one stanza of which remains in my memory. It went:

> But think of the joy
> In the hearts of the Pews,
> The anti-Earle Drexels
> Have no anti-mumps views.

Like Elizabeth Sloane, Helen Walker was a reliable hand when it came to checking a perfectly capitalistic fact. The girls had been thoroughly trained by Patricia Divver, the chief of research, to recognize the difference between opinion and factual truth in business stories. Pat, who had a way of softening up big business executives who came complaining about uncomplimentary first drafts, didn't need women's lib to make her way in the Luce empire. She was both astringent and mollifier in a strange proportion. When I did a bad first draft, she was frank to tell me that it was a "turkey"—but she would soften her criticism by offering very worthwhile suggestions for improvement. The editors and writers deferred to her, the researchers took her word as law. She had an earthy streak, and enjoyed a ribald story, but even as she dominated a man's world she kept her femininity. Her formula for soothing her emotions after a tough office fight with the managing editor was to go out and buy herself the most expensive hat she could find.

When it came to the newer type of *Fortune* story that attempted to deal with foreign affairs, the line between opinion and fact was not so clear, and the passions that were more and more evident as the war came nearer made for some interesting arguments. Here the checking function of the researcher, who was supposed to attest to "truth" by putting a dot over each word, became blurry. I did an article called "Great Britain's Europe" which bothered Eric Hodgins, who had become *Fortune's* publisher to make way for Mitch Davenport as managing editor. The article, which was geopolitical in its assumptions, set Britain's traditional policy of divide-and-rule on the European continent (the better to preserve her own discontinuous maritime empire) off against the thesis of General Haushofer that it would be to Europe's interest to become a continuous continental power. Hodgins thought the article was anti-British; I contended it was an objective statement of two clashing geopolitical views. I wasn't contending that Hitler should dominate continental unification. How could any checker mediate our differences?

By this time I was in rebellion against writing about the foreign scene without leaving Manhattan Island. I had done a long article about Venezuela without going there, and was asked to do a re-write job on an article on Puerto Rico. When I complained that Arch MacLeish and Wilder Hobson had gone to Japan before doing a Japanese issue, whereas I had had to do an article on the internal condition of Hitler's Germany from notes collected by Ernestine Evans and had gone on from that to other foreign stories researched by other people, my unwonted recourse to lachrymose tones had an almost startling effect. I was allowed to spend a month in Puerto Rico, and ended the trip with a fascinating visit to interview Muñoz Marín at his headquarters in the mountains, where the island's great hero was trying to recover, as he put it, from the fact that he had failed to eat 80 thousand tomatoes in his life. Muñoz's Popular Party had just won its first election, and I had caught Puerto Rico at the moment of its passage from U.S. colony to self-governing commonwealth status. I am sure the article on Puerto Rico was much better than the one I had done on Venezuela, and I was gratified that it met with the approval of Rex Tugwell, who had been our proconsul in the island, which he called "the stricken land." But most important to me, at the tag end of 1940, was my discovery from looking into Puerto Rican defense troubles that the United States could be vulnerable to foreign enemies. Our navy and air force were having difficulty policing the whole arc of the Caribbean, and it was not far-fetched to think of Nazi sabotage blocking the Panama Canal. It was important that Borinquén field in Puerto Rico should support our air reconnaissance without worry that revolutionists would seize the island. The fact that Muñoz Marín wanted island self-government within the American system was greatly reassuring.

Although I was still an isolationist of the Taft-Hoover variety, and, with Frank Hanighen, still one of the sponsors of Sidney Hertzberg's *Uncensored*, a weekly inside-stuff sheet that tried to tell the full truth about the war, I was becoming uneasy about the theory that we were adequately protected by the two broad oceans. It still seemed silly, however, when Franklin Roosevelt tried to scare Kansas City with the prospect of Goering's bombers. The 1940 election brought the wartime divisions home to *Fortune* in a particularly poignant way, for Mitch Davenport had quit his job to act as speechwriter and adviser to Wendell Willkie, whom he considered to be the internationalist answer to an enigmatic Roosevelt. Mitch's intellectual romance with Willkie made a long and amusing story. At the time of the TNEC hearings, Tommy Corcoran had arranged to have Davenport and me spend a day at Hyde Park. Mitch had all sorts of ideas about bringing business and government together, and he was bursting in anticipation of outlining them to the President. We were greeted at the door of the President's ancestral country seat by Eleanor Roosevelt, who looked trim in a riding habit. "I am Eleanor Roosevelt," she said. We didn't know whether to laugh at this as mock modesty or to take it for what it was probably supposed to be, a gracious lady's attempt to make us feel at home. Later, when we were introduced to the President's mother, who spoke to "Franklin" in severely imperialistic tones, we could see the reason for Eleanor Roosevelt's self-effacing attitude in the Hyde Park atmosphere. The lunch that followed the introductions was interesting enough to me, but it was a disaster to Mitch Davenport. Try as he might, he couldn't get a word in edgewise. The President monopolized the conversation, if it could be called that, with a continuous monologue. With no attempt to conceal his disgust, Davenport went back to New York, started his "business-and-government" editorials which presented some of the opinions he had ached to present to Roosevelt, and took up eagerly with Wendell Willkie, for whom he wrote a noteworthy article in *Fortune* that started Willkie on his political career. It is titillating to think that if the President had only given Mitch Davenport a half-hour forum at Hyde Park, Wendell Willkie might have remained just a clever Wall Street lawyer who had gotten some fame by fighting the New Deal's TVA on behalf of the Commonwealth and Southern Company utility.

I didn't exactly love Franklin D. Roosevelt in 1940, but I distrusted Mitch Davenport's feelings about America's duty to get into the war and knew that his aim was to project those feelings on Willkie. In the democracy of *Fortune* it was decided that Davenport would do the article supporting Willkie, while I was asked to present the case for Roosevelt. To do this I had to take the President at his word that it was his aim to keep the raging conflict far from America's shores, and that—as he insisted "again, and again, and again"—nobody would be sent to die in foreign wars. As one who was feeling his way toward a competitive business philosophy, I had liked the President's turn from the NRA-AAA ideas of the First New Deal, which seemed fascistic the more I looked at them, to Leon Henderson's proposals for returning America to the Brandeisean ideal of small competing units. So, without great misgiving, I proceeded with the article, which ran along with Davenport's on Willkie. I know that my article had a good reading at the White House, but it did not have the effect I wanted. Arch

MacLeish told me the President had mentioned it to him as being "written from a very peculiar point of view." When I said to MacLeish that I had taken the President at his own word, and had considered that the appointment of Thurman Arnold to the Department of Justice's trust-busting position was certainly symbolic, Arch smiled and remarked, "Well, you didn't exactly nominate him for Heaven."

In Robert Elson's first volume of the official history of Time, Inc., I figure as the *Fortune* office isolationist. Actually, I spent very little time in 1940 and '41 arguing international politics. The work of exploring the exciting, if disconcerting, world of war preparations was too absorbing. With Eunice Clark, the granddaughter of the famous economist John Bates Clark, as researcher, I spent some fascinating hours with Bernard Baruch on the subject of financing the military preparations that would be needed to keep America safe after the fall of France. Eunice Clark, a graduate of Mary McCarthy's Vassar, had grown up as a liberal like the rest of us, and the outsize financial figure which Baruch mentioned as the rock-bottom need for what had to be done almost reduced her to tears. I was pretty flabbergasted myself. We didn't dare take Baruch at his full word in the article that we prepared, using a smaller figure. Later, Baruch accused Harry Luce of losing his nerve about informing the American public about the probable cost of rearming. But it wasn't Luce who had lost his nerve; it was two of his employees who had been nurtured on the anti-militarist feelings of the boom-and-bust interwar period.

The "corporation story" as such tended to give way to a more comprehensive type of industrial reporting as war production began to flush the U.S. economy. Instead of biting off single companies, teams of writers and researchers went out to do linked stories on whole industries. With Marie Hayes, who was later to become John Davenport's wife and the mother of lovely daughters, I made a shipyard survey of the whole East Coast. We watched as giant steam shovels dug out a building basin for Ugly Duckling cargo carriers at South Portland, Maine, and moved on up to the Bath Iron Works, which specialized in destroyers. Bill Newell, the boss of the Bath company, exuded a confidence that did not seem to consort with the bad news from the war zones of Europe. "We can build anything," he said, "just get us the orders." He took a great delight in initiating a tyro into the mysteries of maritime construction, explaining templates and expanding on the functions of sheer and camber. We went on to places like the Bethlehem Ship Company's Sparrow Point yard in Maryland with a growing sense that if America were to be drawn into the war as an active participant, it would be capable of out-building—and outlasting—Hitler.

Another enlightening assignment took me through virtually every factory in Bridgeport, Connecticut, and its industrial environs. Bridgeport had 20,000 new people, many of them exanthracite miners from Pennsylvania; and its 50 machine shops had huge backlogs of work. (All of which prompted me to wonder, in an article written for the isolationist *Progressive* of Madison, Wisconsin, what the town would do after the war. Thus my reversionary mood, based on what had happened after World War I. As it turned out, my worries were needless.) Just outside of Bridgeport in the Bullard factory I got my first glimpse of a Bullard mult-au-matic turret lathe, which I later saw doing the work of five separate machines on the floor of the United Aircraft Pratt and Whitney airplane engine division in East Hartford. There were even bigger marvels to be seen in the Detroit area, which a *Fortune* expedition invaded to catch the automobile industry as it converted to war production. With John Davenport I listened as K.T. Keller, the President of Chrysler, tried to tell us something about the difficulties of adapting assembly-line space from cars to tanks. Difficulties or not, none of the automotive tycoons entertained any doubts about the ability of Detroit to win the war almost single-handedly if Washington were really to give a go-ahead signal. And when we saw the Ford bomber plant rising in a field at Willow Run, out near Ypsilanti, we could see the reason for Detroit's confidence.

Later, when Michael Straight, the publisher of the *New Republic*, ascribed the magic of American war production to something in the "earth," and not to our native breed of enterprisers, it made me angry. True enough, the automobile workers had a lot to do with Detroit's wartime performance. The plan offered by Walter Reuther for converting idle automobile capacity to bits-and-pieces production for the aircraft industry had some merit, if only because it pointed to the need for pooling the tools and skills of some extremely competitive companies. But there were limits to the Reuther idea that Detroit manufacturing could be run by a committee, with labor and government in a position to outvote management. Roosevelt listened to Reuther, but he gave more attention to Bernard Baruch, who had created the War Industries Board in World War I and provoked Hindenburg to say something about America's "pitiless industry." The result was a War Production Board for World War II, with an automobile division presided over by Ernest Kanzler. With a chain of command established, Detroit performed mightily. I took issue, in a *New York Times* review of Mickey Straight's *Make This the Last War*, with the idea that our war production was something that happened in spite of our industrialists, and was gratified when James Forrestal found time in his busy Washington day to let me know that the review was all right with him.

Mitch Davenport had left *Fortune* for the Willkie campaign, and Ralph D. Paine, the son of the historian, had taken over. Del Paine warned me that I was going "against history" in maintaining my sponsorship of the anti-war newsletter *Uncensored*, but I still held to the position—which also happened to be that of William Allen White, head of the Committee to Defend America by Aiding the Allies—that active fighting participation in Europe should be limited to the European countries. I was, however, becoming absorbed in the subject of logistics, which must have amused Del Paine. In any event, I was assigned to do articles about army training camps, and then turned loose on a fictional essay called "Troop Transport," which told the story of the preparation and the dockside loading of a mythical force destined to beat a foreign enemy to the punch by seizing a South American vantage point. The essay went all the way to General George Marshall, who read it and returned it with a tacit approval. Later, after I had written a *Fortune* article on the "War of Distances," I got an ecstatic comment from Harry Luce. "Yes," he said, "every little goat track is in it." Far from being resentful of my opposition to his "The American Century," Harry Luce was willing to use me for his own purposes. I suppose this was a sign of his own confidence that he could convert anyone to his way of seeing things given time and patience. He had the same patient attitude toward Joe Thorndike, who was the managing editor of *Life* before he left to start the *American Heritage* publications. Joe, another child of the interwar period, had a sour taste in his mouth about war because of the stupidity of the generals who had allowed World War I to bog down in the murderously static four-year struggle of the trenches. But one day Joe woke up and exclaimed to John Billings that World War II was a war of *movement*. With Joe's change of attitude, Luce had landed one fish. And, however slowly, he was ultimately to land me.

My change did not come without assistance, however. First of all, there was the influence of Dorothy Thompson. I had met her in the '30s, on a boat to Bermuda. She was traveling with Mrs. Edwin Kuh, the sister-in-law of Ferdinand Kuh, the well-known correspondent, to join her husband, Sinclair Lewis, for a vacation before starting her column in the *New York Herald-Tribune*. My wife Peggy and I saw something of the Lewises at the St. George Hotel, and we were both amused at Red Lewis's prideful deference toward Dorothy, the new "pundit." Between praising his wife and trying to extract details about hotel keeping from the staff of the St. George (he had just written his *Work of Art* about a hotel keeper), Red had no time for his besetting sin of self-pity. Red's attitude toward Dorothy was to change later, as we were to see for the first time during an uncomfortable evening in the Lewis home in Bronxville. We had been invited to dinner, along with the Clifton Fadimans, after Lewis's anti-Fascist *It Can't Happen Here* had come out. Kip Fadiman and I had liked the book, and had said so in reviews; the other reviewers were less appreciative of Lewis's first fictional capitulation to his wife's influence. Whether he blamed the response of the critics on Dorothy we did not know; it was more probable that his ego, which was always vulnerable to even the most innocuous slight, had been hurt by somebody's denigrating phrase. Possibly he was just in a letdown period between books. Anyway, he was in a thoroughly bad mood, and before the dinner was over he had to be helped upstairs. Dorothy held up bravely, kept the conversation going, and was entirely willing to take issue with any statement that America could sit out an anti-Fascist war in Europe. Over the next few years Lewis would sit in a corner at New York parties, looking like a sick crane while Dorothy held forth. He seemed happy only when he was with people who were willing to listen to him without any desire to take the spotlight for themselves. I heard him give a great mimetic monologue at the Hotel Brevoort one night, imitating William Allen White on the subject of the "Yanks aren't coming— just yet." Again, on another trip to Bermuda, my wife and I and our friends, Dr. and Mrs. Lawrence Sophian, were instructed by Red in something he called the cliché game. He offered to provide the proper cliché answer to any question, and kept it up with infinite ingenuity and great hilarity until two o'clock in the morning. It was better than *The Man Who Knew Coolidge.* Red was drinking a little bit, yes, but nothing like the amounts that were generally attributed to him. He didn't seem to mind at all that Dorothy wasn't with him. It was a doomed marriage between two people of talent and even genius who couldn't square their public and private lives, although Dorothy gave it a real try. In the early years of the marriage, Red Lewis got a letter from a woman offering to help him. Dorothy, sensing a come-on, answered it by saying, "I take care of all my husband's needs, and when I say all I mean all."

Dorothy Thompson could be overpowering. But she could be humorous and she could be kind. She regarded me as a personal reclamation project. When my *American Stakes* appeared she devoted a column to it, an unusual thing considering that she was expending syndicated space on a mere book review, and this of a work whose thesis she had no interest in advertising. At her prodding I read the works of the English geographer, Sir Halford Mackinder. Sir Halford divided the globe into two unequal parts. The big part was the World Island, which included Europe, Asia, and Africa. The rest of the world—Australia, North and South America, the Pacific Islands—held its freedom by virtue of the fact that the peninsula countries of Western Europe had never allowed any single power to dominate Central and Eastern Europe, which Sir Halford called the Heartland. If the Heartland were ever to fall to one great power—a Nazi Germany, a Communist Russia—Western Europe and Africa would be under the fist of a blackmailer, and Australia and the Americas, as the "fringe lands," would be outflanked.

This was heady stuff, and for the first time I could see why the isolationist position would be untenable if the British fleet were to be destroyed and the Heartland possessor left free to take to the oceans. (Parenthetically, what bothers me now is that I never run across a college or high school student who knows anything about Sir Halford Mackinder, let alone Dorothy Thompson. The young of the '70s, and earliest '80s have been quite as oblivious as I was in the '30s to the possibility that the world can be cut in two by a malevolent power.)

Willi Schlamm was the second important influence in tempering my anti-war position. Willi, who had grown up in Vienna, had joined the Communist Party in his teens. His first disillusionment with Communists, at least of the Russian variety, came in Moscow when some sophisticated older hands tried to provide him with girls, an essay in pimping that didn't seem to consort with his idealistic ideas about morality in waging the class struggle. As a Viennese Jew, Willi was keenly aware of the meaning of Hitlerism long before the Nazis took over in Germany and forced the Anschluss with Austria. After all, Hitler, too, had come out of Vienna, and had soaked up the peculiarly virulent anti-Semitism of the Hapsburg capital. As editor of Carl Ossietsky's *Die Weltbuehne*, Willi had gone with the publication to Prague, where he remained a thorn in Hitler's skin until Munich. When it became apparent that the Czechs were doomed, Willi took flight over Germany to Brussels and Paris, carrying a vial of poison in his pocket in case a forced landing were to plunge him into the hands of the Gestapo. He and his wife Steffi eventually wound up in New York, where he was relatively unknown. Fortunately, Edmund Wilson had read Willi's book on the Stalinist perversion of the Russian Revolution, *The Dictatorship of the Lie*, and had commented on it in a piece in the *New Republic*. With this introduction from a respected American critic, and with his anti-Stalinist and presumably social-democratic credentials in order, Willi caught on as a columnist for Sol Levitas' *New Leader*. He learned a good colloquial English, richly flavored with New York idiom, by spending time at the movies and by listening assiduously to New York's intellectuals. I had read Willi in the *New Leader*, and was impressed with the speed of his American acculturation. When I was assigned by *Fortune* to do an article, for a special background-of-war issue, on how America must appear to the Nazis, I had what I thought was a bright idea. I would try to put myself into the skin of a German agent who considered it his duty to tell Hitler that the U.S., though it had an undoubted ethnical diversity, was not about to break into pieces as the Austro-Hungarian Empire had done in World War I. I needed a collaborator for the job, one who could Germanicize the turns of phrase without destroying the analysis, which would be my own. *Fortune* was willing to hire Willi for this one assignment. He came, he turned the article into a notable one, he made friends in the *Fortune* office, and he was soon the newest member of the staff. He began by specializing on labor stories, but it wasn't long before he had teamed up with Herrymon Maurer, who had grown up in China, as the "Vienna-Chungking Axis" in the *Fortune* office. Willi and Herrymon were both gung-ho about beating Germany and Japan, and, if I wasn't quite converted to the idea that we belonged in the war on a full-fledged fighting basis, I was certainly infected by the Vienna-Chungking enthusiasm. I read Willi's new book, called *This Second War for Independence*, with respect both for its argument and for a very passable English which Willi said had been labored over by Ben

Mandel and Eric Seligo. Willi was always willing to concede that Goering had no bombers that were capable of crossing the Atlantic with significant pay-loads, but he didn't regard the U.S. invulnerability to physical conquest as definitive. Hitler, he kept saying, had perfected the technique of taking the world bite by bite, like eating an artichoke. We would not be invaded, Willi said, we would be surrounded by other nations conquered from within. Our credo, "We shall fight like lions—but only on our own soil." was, so Willi insisted, "the most essential of all democratic credos" for a totalitarian victory.

Willi was full of paradoxes, aphorisms, and startling juxtapositions. The French, he said, refused to lose their cool heads until they had lost their warm blood. As Willi wrote, they were defeated not in Flanders but in the schoolrooms of Paris, where the intellectual professors debunked everything but themselves.... In due time Willi moved upstairs to become Harry Luce's European-affairs advisor. His rapid rise provoked jealousies—but that is another, and later, story. Before his downfall at Time, Inc., which came after the victory had posed what seemed entirely new problems for the Luce publications, Willi was a vivid part of our anti-Stalinist group which was determined to keep the local Newspaper Guild unit from becoming an arm of Soviet policy. Naturally, after Hitler had attacked Russia, the in-office fight had to be muted—which explains why Willi couldn't get Luce to make journalistic capital of such Soviet atrocities as the massacre of the captured Polish officers in the Katyn forest. Willi didn't approve when Elmer Davis, the chief of War Information, decided to sit on the Katyn story until after the war, but he went along with Davis when the decision had been made. None of us could tell the full truth while "there was a war on"; unlike the modern breed of reporter or war photographer, we were patriots first and journalists second. *Life* magazine in those days, would certainly never have paid a photographer $30,000 for Mylai-tragedy pictures. Indeed, if such a purchase had been suggested, Willi would surely have told Harry Luce to say "no," and Harry Luce would just as surely have said, "Willi, you are right."

Chapter 8

I left *Fortune* in the late summer of 1941—and yet I didn't leave it. Officially I had become an Associate Professor of the Columbia University School of Journalism, meeting a class of some 40 boys and girls—or young men and women, as they certainly were—for most of every Wednesday. The course was called Editorial Methods, and was to cover every type of newspaper writing save straight reporting. I was free to teach editorial writing, reviewing, background article preparation, and all the permutations of feature work in general.

I had wanted to take on the teaching job in addition to remaining on the *Fortune* staff, but the answer was that the rules precluded this. "When you work for *Fortune*," said Eric Hodgins in an uncomfortable meeting in the publisher's office, "your entire vasomotor system must be at its service." The rule seemed entirely arbitrary to me, for during my six years on the staff I had continued to do a monthly book-criticism page for *Scribner's* and *Harper's* magazines. Hodgins had known about this, but tacitly accepted my theory that reading and reporting complemented each other. Teaching, however, was something else again, and he didn't see how it would be any help to *Fortune* work. When I reminded him that Arch MacLeish had been a poet in residence at Princeton, he brushed it aside with the statement that Arch had merely to sit around with the students after hours; it didn't take a whole day out of the week.

As we talked it over I found myself becoming more and more stubborn. I had been a workhorse of the staff, sometimes doing as many as three articles for an issue, and I had Dean Carl Ackerman's word at Columbia that if a *Fortune* assignment demanded my absence from any particular class, he would arrange to excuse me. So I put it up to Luce. Strangely, he said he detected "MacLeishism" in my attitude (MacLeish had never made it a secret that he considered his poetry and play writing more important than his journalism, although this did not keep him from being a good journalist). The truth was that Harry Luce was intensely proud of the institution he had created and couldn't stand to see it given second place by anybody. No doubt he felt he had to uphold Hodgins on the rules. He softened, however, as we talked, finally dismissing me pleasantly with a cryptic statement that we could "meet in the marketplace." Del Paine, the *Fortune* managing editor, translated this to mean that I could go on doing *Fortune* articles on a piecework basis and proceeded to outline a series of articles on U.S. labor in a wartime world. I was not to apear on the *Fortune* masthead, but the articles were to be signed.

So I went off to Columbia with an assurance that I could both teach on a part-time basis and continue to make a living. Exuberant, I bought some Time, Inc., stock on the day I officially left, which amused Del Paine no end. The new arrangement turned out to be a blessing, for it enabled me to be fluid as America, stricken at Pearl Harbor, moved actively into the war. I was to spend the next three years doing a variety of things—teaching, working on a per-diem basis for Wild Bill Donovan, the organizer of OSS, writing the labor series for Paine and a labor-and-the-war column distributed to newspapers by Freedom House, and returning to the *New York Times* to split the daily book review page with Orville Prescott. Meanwhile I started doing profiles—or close-ups—for *Life* magazine, and in 1944 I was to go to Washington as *Life*'s political "text man" on a full-time basis.

The kids at Columbia were a revelation. The last time I had had any extensive contact with the younger generation was in the middle '30s, when I had done a Youth in College article in *Fortune*. Like the rest of the country, college youth during the depression were willing to take a lot of New Deal measures on faith. But the 1941-42 class in Columbia Journalism and the two subsequent classes that I taught before going to Washington had lost some of the commitment of the high New Deal years. They did not necessarily believe in the business system, as I had come to believe in it, but they had no great faith in the ability of government to plan a nation's economic life. Their attitude was thoroughly critical, though in an open-minded way. They were, in short, first-rate journalistic material, and a large number of them were to become successful mainstays of the news business in the decades after the war.

The most vividly remembered of the students was Marguerite Higgins, who didn't need any women's lib movement to make her one of the most resourceful war correspondents of her generation. She had a deceptively demure, almost school-girlish, look, which she used at a later date to open doors in a way that her male competitors in Korea and West Berlin regarded as totally unfair. Since she knew where she was going (she informed her classmates without any boastfulness that she would someday be as well-known as Dorothy Thompson), she needed no teacher to prod her to develop native abilities. In this she was like other self-directed kids at the journalism school. The most talented of them all was Murray Morgan, a West Coast boy who could have done almost anything. But Murray had an antipathy to great cities. He said he was going back home to the Northwest after graduation and become a local journalist, which to the best of my knowledge he did. So Murray, the leader in his Columbia peer group, is less famous today than others in those journalism classes of the early wartime years. Others went further because they had more drive, or less regional commitment to trees and the open air, but maybe Murray Morgan has had a happier life.

The distinguishing thing about most of the kids was that they wanted to be journalists, not world-savers. Al Otten, now London correspondent for the *Wall Street Journal*; Flora Lewis, foreign-affairs columnist of the *New York Times*; Elie Abel, who had a great career as an overseas correspondent, a Washington bureau chief, a TV newsman, and a book writer (he did the first real study of the Cuban missile crisis) before becoming the School of Journalism Dean; Stan Levy, the *Times* labor expert; Carl Hartman, who served the AP in Bonn; Al Rosenthal of the *Herald-Tribune*; Milton Stewart, who went into Wall Street and became a spokesman for small business after serving Governor Averell Harriman in Albany; Edie Efron, who as staff writer for *TV Guide* was to anticipate Spiro Agnew in exposing TV bias in election-year and military reporting; Nona Balakian, a *Times Book Review* editor; Woodrow Wilson Wirsig, who deserted journalism for public relations—these were only a few of a capable bunch who were not simpletons, as their shell-shocked predecessors on the campuses of the mid-'30s had inclined to be. Their loyalty was to the story, so, though they were too close to the Depression to be interested in the idea that America had had a history before 1933 or a President before F.D.R., they never became ritualistic liberals. Nona Balakian, with a commitment to literature, became a most discerning editor as well as a stimulating critic. I learned more from the students than they learned from me. After I had become a syndicated columnist and started to attend national political conventions, Maggie Higgins and Al Otten, presumably taking pity on an old teacher who needed his rest, helped me with a bit of shared information here and there, even though I was a competitor for their public or their space.

Maggie Higgins was not the best writer in her class, but she had a go-for-broke attitude that made up for her sometimes shaggy sentences. She always reminded me of my favorite ball player, Pete Reiser, who could have become the second Ty Cobb if he had not wrecked his body by running into Ebbetts Field concrete in pursuit of fly balls. Just before Pearl Harbor I had asked the class to do a 750-word background piece on the chances for peace in the Far East. The watchwords were those of traditional Pulitzer journalism, "terseness and accuracy." When Marguerite Higgins turned in a 20-page paper I thought that this young woman would never make it in a city room. I started to give her a zero, but my eye was caught with some information about Oriental history and psychology that I had never seen in print before. I read on, fascinated. Later, after telling Maggie that she had missed the assignment, but that I was giving her a good mark anyway, I asked her how she had come by so much knowledge of the

Far East. She said she had been born in Hongkong of an Irish father and a French mother, and had spent some of her childhood in such outlandish places as Indochina.

Insofar as she had any ideological commitments, Maggie Higgins was a liberal. But she was reflective, and when events exposed the liberals as shortsighted, or unfair, or ridiculous in their prophecies, she turned against them. Like Joe Alsop, who had lived in China, she had no inhibitions about returning again and again to Vietnam (she made ten trips before a tropical disease picked up from an insect bite killed her), and her knowledge of Oriental affairs kept her from swallowing the notion that there was ever a Diem-inspired plot against the Buddhists. She quickly spotted the phony quality in the Buddhist "saint" Thich Tri Quang. It infuriated her when an editor in the home office of the *Herald-Tribune* in New York would question one of her facts merely because the *Times* had a different version. (Maybe this had something to do with her switch to *Newsday*). To her, Thich Tri Quang was an evil man consumed by his lust for power. She was most disapproving of the State Department plot to get rid of Diem. When, for newspaper column purposes of my own, I called her up to get her opinion of the damage done by the assassination of Diem and his brother, and the purge of their adherents, she put it into American terms by saying, "It's as if the U.S. President, Vice President, Secretary of State, Secretary of Defense, and Secretary of the Treasury, along with the governors of Pennsylvania, New York, Illinois, and California, plus the Speaker of the House and our most important Senators, plus the mayors of New York, Chicago, and Los Angeles, had all been killed. There's no administrative personnel left in Vietnam."

I was taken aback by the breathlessness of her condemnation. But the next few years in Vietnam bore her out. She kept on writing columns after she was ill, pushing herself because someone, not the David Halberstams and such who cared little who took over in Vietnam, had to get the eye or the ear of Lyndon Johnson. Mayor Sam Yorty of Los Angeles, who was one of Maggie Higgins' great partisans, mailed her book, *Our Vietnam Nightmare*, to L.B.J.; whether the President read it or not, Yorty never knew.

Before teaching at Columbia I had always thought that schools of journalism were useful to the end of placing people in jobs, but I had insisted that ordinary college courses in government, history, economics, and foreign languages were a better preparation for a newspaper career than listening to professors who had a trade-school attitude. Bob Hutchins, the President of the University of Chicago, was quick to taunt me with inconsistency when I told him that I was taking the Columbia job. I had done a story for *Fortune* on the University of Chicago, and had listened to Hutchins's complaints that he couldn't get the great books of the world read by his own undergraduates. His faculty, he said, had all the power. Ironically, I discovered at Columbia that a trade-school course on methods that had no prescribed content could be used to achieve the ends which Hutchins despaired of introducing at Chicago. When giving out an assignment in book reviewing, I would see to it that some of the class read and reviewed Walter Lippmann or Max Lerner and others did the same for Isabel Paterson or Albert Jay Nock. This assured a lively by-the-way controversy over attitudes toward government planning. I told Hutchins that in a trade school which was not overly concerned with substance, one could introduce all the substance in the world. I don't think I persuaded one of our truly great educators that I had found the right milieu to teach the classics that were more and more being ignored in the liberal-arts curricula, but Hutchins, as a student of irony, must have been amused by something that I called the Chamberlain Paradox. I never told Dean Carl Ackerman or the students what I was up to, and maybe my efforts to get the kids to read some good books while they were learning about methods of presenting facts and ideas were not appreciated. On the other hand, some of the reading may have stuck. The arts of insinuation are always useful to teaching, and one sometimes gets his way more easily by not making an issue of it.

My growing libertarianism had been particularly stimulated by Isabel Paterson, an old enemy of the '30s who thought I was being used by the Communists during my first stint at doing the *Times's* book column. Isabel's *The God of the Machine* hit me like a ton of bricks when it came out in 1943. Her explanation of "the long circuit of energy" that is unleashed by capitalistic voluntarism checked with everything I had learned while doing business stories for *Fortune*. When I reviewed her book favorably, she was genuinely surprised that she had made a convert out of human material which she had once considered hopeless, and she thanked me for my "integrity and generosity." (Later, she was to take back some of her praise when I tried to get her to write at pittance rates for the *Freeman*, but that is another story.) I took particular pleasure in assigning her book for review to the journalism students, for it represented everything that was unfashionable in the Rooseveltian era.

Edie Efron, one of the more promising kids in the 1942-43 class, doesn't recall being touched by libertarian ideas in the Editorial Methods course, but she must have absorbed something from the idea that I tried to spread that the Zeitgeist was not sacrosanct. Edie had grown up in the radical New York atmosphere of the '30s; her uncle was Joshua Kunitz, one of the *New Masses* editors and a prominent Left-Wing poet; and she herself tried hard to be a Communist at Barnard. Her career in Left-Wing activism came to an end on a Harlem park bench for strictly esthetic reasons. She had undertaken to sell the *Daily Worker* on a Harlem street corner without knowing much about the contents of the paper. When trade was slow one day, she took time out to read what she was hawking and was horrified by the sloppy prose. Unwilling to foist any more papers on the Harlemites, she destroyed what she had in hand. Then, scared to admit what she had done (she was not intellectually prepared for a confrontation with the "Party"), she explained that she had sold out her consignment and took money from her own pocket to pay for it. In later years, after living in Haiti where she observed the connection between work and the opportunity to eat under the raw circumstances of a primitive economy, she lost what remained of her radicalism. Ayn Rand's objectivist libertarianism touched her, but she ascribes her conversion to rationality to watching cause and effect at work in the barbaric Haitian setting.

I like to think, however, that she had gotten an inkling of what the free economy can do by contact with Isabel Paterson's theories in a Columbia journalism classroom long before she went to Haiti, and long before she had read Ayn Rand's *Atlas Shrugged*. At any rate, it was in Edie Efron's capacity in 1970 to be the first to anticipate Vice President Spiro Agnew's attack on the chronic Left-Liberal bias of TV.

Edie's interview with Howard K. Smith on the one-sidedness of TV-radio news commentary was published in *TV Guide* two months before Agnew sounded off. Then, just to prove how obviously right Agnew had been, Edie did a blockbuster of a job analyzing scores of transcripts of the election coverage of 1968. Agnew will always get the credit (or the ignominy) for having informed the TV news-commentary public that their king was a monarch without clothes, but it was Edie Efron, Columbia Journalism '43, who broke the barrier and then proved the case.

In taking on a *Fortune* assignment to write five articles on the labor movement in wartime, I had a voluntaristic hypothesis in the back of my mind that I wanted to test out. We had a union, a unit of the New York Newspaper Guild, at Time, Inc., that was not a compulsory affair, yet it had no difficulty in getting members. True, it was dominated by the fellow-travelers, who did the Communists' bidding at one remove, but the situation was not hopeless. Our own anti-Communist cell, consisting of John Davenport, Calvin Fixx, Bob Cantwell, and Whit Chambers (with Whit telling us what to expect from the hard core of fellow-travelers after ten o'clock at night when the innocents had departed to catch commuter trains), could exercise a pull toward common sense; and an occasional natural anarchist like Jim Agee could get up and denounce all people who enjoyed prolonging meetings. The *Time* Newspaper Guild unit had been started by Wilder Hobson, Dwight Macdonald, and other free-lance liberals and radicals, and after Hobson's presidency Joe Kastner, who long presided over the *Life* copy desk, was the somewhat beleaguered head.

Joe had to get along with the Left, though he never seemed quite comfortable as a union boss. The fact that the union flourished without becoming a union-shop monopoly (it eventually escaped from the clutch of the fellow-travelers when our ties to wartime Russia weakened) made me think that labor as a whole could organize without compulsion. I thought the war, which had brought the unions and management together for the common purpose of producing to defeat Hitler, might be used to create a free movement that could brgain for security without coercing the occasional individual worker who had a philosophical or a psychological objection to accepting union membership as a condition of holding a job. And I also thought that if labor and management could get along one way, they could see the virtue of profit-sharing arrangements that would by-pass the need to strike.

With such naïve thoughts in mind, I set forth to do separate articles on the coal miners, the steel workers, and the automobile union. The first thing I did was to get the "feel" of the miners. My researcher, merry Elida Griffin, insisted on donning work clothes and a safety helmet and going into the mines. She was permitted to do it, for Mrs. Roosevelt had already set a precedent by going into "the picks," but it was obvious that the presence of a woman underground made the miners uneasy. They were a special breed, without much care for the outside world or for changing attitudes that encouraged what was to become known as women's lib. Since the coal patch was an isolated community, it engendered an orthodoxy that expressed itself in solidarity slogans. Kyle Crichton, who had come from the coal fields to become a Scribner's editor before his reincarnation as Robert Forsythe ("So Red the Pose") of the *New Masses*, had told me that miners actually like mining. It was true. Their work, as I later wrote in a foreword to McAlister Coleman's *Men and Coal*, was dangerous, but its circumstances produced pride, not apathy.

Working in an oak-supported room in a steady 65-70-degree Fahrenheit temperature under the perpetual menace of the overhanging rock, the miner set his own pace. The rhythm of the Joy and Goodman loaders was set by the men who drilled the holes for the "cardox" (carbon dioxide gas) explosives, and by the follow-up crews who moved in after the coal extraction to clean up the loose slate and put in new oak props. Save in the strip mines, mining was no dull routine.

I could see that men who were up against a coal seam for eight hours of the day, and who came home to a community consisting only of miners and a few merchants, would not care in the least for outside public opinion. They followed their leader—the great John L. Lewis. Their sense of "otherness" was a great cohesive, and when they struck they did so as a willing body. "No contract, no work" was a distinctive miner's slogan. To argue about the danger to individual rights that was inherent in the closed or union shop was meaningless to Mr. Lewis's men, for as long as John L. stood up for them they could not conceive of needing an abstract freedom. Things would change, or course, when Lewis died and the miners lost their identity symbol, but in any case, I did not find much encouragement for my philosophical thesis in the Appalachian country.

The steel union was different. Steel had been organized by the coal miners, with Lewis and the faithful Phil Murray taking the lead. But in the early '40s it was anything but a monolithic union. What surprised me was the philosophic breadth of some of the younger men at union headquarters at Pittsburgh, notably Harold Ruttenberg and Joseph Scanlon.

Harold Ruttenberg had grown up in a coal town, where he had been witness to what he considered an avoidable mine disaster, and his young manhood, as he told me, had been dedicated to hating rich people. But in 1942, touched by the mellow philosophic influence of Clinton Golden, vice president of the steel union, he was moving out of his earlier crude class-struggle phase. Together with Golden, Ruttenberg was preaching the new gospel of productivity sharing which, indirectly, led to the creation in 1943 of the War Production Board's joint labor-management committees for speeding the war effort on the factory floor. Ruttenberg had great hopes that the cooperative wartime attitude of the labor-management committees would continue on into the peace. He could see no reason why representatives of both management and the union could not pool their knowledge in a peacetime economy, cooperate on programs of cost cutting, and share the resulting profits after making an allowance for lower prices (and therefore expanding sales) to the consumer. Ruttenberg had the Henry Ford economics in his bones.

Joe Scanlon, an open-hearth worker from Mansfield, Ohio, who had studied cost accounting, worked out a formula for productivity sharing in a small, shaky company, and its success emboldened Golden and Ruttenberg. Scanlon and I hit it off well, for we had a mutual friend in Louis Bromfield, who was then plowing his profits from novels into some exciting soil-renewal experiments at his farm at Pleasant Valley near Mansfield. After the war I was to pick up the trail of the so-called "Scanlon Plan," which really worked whenever it was tried. Unfortunately, the "coal" mentality of Phil Murray, a thoroughly decent fellow who had tenacity but who lacked creative daring, could not follow Golden, Ruttenberg, and Scanlon in their enthusiasm for "codevelopment" in the steel industry. He thought the "Scanlon Plan" premature. Both Scanlon and Ruttenberg had to quit the union after 1946 in order to proselytize for their ideas. Ruttenberg took a job running the Portsmouth Steel Company for Cyrus Eaton, made some money on stock options, and then bought the Stardrill-Keystone Company, a well-drilling outfit which operated all over the world. Scanlon moved to New England, where he taught a course at M.I.T. in the elements of union-management productivity sharing.

When the U.S. labor movement lost the inspiration and the services of these two young men, it lost a great deal. But this was still in the future as I moved on from Pittsburgh to Detroit to look at the automobile-workers union.

Walter Reuther, the Red Head who did good work in fighting the

Stalinists in the UAW, had ideas for union-management cooperation that, superficially considered, sounded very similar to the Ruttenberg-Scanlon ideas. But Walter was, at bottom, an incurable socialist. He always wanted to bring the government in as a third party, which would have resulted in a labor-state dictatorship. Back of his suggestions there always lurked the idea of "encroaching control," or, as Eddie Levenson, his press man, put it in a moment of confessional honesty, "building the new society in the shell of the old." Walter was always cloudy about details of investment and incentive when he elaborated his grandiose plans for turning bomber plants into factories for making prefabricated housing. Despite the fact that Reuther was preferable to the Stalinist "gruesome twosome" (George Addes and Dick Frankensteen) in the UAW, I could only reflect that John L. Lewis was right when he scoffed at Walter's economic thinking as half-baked Marxism. Lewis himself was no voluntarist, as I had quickly learned in some fascinating interviews with a volcanic presence, but he at least conceded much virtue to Adam Smith economics. Lewis was an intimidating figure to question; he positively enjoyed frightening a too inquisitive prober. "I'm scared of that man," said Roosevelt's Secretary of Labor, Frances Perkins. Once, when I was interviewing Frank Murphy, the labor governor of Michigan, in his office in Lansing, I noticed that he had hidden a picture behind his couch. It was a portrait of John L. Lewis. Murphy had put it there, so he laughingly told me, because he expected a visit the next day from Frances Perkins and didn't want to ruffle her.

In his social hours Lewis could be most pleasant. I encountered him with Alice Longworth at Washington parties. He wanted it known that he was no enemy of capitalist technological progress. He admitted to being disingenuous about this; his idea of preparing the way to "sharing productivity" was to let the mine owners put in the most advanced machinery. Then, roaring that there was "blood" on the owner's hands, he would proceed to milk most of the value of technological improvement for his own men. He willingly saw older miners displaced by automation, but he tried to make it up to them from a big pension fund. He left the mines in good technological condition when he died. Unfortunately, he also left his union without much power of democratic renewal.

Lewis's criticism of our wartime economics was cogent: he argued that the ending of war controls would suddenly reveal what had been a gigantic hidden inflation, and he wanted his miners to "get their's" at a time when management was benefiting from cost-plus contracts and the easy depreciation of new plants. Though his wartime strikes were hardly patriotic, they were "pulled" at cannily-considered moments when coal inventories were big enough to maintain war production. Thus, slyly, Lewis avoided being irretrievably branded as a public enemy. Reuther tried to form public opinion; Lewis scoffed at it even when he maneuvered to avoid stirring it up against his men. Neither Lewis nor Reuther was interested in voluntarism when it came to union membership, nor were they for letting profit sharing distribute the "take" of industry in a strikeless world. Acquaintance with their methods and their philosophies helped disillusion me with great labor personalities and "big" labor in huge corporative industry—but I continued to have hopes for voluntary unionism and for labor-management cooperation in small plants.

I tried to sum up the case against the closed shop, and its "union shop" sub-variety, in two *Fortune* articles, one devoted to exploring the issue itself, and the other on Will Davis, the head of the War Labor Board. The really significant strike history of 1941, I noted, had been over the question of union control of the labor supply. In its efforts to impose compulsory dues (in reality, a tax) on a man to hold a job, the CIO was, whether it realized it or not, aspiring to a function of government. A dissident union man, possibly resenting the political deployment of his own share of the union treasury, had no recourse if he were denied the opportunity to quit the union. The right to "opt out" is the only check a union man has on his leadership. As I saw it, the open union and democracy were intertwined; neither could exist without the other.

This philosophy was later espoused by Reed Larson, the indefatigable director of the Washington-based Right-to-Work Committee, who has been doing such yeoman work on behalf of labor itself to maintain and extend the Right-to-Work laws that we now have in 20 states, none of which specializes in or even tolerates the union busting that is such a bogy to the AFL-CIO.

In studying the history of the European labor movement, I learned that Sweden and England, the two countries of the celebrated "middle way," had finally been forced to meet the question of the closed shop when they were confronted with syndicalist-type general strikes. The Swedes drew back from an abyss in 1909 when their country was on the verge of a revolution that nobody really wanted. England did the same thing after the general strike of 1926. The deal in each country depended on a particular north-of-Europe common sense. Management, for the sake of efficiency, reserved its right to hire and fire at its own discretion and to employ workers belonging to any union or to no union. But, in exchange for the recognition of the right-to-work principle, the employers' associations voluntarily relinquished the old habits of union baiting. In an America that had been chastened by the sit-down strikes of the '30s, the Swedish and English formula for labor peace would surely work, but it was a question whether the old combattants in the U.S. could be brought to see it.

Astoundingly, Henry Ford the Elder broke with all his principles in giving way to the union shop, a modification of the closed-shop principle that allows management to hire anybody provided he is willing to join the union after a stated interval. Theoretically, the union shop does not bind management to accept the union tyranny over the worker that is inherent in the closed system (closed unions lead imperceptibly to rackets). But as I wrote in *Fortune*, the union shop "can effectively prevent management from hiring the type of person who resents compulsion—in brief, the very sort of independent human being who might ordinarily forge ahead to the foreman or upper-executive class if he is left to work out his own career." If such people were to be forced out of the mass production industries, so I wrote, the U.S. would become a stratified nation, with "classes" reduced to fixed categories on the European order. It was incomprehensible that Henry Ford should sell out his ingrained Americanism, which he had always flaunted, to trade a basic management prerogative away for a little temporary peace. It was *"cherchez la femme,"* so I was told; Henry's wife, frightened by the turmoil at the Ford River Rouge plant, had induced her husband to do the most unFordlike thing of his life.

The Allis-Chalmers strike in Milwaukee dramatized political danger that might develop under closed- or union-shop conditions. During the period of the Stalin-Hitler Pact, the Communists in the United Automobile Workers Union were doing their best to sabotage any production that might help Britain to keep the war going. The Allis-Chalmers unit of the UAW was a notorious example of fellow-traveler or even Communist control. The strike in Milwaukee lasted from January to April and eventually ended in a compromise settlement, with the company promising to discipline workers who tried to disrupt the union. If the Communists had won a complete victory at Allis-Chalmers, it might not have been fatal during the period when the U.S. was allied with Stalin against the Nazis. But in the Cold War period it would have been another matter.

The Roosevelt government kept blowing hot and cold on the issue of union compulsion. And the pragmatic and thoroughly likeable Will Davis, the patent lawyer who headed two successive War Labor Boards, did not improve things by his policy of settling each separate case on its merits without regard to principle or precedent. If the government needed ships in a hurry, as it did at the Kearny yard of the Federal Shipbuilding and Drydock Company, it would take over the plant itself and force both management and the union to wait. But on the Pacific Coast labor got a closed shop in 39 shipyards. When John L. Lewis failed to get a union shop in the captive coal mines owned by the steel companies, he was nonplussed that Will Davis's board had not followed its reasoning in the case of the shipyards. The whole issue was left at sixes and sevens during the war, as it still is.

After immersing myself in Will Davis's troubles, and watching the man wrestle with his "principle" of getting something over with so that he could pass on, I thought I had a final solution to his difficulties. Theoretically, the state itself could regulate a union's intramural activities, overseeing elections to keep them honest, and sending government accountants to inspect the union's books periodically. But this would be just one more step toward the corporative state that is fascism. Why not, so I asked Will Davis, why not adapt a maintenance-of-membership compromise, hinted at in the Federal Shipbuilding case but not fully worked out before the government stepped in to take over the works in its ham-handed fashion? Maintenance of existing union membership could be granted in order to assure labor that there would be no union busting on the part of management. But let it be maintenance of membership only for the duration of a specific collective-bargaining agreement. Every man could be asked personally to sign the collective-bargaining agreement, which would preserve the traditional conditions of contractual sanctity and freedom. The individual would pay his dues while the contract was in force. But when the contract had lapsed, the individual worker would be released from his union obligations. He would be free to join or not to join for the period of the next contract. Thus he could hold his own personal veto over his union boss's behavior.

My solution seemed to appeal to Mr. Davis if the look on his rumpled face—the face of "an overtrained trombone player"—meant anything. But he gave me no direct answer, and the idea came to nothing. I still don't see why it couldn't be made part of an overall voluntaristic settlement of our labor-management troubles. Put together with profit-sharing, it would end the eternal bickering that goes on as our César Chavezes try to extend the sphere of compulsory unionism into the farm regions and our George Meany successors still strive to turn the unions into little replicas of the one-party state.

I kept trying out my ideas in a series of columns which I did for Freedom House in 1942 and 1943 for free distribution to various newspapers. But all I ever earned for myself was an entirely undeserved reputation for being anti-union. Freedom House, which had started my column as an "antidote to Westbrook Pegler" (with whom, incidentally, I had no quarrel beyond objecting to his latter-day one-note quality), must have been disappointed. However, like Martin Luther, I could "do no other," even though I have absolutely no taste for fanaticism of any kind. What I was looking for was a compromise to appeal to both sides, and it is the two sides, in my opinion, that remain fanatically stuck with unworkable ideas that lead to the betrayal of freedom of the individual.

Chapter 9

One thing at the back of my mind which made me anxious for a less binding tie with *Fortune* was a desire to write more books. I had had many pleasant conversations with Professor Albert G. Keller of Yale about writing a biography of William Graham Sumner, the pioneer American sociologist who had defended the "forgotten man" (the average taxpaying citizen who takes care of himself and his family), only to have Franklin Roosevelt purloin the phrase and apply it to the world's chronic losers. "Billy" Sumner, who had thundered in an iron voice to generations of Yale undergraduates, had meant a lot to my father, and Keller had passed along some of his no-nonsense attitude to students of a later period. As an opponent of the Spanish-American War who had written a magnificent essay called "The Conquest of the United States by Spain" (meaning that we had gone over to Spain's values in defeating her), Sumner was in tune with the "stay-out-of-war" groups of the '30s. He was also a continuing influence for a traditional individualism that was even then asserting itself against the New Deal.

I had read most of Sumner's essays, but had regarded his defense of individualism as a last-ditch battle in a lost cause. His *Folkways*, however, had been formative in impressing me with the relativity of cultures, and I had done the article on it for Malcolm Cowley's symposium, "Books That Changed Our Minds." Sumner was a paradox: in his essays he knew what was right, and there was no relativity about it. But his study of the mores in *Folkways* seemed to prove that there is nothing right or wrong but that thinking makes it so. This was heady doctrine for the rebels of the '20s, and it had done its damage in a period of moral let-down. Though Keller was one of the great admirers of *Folkways*, he did not like the consequences of moral relativity. He told me of the work which Sumner had started on a cross-cultural survey that was still in process of completion. Such a survey would, so Keller surmised, establish continuities and constants as well as disparities in human adaptivity. Presumably, the determination of constants would justify the unrelenting Sumner of the essays, whom I was coming more and more to prefer to the author of *Folkways*.

Pearl Harbor rudely dashed my plans for doing a Sumner book, even as the depression of the early '30s had stopped me from doing the biography of George Henry Lewes. Like many others who lived through December 7, 1941, I have a clear memory of how the news of the bombing broke. I was sitting at a card table writing a review of a book by Max Eastman and contending with Micky, our philosopher cat with the indistinct tiger markings who enjoyed stepping on the typewriter keys. The radio was on in another room, and I knew that something terrible had happened even before my wife broke in with the first details of the Pearl Harbor debacle. I put the cat on the floor and finished my review, but the dream of mixing teaching, book writing, and occasional journalism had gone up with the smoke from burning battleships half the world away.

Hank Brennan, who had been the art editor at *Fortune*, was busy recruiting for something he called the Visual Presentation Group for Colonel Wild Bill Donovan's Office of War Information, the organization that eventually became the Office of Strategic Services, or OSS. Though I was not a lay-out man, or a visual artist of any sort, I had had experience in interpreting charts and graphs for *Fortune*, and Hank thought I might be an asset to his group. We had lunch together in Washington with Atherton Richards, one of Wild Bill Donovan's personnel people, and I accepted a part-time per-diem job which would take me to Washington a couple of days a week. I could do this and still carry on at Columbia and do wartime journalism in New York.

Before I could be passed for government work, however, I had to be investigated by the FBI. One freezing day in Connecticut there was a knock on the front door. A young man with a Deep South accent explained that his car had slid off the road opposite our house and he couldn't get it back on. My wife and I went out with a pailful of ashes and a couple of shovels to help the poor fellow, who knew nothing about coping with Northern snows. When we had gotten the car back to a place where it had traction, we invited the stranger in for a cup of coffee.

Without asking our names he explained why he had come to our road. He worked for the FBI, and was trying to find out something about a man named Chamberlain who must be a neighbor of mine. He showed us his FBI credentials, and waited for us to open up. Peg and I couldn't have been more amused as we assured him that Mr. Chamberlain was indeed a good patriot and an honest man. The strain of remaining deadpan was too much for Peg, however. The poor fellow was a picture of embarrassment when she told him that we, not our neighbors down the road, were the Chamberlains. He stammered and apologized, thanked us again for our help with his car, and then went off to ask questions of some people whose names we had given him. I never told J. Edgar Hoover, whom I later came to know under friendly circumstances, the strange lapse on the part of one of his agents, which could have been due to confusion because of the difficulties any Southerner would have had in coping with winter weather in New

England. I admired Mr. Hoover, and had nothing against the FBI, so I was careful about telling the story of my "investigation" to possible FBI detractors. Nobody ever showed me my "unevaluated" dossier at FBI headquarters, but presumably the fact that I had remained a "keep out of war" advocate after Hitler had attacked Russia had proved to the government's satisfaction that I was no Communist, nor even a Communist sympathizer. So I was passed to do a job for Bill Donovan.

After going through the mill of an FBI investigation I was somewhat surprised by the names on some of the doors at Donovan's COI headquarters in one of those old "temporary" wooden World War I buildings in Washington. Dan Gilmor, the publisher of the Popular Front *Friday Magazine*, and David Zablodowsky, whom I had known in literary New York as a fervid Communist sympathizer, were on Donovan's payroll. But this was a post-Stalin-Hitler Pact period, and on reflection I could see why Wild Bill should not be unduly worried about bringing the old Popular Front into his establishment. (As Wallace Carroll was to say later, "We're in this with Russia.")

Donovan adhered to the rule of "the enemy of my enemy is my friend," so it mattered little to him that he had taken on ex-Popular Fronters who could be counted on in any case to give full measure in fighting Fascism. The rule, of course, was applied in Washington unevenly; Malcolm Cowley, who had had his own pro-Stalin period in New York but who was a most dedicated enemy of Hitler, got into trouble with his employers at the Office of War Information and was deprived of a job which he would surely have broken his neck to carry out.

The secrets were well kept at Donovan's headquarters. I saw something of Walt Rostow, but never knew what he was doing. Sherman Kent, a Yale professor of history whom I had known in New Haven, came and went, but it was not known to me until after the war that he had had a major hand in the North African invasion planning. He went on to a permanent career in the CIA. Our own Visual Presentation Group was engaged in less hush-hush work; we were handed the task of putting material from the so-called One Hundred Professors into chart-and-graph form so that busy VIPs such as General Marshall and Harry Hopkins could take in important information at a glance.

Our first project was to prepare an easy-to-assimilate booklet on comparative strengths along the Russo-German front. We went assiduously to work, but by the time we had something put into final form the Nazis erupted and the whole Eastern front changed. A good managing editor with a competent staff could have whipped the material into usable shape within a week, but government procedures were not those of the normal marketplace.

Everything that the Visual Presentation Group did had to be reviewed and then reviewed again. So, after six months, Colonel Donovan or someone under him decided to junk the whole procedure. The stuff from the One Hundred Professors presumably was used in unedited form. Maybe the unprocessed material was helpful to Marshall and Hopkins, but if they learned anything at all from it I am sure they got it second-hand from Bill Donovan by word of mouth.

When the office of the Coordinator of Information was reorganized to become the OSS, with per-diem work an uncertainty, I had to choose between applying for full-time status or wait for another Hank Brennan to think of me for some special connection. The experience with bureaucracy in trying to get the Visual-Presentation product to press in time to be useful had not been encouraging. Wild Bill Donovan, of course, was not a bureaucratic type; he carried out his own exploits without interference, and many of his trusted lieutenants, as I was to learn when I did a long article on OSS for *Life* after the war, were molded in his own image. But there was no special dispensation for office-workers in Washington; they had to "go through channels" even in Donovan's relatively free-wheeling establishment.

With other commitments piling up, and with *Fortune* wartime assignments becoming more and more interesting, I decided against trying to become an OSS bureaucrat. Office routine had always driven me to revolt anyway. I had always found exhilaration in balancing several jobs, and I had certainly worked out a blend for myself that gave me plenty of variety. I was doing the book column for the *New York Times* again, splitting the assignments with Orville Prescott. But reading was something for trains, evenings, and week-ends. During most of the week I was busy covering labor for *Fortune* and the Freedom House column, or communing with the Columbia Journalism students and correcting their papers, which I found for the most part an enjoyable occupation.

I had good relations with Charles Merz, the editor-in-chief of the *Times*, and with Edwin—or Jimmy—James, the managing editor. Charlie Merz was a liberal, in the old *New York World* tradition, but he was also an ironist with a good sense of the ridiculous. His *The Great American Bandwagon* had made excellent Menckenian fun of the "joiner" impulse that has had such a free play in American life, and it is a pity in a way that Charlie Merz had ever permitted himself to be absorbed into editorial anonymity. After the collapse of the *New York World*, for which he had written editorials under Walter Lippmann, Charlie had sold all his stocks and took himself off on a year's tour around the world. The 1929 collapse occurred when he was somewhere in Asia, his money safely out of the market.

Any other person would have boasted of special foresight, but this was not Merz's way. Actually he did have foresight; in 1933 after the Roosevelt "hundred days," he advised me to buy certain stocks, and I made my first Wall Street venture under his tutelage.

Merz disliked pomposity, and he took quiet enjoyment in pricking the pretensions of even his closest friends. He had been hired by *Harper's* at

one time to complete a world affairs review-of-the-year book for Walter
Lippmann, and had found in the papers a Lippmann directive to an
editorial researcher requesting some "facts" to support a preconceived
opinion. Charlie Merz showed me the directive with a most wicked grin.
He particularly relished telling stories about Francis Hackett's jealousy of
Lippmann. Hackett had once coveted a desk in a Chelsea shop window.
When Lippmann bought the desk, Hackett was convinced it was done to
spite him. "He knew I wanted it," Hackett told Merz.

My wife Peggy and I exchanged visits with Charlie and his delightful
wife Evelyn, and it was easy to see how domestic happiness had combined
with events to make Charlie perfectly contented with the anonymity of
editorializing for a good, grey page. He had a quiet sense of artistry that
expressed itself in such things as putting up new wallpaper in his apartment. I always felt that the world had lost a successor to Mencken when
Charles Merz elected to become the voice of an institution. But Charlie did
not believe in cultivating an ego. He often laughed at his early *New
Republic* days when he had taken seriously the claims of North Dakota
farmer-labor politicians to be the prophetic voice of the future.

When my wife Peggy died at the young age of 49, I received a most
sympathetic note from Charlie Merz despite the fact that I had not seen him
for a decade and had come to differ with him publicly on the subject of
Senator Joe McCarthy, who seemed to me a well-meaning patriot even
though he lacked both verbal finesse and a sense of arithmetic. Before
reverting to his *New Republican* attitude in the McCarthy period, Merz
had had many misgivings about contemporary economic radicalism. He
liked my attitude toward some of the books on economics that carried
liberalism to insane extremes, and said he hoped I would be around after
the war to play Sancho Panza on the daily *Times* book page to the Don
Quixotes of the economic realm.

As for Jimmy James, he continued to let my review copy go through
unedited. I was on a free contract basis with the *Times*, getting paid so
much for each review, and when I came down with acute appendicitis in
early 1944 and had to miss a few reviews, an outraged James went to bat for
me with the *Times* accounting department to keep my payment checks
coming until I was out of the hospital. It was this sort of thing that made
Jimmy James beloved of his staff in spite of his grumpy exterior. I got along
with James's enemy, Lester Markel of the Sunday Department, too. I
couldn't agree with his opinions about Russia or New Deal policy, but I
appreciated the nice things he had to say about my book column, particularly a rhymed review I did of the seed catalogues. It was Markel who had
suggested that the *Times* rehire me for daily reviewing when he learned
that I had left a staff job at *Fortune*, and I felt a loyalty to him as a
benefactor even though I disliked his philosophical drift. So, with good
personal relations all around, I might have had a third career with the

Times. I had some exploratory talks with Iphigenia Sulzberger, Adolph Ochs's daughter, about doing a semi-official biography of her father, but they eventually came to nothing, and Gerald Johnson of Baltimore got the job after the war.

My trouble was a growing conservatism that cut across publisher Arthur Sulzberger's increasing enchantment with ideas that would have horrified Rollo Ogden, who had been Merz's predecessor as chief of the editorial page. Henry Hazlitt, who did economic editorials and a Sunday economics feature, was having the same sort of difficulty blending his classical liberalism with Sulzberger's belated New Dealism.

Sulzberger, a thoroughly decent person, did not welcome crude breaks with anybody, and for a period the *Times* editorial page presented some subtle discords as the older liberalism contended with the new. Through all this period Simeon Strunsky, with whom I had many a delightful conversation, carried on his "Topics of the Times" column which poked considerable fun at the newer radicals. Sulzberger was continually beset by Lester Markel, who wanted to bring Donald Adams's *Sunday Book Review* section under direct control of the Sunday Department. But Adams, who had taken violent personal issue when Markel referred to William Henry Chamberlin, the disillusioned expert on Soviet Russia, as a "discredited" man, would not serve under Markel.

For a number of years Sulzberger refused to make the indicated move against Adams, but eventually he succumbed. He could not, however, bring himself to fire the redoubtable Donald, a man of complete integrity. A compromise was reached that turned over page two of the Sunday review to Adams for his own column, "Speaking of Books," and any column of selections which Adams personally submitted. The arrangement rankled with Adams for years, but he made the best of it, producing some worthy books in his semi-retirement and providing an "against the grain" offset in the Sunday review itself to the "liberal" outlook that dominated the rest of the section under Robert Van Gelder and Francis Brown. Adams never forgave Lester Markel, and he was, at the time of his death, contemplating a book that would blow the gaff on Markel's role in what Adams complained was the *"Gleischgeshaltung"* of the *Times* Sunday edition.

I saw Don Adams at a Dutch Treat Club luncheon shortly before his death. He had promised the Dutch Treaters a block-busting speech on current newspaper practice, which presumably included the practice of the *New York Times*. But the speech turned out to be incomprehensibly affable. Whether Don ever wrote any of his promised exposé I do not know; he was not vindictive, and he probably kept putting it off. But Gay Talese, whose book about the *Times*, *The Power and the Glory*, is one of the best novelistic treatments of office politics that I have ever read, could have interviewed Don Adams and learned much that escaped him. Talese is great stuff when he writes about what he has personally observed; his

account of the manuevering between the *Times* home office in New York
and the Washington bureau is real close-in reporting done with a born
novelist's flair for the telling detail. But the real story of the fight for the
Times's soul is not in Talese's book; it happened just before he came on the
Times.

The fight was a muffled part of the Cold War, with the appeasers
winning the ultimate victory. True enough, nobody in the *Times* hierarchy
ever thought of it that way.

Scotty Reston, who had Sulzberger's ear, had so much common sense
himself that he couldn't bring himself to believe that the rulers of the
Communist world would persist in their ideological madness. He had taken
Hitler's blueprint for world conquest seriously, but he never thought Marxism was just another type of fascism. The stalwarts who would have
opposed letting the Soviets creep up on us in atomic potential, and who
would have resisted such things as premature use of the Pentagon papers,
were unable to hold their own in the atmosphere of the *Times*, and they
never managed to choose their own successors.

You will look in vain in the index of Gay Talese's book for the name of J.
Donald Adams, yet it was Adams who stood off Lester Markel for years to
keep the *Sunday Times Book Review* a relatively objective journal. Hanson
Baldwin, the *Times'* military expert who opposed the general drift of the
paper during the Vietnam struggle, gets cursory mention, but Simeon
Strunsky, who did the "Topics of the Times" column as a steady feature
before it was degraded and turned over to aspiring copy boys for trial
flights, is apparently unknown to Talese. As I have recorded, it was
Strunsky, the ex-socialist, who had saved me in my run-in in the '30s with
Walter Duranty, and this grand old man seldom missed a chance to fight
the pro-Soviet bias of some of the newer *Times* men.

Henry Hazlitt, who left the *Times* in the '40s to do the business-tides
column in *Newsweek*, is another unknown to Talese. Yet Hazlitt labored
long and hard to keep Arthur Hays Sulzberger from being seduced by the
economics of Henry Wallace. He got his reward by being regarded by the
Times as a non-person when he testified before Congress on the subject of
his book, *American Dollars Will Not Save the World*. The *Times* reporter,
who must have known that Hazlitt was an ex-*Times*man, gave him not a
line.

The *Times* was changing when I left it for the third time in 1944, but it
was not until Edwin L. James had died that its Leftward drift became
rapidly pronounced. The shift swung around the enigmatic figure of
Turner Catledge, who succeeded James as managing editor.

I had known Catledge in the '30s, and a more unlikely revolutionist
cannot be conceived. All of his younger instincts were conservative. He had
first come to fame in the '20s during the time of the Mississippi flood when
Herbert Hoover, who was directing flood relief, was impressed with his

skills as an observer and delighted by his flavorsome way of expressing himself. It was Hoover who first recommended Turner Catledge to Adolph Ochs.

Catledge had been hired on a moonlighting proposition to brief *Fortune* writers during their trips to Washington, and I was charmed by his inimitable imitations of the Southern senators whose company he frankly preferred to that of the New Dealers. He particularly delighted in a take-off of South Carolina's Cotton Ed Smith, who had walked out on the Democratic Convention in 1936 rather than listen to a Negro minister. "Jesus Christ, black as melted midnight," said Cotton Ed as he departed.

Catledge didn't exactly approve of such crudity, but he retailed his anecdotes of Cotton Ed with marked affection. Senator Pat Harrison of Mississippi was another of Turner's friends, as was South Carolina's Jimmy Byrnes. Turner would not have gone against Jimmy Byrnes' decision to fight the Cold War as Secretary of State under Truman. But a certain type of instinctive conservative changes as the social atmosphere changes. Turner Catledge, as managing editor of the *Times*, would naturally suport a new status quo. Despite his distaste for Roosevelt's methods, and for the Happy Hot Dogs who had been spotted around Washington in the '30s by Felix Frankfurter, Turner had gone along with changes in the national atmosphere. As he regarded it, there was nothing ideological about thinking that the U.S. was rich enough to take care of its poor.

Turner Catledge helped create the modern *New York Times*, vastly improving its writing and reporting techniques. In many ways the modern *Times* is a much better product than it was when Henry Luce called it "the world's greatest unedited newspaper." But Catledge's ambitions for the paper were limited by his lack of judgment about deeper philosophical matters. In running the paper he made many changes that he thought of as technical and administrative. Arthur Krock, a good judge of reportorial talent, had brought Turner along in the Washington Bureau, and Catledge was always loyal to Krock as a person, even as he was loyal to Edwin L. James when he was his assistant in New York. But it is significant that Catledge speaks in his book (*My Life and the Times*) of his long friendship with Arthur Krock without raising the question of Krock's own philosophic conservatism.

When Krock finally gave up his column and ceased to be a Washington influence, Catledge spoke of Tom Wicker, who took over in the capital, as a brilliant reporter. Wicker may have been a good newsman when covering spot news, but the crowds he saw in the Chicago streets during the Democratic convention week of 1968 were not the crowds I saw. Both as a Washington bureau chief and as a columnist, Wicker favored causes that Krock regarded as menaces to the Republic. Strangely, this never bothered Turner Catledge. Turner was never responsible for the *Times* editorial page, but he does not comment in his book that, for *Times* readers, the

descent from Krock to Wicker meant a disastrous loss of balance. No one
has replaced Arthur Krock, either by coming up through the Washington
news room or from outside. The *Times* has obeyed a sound impulse in
starting its opposite-the-editorial page, but even this effort to accommodate the critics of its policies does not compensate for the disproportion
that has only William Safire to balance the Anthony Lewises and Tom
Wickers of this world.

Turner Catledge's own uncomplicated brand of Democratic liberalism
put blinders on him. The changes in *Times* personnel that he presided over
tended toward a uniform pattern; when someone went, for reasons of
tightening the organization or improving the style, the result was almost
always to replace a conservative with a liberal. When the nightside
"bullpen editors," Raymond McCaw and Neil MacNeil, were replaced, the
conservative judgment disappeared along with them. MacNeil saw it coming, and kept me informed from time to time about the changing climate of
the city room which I had regarded as my first real New York home.
Catledge worked with many good reporters, and he is just to most of them;
but Hanson Baldwin, his first-rate military correspondent, gets even less
respect in Turner's reminiscences than he does in the Gay Talese book.

Ruby Hart Phillips, the veteran *Times* correspondent in Havana, tried to
warn her home office that Fidel Castro was not the Robin Hood that
Herbert Matthews, always a romantic about revolutions, supposed he was.
But the index of Turner Catledge's book does not contain Ruby Hart
Phillips's name. Turner remains a vaguely uneasy apologist for Matthews,
who, in selling the *Times* on Castro's claim to being the Cuban Messiah,
also sold the U.S. public on it. When Castro turned out to be a Leninist,
self-proclaimed as such, the *Times*, worried about its "credibility," ceased
to use Matthews as a reporter on Latin America, though it still welcomed
him as an editorial writer. Catledge had to serve as the instrument of
Matthews' banishment from the newsroom, but he still wonders whether
Matthews was "more sinned against than sinning." He missed the main
point, which is that a more philosophically aware managing editor would
have known what Alice-Leone Moats had already published about Castro
before Herbert Matthews "discovered" him. Writing for Bill Buckley's
National Review some 18 months before the fall of Batista, Miss Moats,
working from her Mexican police sources, told her readers that Castro was
a Communist pawn long before his eruption from the Sierra Maestra.

Because it was "news," Catledge broke Tad Szulz's story of the Cuban
exiles' training for the Bay of Pigs invasion. Though it might be argued that
this was a more dangerous breach of security than printing the Pentagon
Papers, Catledge justifies his decision by quoting John F. Kennedy as
telling him that "if you had printed more about the operation you would
have saved us from a colossal mistake." Given Turner Catledge's view of
the proper news treatment of the Bay of Pigs, it is hardly surprising that it

was Charles J.V. Murphy of *Time* who got the story from sources close to the CIA and the Pentagon of the disastrous White House backing and filling about supplying the needed air cover for the Bay of Pigs landings. When and if Dick Bissell of the CIA writes his memoirs, it will be the White House, not the "military," that will look bad. And Murphy will look like a better reporter than any that Catledge put on the job.

The "cultural" daily *Times*, never very distinguished in Adolph Ochs's day, continued to improve under Catledge, who detailed Alden Whitman, a copy editor wth a good background in the arts, to do the more important *Times* obituaries. From the standpoint of literature, this was a brilliant stroke. But, again, it suffered from philosophical drawbacks. It saddened me that the *Times* obituary for John Dos Passos repeated all the clichés about Dos's "failure" as a writer after turning "conservative." Aside from the fact that Dos always remained a libertarian, he had had a great second career as an historian and biographer in his later life. He had instructed a whole new generation in the ways of the Founding Fathers with his books on the lost world of Thomas Jefferson. You could not, however, have learned this from the *Times* treatment.

The news sections of the *Times* have been better under Abe Rosenthal, who is a sophisticated man about the climate of post-New Left America. I had his promise in a letter that he intends to fight to the end against the impulse of young advocates of "commitment" to make the *Times* the uptown edition of the *Village Voice*. But the *Times* needs competition, and it gets none in a New York that is shockingly bare of newspapers. Along with Henry Hazlitt, with whom I have often lamented what has happened to the editorial point of view of the *Times*, I followed with melancholy interest, sometimes tinged with hope, the course of the newspaper that taught me journalism. Jeffrey Hart, a *National Review* editor and a fellow columnist, says that the *Times* has lost all legitimate claim to being a "newspaper of record." I can't agree with him, for I still find its coverage indispensable in getting leads for my own column ideas. But unless some competition emerges to challenge its domination in its own city, Hart could be proven right in the long run. I would hate to see that happen, for it would be something in the nature of a mortal blow to an old friend. And I suppose I should be humble in criticizing *Times* ideological stances. Maybe Turner Catledge's trouble was that he had taken some of my reviews in the early '30s all too seriously.

Chapter 10

History is full of turning points that fail to produce the expected turns. Or, better, it is full of turning points that collide with the unforeseen. In 1938, Harry Luce, who had never accepted Franklin D. Roosevelt's New Deal with any grace, began to talk of a new Republican era. The slump that had come in 1937, when Roosevelt had had to renew his pump-priming, had led to the "recession within a recession," and the results were felt at the polls in November of 1938 when Republicans gained 11 seats in the Senate and 81 in the House, meanwhile increasing their state governorships from 7 to 18. It was an astounding victory, made all the sweeter to Luce by the emergence of hopeful young Republican liberals such as Harold Stassen of Minnesota and Leverett Saltonstall of Massachusetts.

Pursuing the theory that a real turning point was at hand, Harry Luce willingly promoted Wendell Willkie, a maverick Democrat-about-to-turn-Republican, in the pages of *Fortune*, with managing editor Russell Davenport doubling as Willkie's ghost in an article that bore all the earmarks of a platform manifesto. Willkie might have made the White House on economic issues in 1940 if the war hadn't interrupted the old rhythms of politics, which ordinarily move from reform to frustration and then back to the solid men. During the first years of the war, Luce kept his Republican sympathies more or less to himself, but as 1944 approached he began sniffing the wind. Assured that I was no advocate of a fourth term for Franklin Roosevelt, he let me do a long close-up of Wendell Willkie for *Life* magazine. It was obvious that Harry Luce wanted to believe in Willkie, but the party realists had it set down as a Dewey year, and there was much doubt about the possibility of beating F.D.R. anyway while the war continued.

I was charmed by Willkie's personality, describing it as "alkaline" and exuding "the eupeptic quality of the big, healthy, buffalo-bull man whose digestive juices run freely and whose nights are dreamless." His economic goals seemed clear enough, but there was a blurry quality to his "one world" foreign policy approach. With Joe Barnes, a confirmed Leftist, helping him to write the book called *One World*, it was perhaps no mystery that much of Wendell Willkie sounded like Henry Wallace.

I concluded that Willkie had been spending too much time wooing the *New York Post* and *PM* liberals to make the necessary appeal to the center of the Republican Party. The Negroes, the Jews, the New York literary crowd that listened to Willkie's good friend Irita Van Doren of the *Herald-Tribune Sunday Book Review*, were for Willkie, but it was mostly on a second-best friend basis. David Dubinsky, the boss of the International Ladies Garment Workers Union, told me he thought Willkie was a fine fellow, but his union was nonetheless sticking to Roosevelt. What it all added up to was that Willkie had developed a following that might have supported him if Roosevelt had decided to call it a day after three terms as President. But the liberals would obviously not be voting in Republican primaries throughout the land. Dorothy Thompson, though a liberal herself, warned Willkie to stop campaigning on Park Avenue, but he didn't listen.

My close-up of Willkie, which was skeptical of his ability to go before Midwest Republicans with a clear outline, hit the stands in the middle of the Nebraska primary week. When Willkie saw it, he went through the roof. He dispatched an enraged telegram to Harry Luce complaining of Time, Inc., perfidy. The close-up, which was friendly enough in its detail, couldn't have affected the Nebraska vote to any appreciable extent, but Willkie was an all-or-nothing fellow when it came to demanding personal loyalty. He was more angry at Luce, his old friend, than at me, so I got the impact of the Willkie displeasure second-hand.

With his sharp journalistic judgment, Luce knew—after the first primary verdicts were in—that Willkie couldn't make it. The fact that I had spotted the Willkie weakness put me in line for other close-up assignments when Republican figures were being rated as *Life*-worthy subjects. Eric Johnston, a three-time president of the Chamber of Commerce who was willing to talk to labor leaders and to Franklin Roosevelt, interested me, and I did a close-up of him that appeared while he was touring Soviet Russia with young Bill White of the *Readers Digest* and the *Emporia Gazette*. In personal conversation after his return home, Eric Johnston was clear enough about the Soviets, but for public consumption Bill White turned out to be the realist of the trip. Eric broke the mold for official visitors to Russia by making a speech to the commissars to the effect that the U.S. was unabashedly and proudly capitalist and intended to remain so. But he came back to America with a prediction that the Soviets were only interested in postwar trade with the U.S. Even Harry Hopkins and Averell Harriman knew better than that.

With Tom Dewey looming up as the probable Republican presidential nominee, Luce set me to work on profiles of promising Republicans. I did an enthusiastic study of Herbert Brownell, a Dewey confidante and manager. Luce also put me on the trail of John Foster Dulles, who was slated to be Dewey's Secretary of State. I had read some of Dulles's books, which were highly abstract and gave little hint that the man would, under Eisenhower, become a most skillful practitioner of *machtpolitik*. His criticism of the League of Nations-Versailles system was that it had not allowed for peaceful alteration of boundaries and reparations. This was sound enough in retrospect. It also impressed me as a sound approach when Dulles said the victors in World War II should ask themselves the question: "What can we do to Germany that Russia, England, and the U.S. will stick together on for the next 25 years?" If the question had been asked, we would have had a better peace.

Dulles, as I described him, looked as though he might have just finished contact with a green persimmon, but he had a hidden vein of humor. He spoke of his desire to become Secretary of State, a post which his maternal grandfather, John Watson Foster, had held in Benjamin Harrison's cabinet. He said, however, that if he were to be disappointed by Tom Dewey's failure to win the election, he wouldn't waste away in vain regrets. His job as head of the Federal Council of Churches' Commission on a Just and Durable Peace would, as he put it, give him "an ace in the hole" when the time for the big peace conference arrived.

Harry Luce, the devout Presbyterian, didn't approve mixing card-game terminology with religious-organization matters, so the Dulles remark about an "ace in the hole" disappeared from my copy. The rest of the story ran as written, playing in astounding luck. It hit the stands on the very day that Tom Dewey named Dulles, then pretty much unknown, to confer with Cordell Hull. *Time* magazine routed my researcher, Elaine Keiffer, out of the ocean at Southampton on a week-end to learn the whereabouts of the *Life* research, cribbing even the phrase about the green persimmon for its own story. Dulles said he liked the close-up, but I wonder, in retrospect, whether it did him a great deal of good. A subsequent note from my researcher said that her old lawyer had called her "from John Davis's to say that they had read the piece aloud to each other the night before and they thought you had done a fine job—that you'd showed up Mr. Dulles in his true light as an isolationist . . . he said it was all right to tell you but not to quote John Davis. They felt the piece would do much to hurt the chances of the Republican Party."

This was interesting, coming from the John Davis who had been a Democratic candidate for President in 1924, but it was certainly not my intention to hurt either Dulles or Dewey. What was Davis's "isolationism" was, to me, just Dulles's common sense. In any case, Luce didn't take the Dulles piece as anti-Republican. The *réclame* which the close-up got around the office resulted in a magnificent offer; I could have the job of *Life* "text" man in Washington, doing eight or nine articles a year and paying particular attention to indications of Republican renascence.

Chapter 11

Washington was exciting, the place to be, in the last months of the war, and I played in luck in getting one particular scoop. I hadn't been in the city for more than a couple of months before I found myself listening to a loquacious colonel, a friend of Don Levine's, at a party which Don held at the Wardman Park for his wife Ruth and me, who happen to share the same birthday. The colonel, assuming no doubt that he was speaking off the record, told us about a great "secret" the Republicans had failed to exploit. When Tom Dewey was preparing his campaign for President in 1944, he had learned that the White House had been adequately forewarned of the Japanese attack in time to save our Pacific Fleet from destruction at Pearl Harbor and our bombers from being caught on the ground in the Philippines. The Roosevelt Administration's negligence about passing the warning word to General Short and Admiral Kimmel in Hawaii and General MacArthur in Manila could, theoretically, have been used by Dewey with devastating effect. But with the war still on in 1944 Dewey, a patriot, wondered what disclosure of the great secret would do to our code-cracking in the Pacific. Our cryptographers had broken the Japanese "ultra" code in 1941, and for all that Dewey or his political manager Herbert Brownell knew the Japanese might still be using a variant of their original code in 1944.

I lost no time in sending a memo to Harry Luce about the colonel's disclosures. Luce, of course, reacted as Tom Dewey himself had reacted. He told me to file the information away. It would be useful after the war.

John T. Flynn, of course, was "on" to our 1941 failure to make use of our foreknowledge of the coming Japanese attack, and he had his story ready for post-war use. But he did not know the Dewey angle. Right after the Japanese surrender in August of 1945, Luce told me to get in touch with Dewey, who was on a tour of inspection in western New York. I caught up with Dewey at the Elmira Reformatory after an all-night trip on the Erie Railroad. He asked me to join him in a ride along Lake Seneca to Geneva, the next stop on his tour. In a fascinating hour in which neither of us looked at the beautiful Finger Lake scenery, Dewey told me about the visits to his

117

office of Colonel Carter Clarke, General Marhsall's emissary. It was Clarke who gave Dewey the letters that persuaded him to keep the Pearl Harbor issue out of the 1944 campaign. Dewey said I could use the story of the gagging in *Life*, but warned me that I must not reveal my source.

My *Life* article was by no means as comprehensive as Flynn's articles in the *Chicago Tribune*, but it rated a front-page story in the *New York Times*. Luce was pleased with what he called "Operation Chamberlain," and told me to follow the Pearl Harbor story through the Congressional investigations that were bound to come.

If it is really true that the Japanese never changed their basic code, there is a justification for the wartime suppression of information about our Pearl Harbor negligence. But there was no excuse for the heartless way in which Roosevelt made public scapegoats of Admiral Kimmel and General Short. After all, they had no warning of our code-cracking feat. There was also the double standard involved in Roosevelt's refusal to criticize General MacArthur, who was just as surprised in the Philippines as Kimmel and Short had been in Hawaii.

The big postwar congressional investigation of Pearl Harbor was pushed by Senator Homer Ferguson, the Michigan Republican, who felt sure that he could unearth some evidence that Roosevelt had connived to bring on the Japanese attack in order to get us into the war against Hitler by the back door. I saw Ferguson practically on a day-to-day basis during the investigation in order to do a close-up of him for *Life* called "The Man Who Pushed Pearl Harbor." Try as he might, Ferguson never managed to document his suspicion that Roosevelt had set up our Pacific fleet for attack.

He came closest to pay dirt when Commander Lester Schulz, who had been the naval aide on duty at the White House on the night of December 6, 1941, testified that he had personally delivered the final Japanese intercept to Roosevelt and Harry Hopkins. When Hopkins, after reading the intercept, suggested that we might surprise the Japanese by striking the first blow, Roosevelt said, no, we can't do that. We were, he told Hopkins in the presence of Schulz, "a democracy and a peaceful people." If Roosevelt didn't set us up to be hit, he was obviously prepared to welcome it. In all probability he considered the blow would be delivered in the Philippines, not in mid-Pacific.

It was somewhat damaging when the investigation brought out that the Administration had made an effort to get Admiral Tommy Hart, our naval commander in the Far East and later a U.S. Senator, to deploy some useless reconnaissance ships as decoys to invite an overt act from a Japanese aviator. But this was not quite the unneutral act that Ferguson hoped to uncover. If he had only looked to the Atlantic instead of the Pacific, Ferguson could have proved his case that Roosevelt was prepared without an act of Congress to get us into the war. Roosevelt put an American plane, a Catalina with an American commander, at the service of the British Navy in hunting for the *Bismarck*. There are other examples of illegal activity on Roosevelt's part in two astonishing books, *A Man Called Intrepid*, by William Stevenson, and *Bodyguard of Lies*, by Anthony Cave Brown. If Ferguson had had these books as evidence, his investigation would really have had the town ringing. The Michigan Senator was just one ocean away from his quarry.

Roosevelt, of course, was willing to take his chances. He knew what he was doing. He admitted as much when he wondered to Bob Sherwood if he would be impeached because of the aid he gave the British in the *Bismarck* hunt.

Harry Luce's motive in giving me my head on the Pearl Harbor story was not, as it might have appeared, to sustain a case for isolation. What Luce hoped to do was to use Pearl Harbor to prove the necessity of achieving an honest integration of foreign and military policy and popular understanding. We had no CIA in 1941 to assess the significance of Navy Commander Alwin Kramer's warning that Japanese intercepts, particularly the one that divided Pearl Harbor into sub-areas, might indicate an attack on our fleet.

After my Pearl Harbor articles, Dan Longwell, the *Life* publisher, thought I deserved a break. He suggested that I go to England for a couple of months to do profiles of Harold Laski and other luminaries in the newly ascendant British Labour Party. With Willi Schlamm, who had a special Luce assignment, I set sail in a decrepit Scandinavian tub whose name I have forgotten. Once in London, I discovered that my Homer Ferguson article did not exactly make me a local hero. But I had done a sympathetic profile of Lord Halifax, the British Ambassador in Washington, which helped me dispel the accusation of being anti-British. Labour Party people were cooperative, and I had a fascinating two-months visit to the dubious world of "planning" that was to afflict us all.

My British experience just about completed my conversion to a frankly pro-capitalist philosophy of voluntarism. The British Food Minister John Strachey, whom I had met in New York during his detention on Ellis Island, sent me up to his constituency in Dundee, Scotland, with assurances that I would find something impressive in the "planning" that was turning the old whaling city from a depressed into a development area. But Dundee seemed to me to be something of a Potemkin village, getting special preference along with certain towns in South Wales and on the River Tyne that were, actually, badly situated for marketing and production. I visited Rebecca West at her dairy farm in the Chiltern Hills, and listened to her general approval of the Labour Party "fair shares" thinking. But when it came to specifics no one was more critical than Miss West.

She and her husband were having difficulty with the Labour Party's animus against so-called tied cottages—meaning cottages built by farm owners to rent to farmhands. The Labour Party wanted farm laborers either to own their own homes or to rent them from a kindly government.

But while the ideological argument went on, no cottages of any sort were being built.

Harold Laski talked a good show with me, and so did Herbert Morrison and G.D.H. Cole. But everywhere there seemed to be a passiveness and a caged tightness in the muscles. I put my feelings not only into a close-up of Harold Laski for *Life* but into a long article for the *Yale Review.* The philosophy of "fair shares" was theoretically very moral, but what did it really mean to a shopkeeper who had to add 18 hours of paper work per week to his normal 44 hours of shop tending? Form-filling had become the bane of English life. "The system," I wrote in the *Yale Review*, "imposes its own limitations on British recovery, for the incredibly numerous acts of form filling and coupon cutting, sorting, marking, and counting take time, some of which might better be spent in productive labor—say, in repairing blitzed homes." I added that "if the modern British had more of the blood of their smuggling ancestors in them, if they were not so absolutely bent on fairness and high honor, they could better their overall production and consumption records."

The British excuse was that "planning" and controls were necessary to pull a blighted country out of a condition imposed by five years of savage war. But the West Germans, the French, and the Japanese, all of whom had suffered as much as Britain, followed a different course—and now, 35 years after my visit to England in 1946, the British are trying desperately to go back to the voluntarism that made them the first of the great modern nations.

The nature of the British troubles was underscored for me by Malcolm Muggeridge, an acute observer who spent some of the war years in Washington as a British correspondent. Malcolm, unlike most of his foreign correspondent friends, refused to get his news at the Press Club bar; if he quoted John L. Lewis it was not from hearsay but as the result of a bona fide interview. We went sailing together, and talked about liberal delusions. We also spent some memorable evenings together with his daughter Val and his good, if contentious, friend Freda Utley, whom he ragged continually because of her insistence that hating the Germans would not make for a good peace. "But Freda," Malcolm would expostulate—meaning that talk about the high cost of vengeance should be postponed while fighting was going on. Freda and Malcolm agreed on Russia, but on little else.

Actually Malcolm Muggeridge was anything but a vengeful man. He had a gorgeous sense of humor, which he indulged particularly at the expense of his old friends in the British Fabian movement. When he went back to England it was with a sardonic statement that he intended to get a job that would pay off in all the perquisites that he delighted in lampooning. When *Punch* made him its editor he specialized in publishing great parodies. I don't know what his *Punch* perks were, but maybe the privilege of laughing in gloomy England was a perquisite all in itself.

My British interlude made me impatient with some of the thinking in Washington, which promised to bring the so-called British disease to our own shores. The longer I stayed in Washington, the more I became convinced that a country can only be happy and prosperous by keeping its politicians on a taut leash. I enjoyed doing some never-used profiles of Clare Luce and Martha Taft, who, though deep in politics, distrusted the whole scene. I found I had become permanently incapable of being a purely political correspondent. The politicians with whom I talked, even so enlightened a person as Bob Taft, all had varying degrees of the Chanticleer complex; they thought that their crowing had something to do with the sun coming up. Politicians are needed to deal with the clashing of energies out in the country, or in the world, but, once Potomac fever has caught a man, it takes a real intellectual effort for him to realize that Washington itself does not originate much. Government is much better at applying the brakes than it is in providing the gas or stepping on the accelerator.

So, once the pressure of doing war and war-related stories for *Life* had lessened, I found myself asking for more and more assignments that took me away from Capitol Hill. My urge was intermittent, and not entirely conscious in its beginnings. Life in Washington, with its early springs, was pleasant; though I had the full use of the Time, Inc., office and owed nominal fealty to Bob Elson, the amiable Washington chief who succeeded Felix Belair (who had returned to the New York *Times*), I was not bound by the office in any way. I had discovered a new sport in figure skating through taking my daughters to the Chevy Chase and Uline rinks, and I had a small sailboat on the Potomac. Only the summers were unbearable in Washington, but there were always ways of getting out of town in the hottest months. One summer I talked Dan Longwell at *Life* into letting me do a long close-up of Ted Williams, which meant watching ball games in Boston and talking with players who were split on the proposition that Ted could follow the ball to the very moment of its collision with the bat. Williams did not approve the piece as it came out in *Life*, principally because it touched on such bits of family history as his mother's career as a Salvation Army lassie. I could see his point about nosiness, but the Williams' passion to excel could not be explained without some mention of his origins. Later on, when I came to know John Leonard, now the *New York Times'* cultural critic, at Bill Buckley's *National Review*, where he indulged a youthful aberration by working for a conservative publication, we found we had a common bond in our admiration for Ted Williams' perfectionism. On another atypical hot weather assignment, I rode around the National League circuit with Branch Rickey of the Brooklyn Dodgers in his Beechcraft, making notes for an article that failed to get into *Life* for the simple reason that the Dodgers did not win the pennant. Rickey was a phenomenon, a baseball man with superlative brains; if he had lived long enough to use a computer in making trades, the Lord only knows what sort of perpetually-winning baseball dynasty he might have put together. Even without a computer he did well enough; he had put a statistician to work on his crack outfielder, Dixie Walker, to work out the pattern of his hitting, and when the statistician disclosed that Walker was getting fewer "pulled" hits and more straightway or even late hits, which portended fading reflexes, he did not hesitate to trade him. We had a sore-armed pitcher named Dockham, as I recall, in the Beechcraft on the way from New York to St. Louis, and I watched with considerable amusement the bewildered look on the pitcher's face as Rickey tried to tell him that it was good for young ballplayers to get low salaries for starters. Rickey's theory was that low pay made a young player hungry for a World's Series check and led him to superior performance that could be turned into a high salary later on.

Traveling with the Brooklyn club was particularly interesting that year, for Rickey had just brought Jackie Robinson up from Montreal to be the first black ballplayer to crack the color line. Jackie, who was playing an unfamiliar position at first base, was under strict orders from Rickey to take any and all insults and even physical provocation without protest. It was a special ordeal for Robinson to play in St. Louis, which had its extra quota of prejudiced Southern ballplayers, yet he adhered grimly to Rickey's instructions. I was sitting in a box with Dodger centerfielder Pete Reiser, who was recuperating from a head injury, when a St. Louis player tried in an obviously gratuitous way to hurt Robinson on a play at first base. Reiser's impulse was to get out of the box, injured head and all, and go to Robinson's aid, but, after starting up, he too, remembered Rickey's orders. He took out his anger by explaining to me in gory detail just what he would have done to avenge himself if he had been in Robinson's place. Reiser, who was suffering at the time from recurring headaches because of a collision with the Ebbets Field wall, was probably the gamest ballplayer who ever lived; he ruined his body—and his great natural ability—by attempting the impossible both in the outfield and on the bases. The team needed him so desperately for that particular St. Louis series that Burt Shotten, the manager, called a meeting in a hotel room with Rickey to try to force the club's trainer to give Reiser a clean bill of health regardless of the headaches. The trainer stood out adamantly against Shotten's continued muttering that "we gotta get him in there or we ain't going to win." In the end Rickey agreed with the trainer that it would be wrong to play Reiser as long as the headaches persisted. I always thought Rickey let me sit in on the meeting just to prove to me that there are some things that baseball magnates won't do to make a dollar. Rickey was one of the slyest men who ever lived, but in all fundamentals he was a man of honor.

I was depressed when *Life* failed to use my Rickey article. But Russell Lynes, a ball fan, bought it for use in *Harper's Magazine*, and it was subsequently picked up from there by the *Reader's Digest* and by a Japanese publication, which meant that I got paid for it four times.

With summer respites, such as the Rickey trip, I could have gone on living in a tree-shaded house in Georgetown, across the street from Drew Pearson, for the rest of my working life if it had not been for the libertarian twist in my thinking that rejected the idea of dealing only with characters who either pushed or served the centralizing political tendencies which I had come so much to distrust.

In June of 1945 I wrote a long piece about the change in tempo in the White House that came with Harry Truman's ascension to the presidency. It seemed to me then that the statement of Truman's grocer, Mr. C.B. Pinckney, that Harry "is a man who everlastingly knows the price of a can of peas," portended a return to an older America in which the ninth and tenth amendments to the Constitution would become visible once more as the states and individual citizens began to function for themselves. Harry Truman did turn out to be a good President, maybe even one of our greatest, in his plucky resistance to Stalin's immediate post-war designs to take over Mediterranean Europe. But on the domestic front Truman was a disappointment. His Fair Deal was just another version of the New Deal as the Democratic Party proved to be an impossible vehicle for returning the country to individuals in voluntary association.

Why did I spark to the opportunity to spend time in Georgia writing about its unusual Governor Ellis Arnall? I had been piqued by statements attributed to him that he had no desire for Washington preferment. Arnall, though he was an accomplished politician who might have made it big in Washington, was a true decentralist who wanted to see the doctrine of states' rights complemented by an equivalent doctrine of local power. His effort as governor was to invoke state power to make centralized federal power unnecessary, or at least unburdensome, and to this end he pushed a big suit to force the Interstate Commerce Commission to change the freight rates that favored the North on the shipment of class goods. His argument was that if Georgia could become a producer of finished goods as well as a source of raw materials, the "race problem" would tend to disappear in the growing prosperity.

Arnall was a supporter of Cason Callaway, a retired textile tycoon who thought he had discovered a way of saving agriculture without running to Washington for money. Callaway had organized 100 corporations known as "Georgia Better Farm Units." Each unit was owned by seven stockholders who had put up $1,000 each toward the purchase and incorporation of a 100-acre farm. The idea was to give individual farmers an opportunity to make a profit from raising crops for the industrial-agricultural businesses of canning, freezing, and dehydrating. Efforts such as Callaway's usually fail to multiply across the board not because they lack merit but because the federal government, with the subsidies made possible by its unchecked taxing power, invariably turns the heads of farmers toward Washington. If the federal government had not been in the business of propping up agriculture in general, the Cason Callaway-Ellis Arnall way of solving farm problems in particular might have had a chance to take hold.

I spent fascinating days in Georgia driving around the state, which was ceasing to be the eroded and beaten land of Erskine Caldwell's novels. And I was beguiled by Arnall's philosophizing, and by his pretty wife's insistence that he was merely a pro-tem politician, into thinking that the Cason Callaways of America, protected by local governors such as Arnall, might really dominate our postwar future. But back in Washington the war of little men to hang on to centralized control of the American economy continued as usual. I filed a report to *Life* in November of 1945 that erred just about as much on the gloomy side as my "Washington in June" piece had erred on the optimistic.

Who remembers today that Harry Truman, who slugged it out against Dewey in 1948 and won an astounding victory, had a lackluster interlude when he went around complaining that he had never asked to be President anyway? Who remembers the crony period when John Caskie Collet, a Missourian ex-county official, ran the Office of Economic Stabilization? Who recalls Chester Bowles's attempts to prolong price-fixing? My November report lamented that the Truman administrators, narrow-gauge men for the most part, had no inkling that such things as prices, wages, reconversion, and stabilization were all subsidiary aspects of production, dependent on the investor's will to risk his capital and the inventor's incitement to come up with new things. The business of getting production going, as the West Germans were to discover in 1948, demanded a departure from the theory that industry should be controlled by politicians—i.e., men skilled in putting on the brakes. What America needed in 1945 was unchecked enterprise, the sort of thing that *Fortune* magazine discovered in Texas and Oklahoma, "lands of the big rich," where cattle multiplied precisely because the U.S. Treasury couldn't seize half a calf at birth and where depletion allowances permitted capital to flow back into the disclosure and exploitation of new sources of oil.

My feelings about returning the country to its productive people were sharpened by conversations with Willis Ballinger of the Federal Trade Commission, and by a chance encounter on Connecticut Avenue with an old college classmate, Professor Aaron Director of the University of Chicago. Ballinger, a student of what had happened to eight free governments in the course of world history when they had allowed production to be choked by directives and taxes, was busy writing a book called, ominously, *By Vote of the People*. Save for Athens and the Third French Republic, which had been overrun by conquerors, six free governments had been destroyed within the framework of the democratic process. Five of them— Rome, Florence, post-Napoleonic France, Weimar Germany, and Italy—

had voted their liberties away. The sixth, Venice, had been done in by a packed legislature which deprived the people of the right to vote.

Ballinger asked me to write a foreword to his book when it was published by Scribner's, and I used my space to lament that the New Deal, which had at one time tried to foster competitive practices under the so-called Temporary National Economic Committee (TNEC) and the trust-busting regime of Thurman Arnold, had returned to the earlier NRA spirit with the post-war battle to continue OPA. Prophetically, I remarked that our tax and control policies were making it impossible for anyone except a rich man like Marshall Field to start a newspaper. (I should have added something about the restrictive practices of the printer's unions.) The stage was being set, I said, for a return to 18th-century mercantilism.

On two points I disagreed with Willis. But he let me say without protest that I disliked his defense of the protective tariff (a breeder of the very rackets which he opposed) and his theory that government can be trusted to break up concentrated wealth or to control its workings by "administrative law." I wanted to see a growth of what I called "mutualizing associations"—producer and consumer cooperatives and profit-sharing industries—which would help people solve their economic problems without bringing government (including Mr. Ballinger's Federal Trade Commission) into the picture.

Ballinger's book did not get any particular *réclame*. Insofar as backing a winner was concerned, I had done better in 1944, my first year in Washington, with another book, Friedrich Hayek's *The Road to Serfdom*. I don't know what Aaron Director was doing in Washington for the government when he ran into me on the street, but we ended up in a restaurant talking about a remarkable manuscript, not his own, which he was about to offer to the University of Chicago Press. Aaron was not strictly an economist, but, as a member of the University of Chicago Law School faculty who specialized in the legal aspects of corporate organization, he shared the economic predilectiohs of the "Chicago school" of Frank Knight and Henry Simons; and, as Professor Milton Friedman's brother-in-law and good friend of George Stigler, he could hardly have avoided a continuing education in the ways of freedom.

Before bumping into me on the street he had had a session with *Fortune* editor John Davenport at the Metropolitan Club. He had hoped, he said, to get Wendell Willkie to write a foreword to the American edition of the Hayek book. The key to Willkie, in Aaron's mind, was John Davenport's brother Russell, Willkie's old 1940 mentor. But Willkie turned the Davenports down, his excuse being that he had too many other commitments. Actually, the changeable Willkie, who had been touring the globe with Joe Barnes, the Leftist character who helped him write *One World*, would not haᵛ been particularly sympathetic to Hayek's point of view, though Hayek could hardly have known this at the time. With Willkie out of the picture, John Davenport had suggested that I be asked to do the foreword. And then, by sheer coincidence, Director had run into me.

The Hayek manuscript, written with knowledge combined with great compassion, seemed to me superlatively good, and I felt greatly honored that Hayek would let me, a mere practicing journalist, do the foreword. I don't think I did a particularly good job of it (my short article on Hayek, written for Kay Jackson's *Free America: A Magazine to Promote Independence*, was much better), but I was glad to have had even a small part in introducing a great thinker on "the constitution of liberty" to the U.S. Hayek, as a leader among the moving spirits who created the Mont Pélérin Society of free economists, has done more than most people to save the West from going the route to full socialism and dictatorship. The Mont Pélérin group, which he, along with Professor Wilhelm Roepke, did so much to nurture, encouraged Ludwig Erhard, a Roepke pupil to remove the dead hand of controls from the West German economy in 1948, and it numbered among its early influential members President Einaudi of Italy. Hayek, after a triumphant appearance in the Town Hall in New York, which helped sell *The Road to Serfdom*, was asked to teach at Chicago; it is a measure of Ivy League shame that he never had a bid to join the faculty of a Harvard or a Princeton.

Life, being a picture magazine, had only a limited tolerance for text pieces designed to prove the case for the free-wheeling economy, so my problem was to find picturesque and pertinacious characters who would exude adventure in addition to exemplifying theory. I went to Pittsburgh to do a profile of Phil Murray, the head of the CIO, with the *arrière pensée* that I would pick up news of Joe Scanlon and his efforts to put "productivity sharing" into the steel industry. Phil Murray had given up his old idea of organizing industry into tripartite labor-management-government councils, the Reutherean gimmick that would have delivered the U.S. business system to a corporate fascism. But even though Phil had rejected socialistic impulses and returned to the belief of his young manhood in the fundamental premises of the American system, he had not bought Scanlon's approach. I had a good time relating Phil Murray to his old background in the coal fields, and, in the course of writing about him, I corrected a number of mistakes about his biography that had become the standard "information" of practically every newspaper morgue in the country. Alas, when the checking department in the *Life* editorial office in New York had finished "correcting" my copy by referring to the old stories, all the old mistakes had been restored. I had to make a hurried trip to New York to purge the copy, but fortunately I managed to beat the deadline. The experience taught me that once something has appeared in print it achieves sanctity, no matter how false it may be.

The search for Joe Scanlon's influence led me to the little Main Street town of East Palestine in Ohio, just over the Pennsylvania border. During the last year of the war, Scanlon had worked out a 50-50 profit-sharing formula for the employees of a small East Palestine company that manufactured welded steel storage tanks. The owner of the company, Cecil Adamson, was a tough, pragmatical man who wondered why the steel-union organization of his shop, which had occurred in the tumultuous '30s, hadn't resulted in a happier productive rhythm. No union baiter, Adamson decided that some incentive should be "organized" into the act of accepting union membership. With the merry, pugnacious Scanlon at his elbow, Adamson asked the still unorganized front office and sales forces to join the union as a pre-condition of sharing the profits. This proved the case to the steel workers on the factory floor that Adamson wasn't using profit-sharing as a trick to weaken labor solidarity.

When the total Adamson Company working force of 100 split a bonus of $4,200 the first month, with gradations according to wage scales, the shop suddenly became alive. All sorts of suggestions began to pour in for improving welding techniques. Workers who had stood around waiting for materials found themselves helping with the loading and unloading; men started to learn extra jobs so that they would be interchangeable in case sickness cut down on the work force. The faster workers helped the slower, and when 1945, the first year of the Scanlon formula, had ended, Cecil Adamson discovered that his plant had registered a 54 per cent increase in production efficiency. The increase in income for the workers had more than doubled the profits of the stockholders.

The rhythm of the company had become that of a winning ball club or a fine symphony orchestra, and the industrial-relations professors started beating a path to Adamson's door. Incidentally, they carried Scanlon off to academia, to teach industrial relations at M.I.T., where he found more scope for proselytizing than he could find under Phil Murray in Pittsburgh.

My Adamson article—"Every Man a Capitalist"—struck fire with a Yankee engineer from Farmington, Connecticut, Ed Hall, who was convinced that if he could only persuade Congressman Wilbur Mills to tie voluntaristic profit-sharing to corporate tax deductions it would solve the whole "social" question for America. Ed Hall became a familiar figure haunting the anterooms on Capitol Hill, but his argument that profit-sharing coupled with tax advantages would put an end to strikes and lock-outs never received enough willing listeners. Despite Scanlon's failure to convince Phil Murray, and Ed Hall's failure to enlist the cooperation of Wilbur Mills, profit-sharing has had its successes. In a recent count, some six million American employees were covered in 77,000 deferred profit-sharing plans, with trust funds exceeding $20 billion. The Council of Profit Sharing Industries swears that the financial performance of profit-sharing companies is superior to that of the non-profit sharers. This could prove everything or nothing, depending on which came first, the chicken or the egg, but I was nonetheless highly gratified when the Profit Sharing

Research Foundation chose, in September of 1971, to hark back to words I had written to the effect that a "progress-sharing" union contract is the only possible way of satisfying both labor and the consumer without saddling industry with fixed costs that, in times of depression, must kill off the marginal companies like so many flies. Recently Mildred Adams McLearn, a contributor to Bill Buckley's *National Review*, has been proselytizing for a profit-sharing capitalism, but, to date, her plan has met the fate of Ed Hall's.

One enthusiast for my "Every Man a Capitalist" article was Spencer Heath, an inventor who had made a fortune in World War I as a propellor manufacturer. Spencer had a theory that if landlords could be prevailed upon to combine their holdings, taking charge of the public services and even the police protection of neighborhoods, they could combine legitimate profit-taking with the offer of superior rental values. Spencer put his thoughts into a remarkable book, *Citadel, Market and Altar*, to which I contributed an introduction. The Heath idea had an extensive future flowering in the growth of condominiums, and provided a pattern that is now favored by St. Louis householders who have formed neighborhood associations to buy up the public streets in front of their homes, closing them off where practicable to through traffic and keeping them free of potholes and winter snows. The Heath defense of voluntarism in urban planning is infinitely extensible. Indeed, *Reason Magazine*, one of our better libertarian journals, has adapted what might be called Heathism to a whole program of "cutting back city hall."

Back in Washington after my foray to steel country in East Palestine, Ohio, I ran into an old friend of the '30s, Joe Borkin. Joe, an irreverent attorney who had once run the "urinal" (so-called because it specialized in "leaks" to the press) for trust-buster Thurman Arnold at the Department of Justice, had carried his passion for a truly competitive business system over into his private legal practice. Joe was selective about his clients; disillusioned by his experience in government, he wanted to work for a list of free-wheeling industrialists and bankers who had no use for the common practices of Wall Street. He found his heroes in the Cleveland and Chicago business and investment communities that were trying to break "Morgan" and "Kuhn-Loeb" control. Joe liked the Canadian-born Clevelander, Cyrus Eaton, who had staged a comeback by getting title to some important Canadian sources of iron ore; he also liked the Chicago investment banking house of Halsey, Stuart. These, so he considered, would be the progenitors of a new trans-Allegheny industrial America that would be unfettered by the Eastern Establishment.

Joe introduced me to a diminutive, white-haired Texan, Robert R. Young, who had gotten control of the Allegheny Corporation, a broken-down Cleveland holding company that had been owned by the Van Sweringen brothers and later passed along to George Ball, the fruit-jar manufacturer of Muncie, Indiana. The Allegheny portfolio contained plenty of dogs, but it also had working control of some good railroads, the center piece being the Chesapeake and Ohio, a sure-thing carrier that could always make money by carrying West Virginia bituminous coal on downhill tracks to Newport News on Atlantic tidewater and to Toledo on Lake Erie.

Young, who had lost a beautiful daughter in an airplane accident and had thus acquired a bias for ground transportation, swore that he would wrest control of some of the more important railroad systems, including the New York Central, from "23 Wall Street," the Morgan bank. When he made his first visit to Thomas W. Lamont to explain his plans for the Chesapeake and Ohio, he had come away feeling, as he put it, that he had been "spanked." Thereafter he always referred to Eastern financiers as "dambankers," very much as his Texas forebears had referred to Northerners as "damyankees." Going against the ancient railroad practice, he offered C & O bonds to the highest bidders, who happened to be Halsey, Stuart of Chicago and Cyrus Eaton's Otis & Co. of Cleveland. This bold act brought an end to the hegemony of Morgan, Stanley and Kuhn-Loeb, the Eastern investment bankers who had long benefitted by the non-competitive bidding which old J.P. Morgan had thought best for the U.S. transportation economy.

Young wrote poetry, some of which was pretty good, but, more important, he also wrote his own ads. One of the ads proclaimed that "A hog can cross the country without changing trains—but YOU can't." Young proposed to change this situation by instituting through passenger traffic by the Chesapeake and Ohio, the Nickel Plate, and allied railroads to spots beyond the normal breaking points in St. Louis and Chicago. He also had a hundred-and-one ideas about making passenger travel more pleasurable and more comfortable no matter what distances were involved. To show me what he had in mind, he invited me to ride on the C & O from Washington to Cincinnati and on, by other Young routes, to northern Michigan. Part of the time we rode in old J.P. Morgan's private car, which Young had acquired. Anticipating an airline practice, Young experimented with first-run movies on his C & O trains. He formed a Federation for Railway Progress to crack the venerable Association of American Railroads, which he called a "broken-down lobby" for the Eastern bankers. He made a case for "train-to-shore" telephones, which were later adopted by the Japanese for their Tokyo-Osaka express. All of this was in preparation for his grand proxy-fight assault on the New York Central, which he eventually took over. The Central, he thought, would give him a real passenger-train challenge.

I wrote a glowing close-up of Young for *Life*, but the fates were against the "Populist from Wall Street." Unable to scrounge out the money to put his passenger-service ideas into effect on the Central, and depressed by the general difficulties of railroad operation under the Interstate Commerce

Commission, Young died a suicide. It was left to Amtrak to try to save the passenger roads in America; but if Young couldn't do the job, it is hardly likely that a government-dominated body will succeed where the energetic banty-rooster from Texas failed.

Joe Borkin didn't have much luck with his other clients. His friend Cyrus Eaton went off in what seemed to me to be a wholly misguided direction when he proposed shipping iron ore from his northern Canadian mines to Krupp in West Germany to be fabricated into heavy equipment for the Soviet Union. The great free enterpriser eventually emerged as Khrushchev's abject apologist. I couldn't square Eaton's eastern pilgrimage with his reputation for being "Cyrus the Great," the hero of a trans-Appalachian competitive capitalism. Discounting the gossip that his wife had snared him into radical chic, the only good explanation was that Eaton, a Canadian, had become sour on the U.S. business "system" for putting monopolist blocks in the way of his ambition. The article I did on Eaton, no panegyric, never made it into print at *Life*, but Bill Buckley ultimately accepted it for *National Review* under the heading of "An Old Man Goes East."

Another of Joe's heroes, Commander McDonnell of Zenith Radio of Chicago, achieved a tremendous success for his company, but he failed for the time being in the one thing that Joe thought might transform the pattern of American life. I went to Chicago to write about Zenith's new "phonevision" patents, which would have allowed Commander McDonnell to establish "pay as you see" TV. The very invention of "phonevision" was a triumph of the creative imagination. McDonnell had gone to Washington during the war to find the "best electronics man" in the government program. He was referred to the person who had devised the proximity fuse. After the war, Zenith devised a system which would have allowed a subscriber to call the telephone company and ask for an "unscrambler" signal over the telephone wire that would permit a TV set to put a movie, an athletic event, or a stage play into the living room. The fee for the entertainment would have been paid with the phone bill. Joe Borkin and I thought that this might reverse the Henry Ford revolution, taking America off the highways and out of the moving-picture theatres, and keep people home at night. We would become a nation of home lovers. Unfortunately, government bureaucracy was too much for Commander McDonnell, for Zenith, for Joe Borkin, and for me. The Federal Communications Commission, duplicating the inanity of the Interstate Commerce Commission, dawdled about sanctioning pay-as-you-see TV for a couple of decades. My only consolation was that Zenith still had a chance of taking America off the smog-generating highways once the FCC relented and see-for-a-fee entertainment in the home had become an easy possibility for everybody. Eventually, of course, cable-TV was to come into its own.

Try as I might, I couldn't find many free-enterprising heroes in government itself. The Ed Stettiniuses, the corporation vice presidents from the business bureaucracies who came to Washington to do government jobs, were, for the most part, seduced in short order by the politicians. The businessman who revelled in a Washington assignment was likely to be an *epigoni* type, the son of a famous father. The theory certainly held for an Ed Stettinius, an Averell Harriman. The self-made men did better— witness Old Joe Kennedy or Jesse Jones, whose Potomac fever was never complicated by excessive admiration for the politicos who had appointed them. Looking for a bureaucrat who could stand out against pressure, I found one in Will Clayton, the cotton broker who had disapproved of Franklin D. Roosevelt's NRA price-fixing and AAA cotton-planting restrictions. Clayton, who had built his Anderson, Clayton and Co. cotton factoring firm into a $43 million giant without asking or giving quarter in a fiercely competitive market, had come to Washington for patriotic reasons just before Pearl Harbor. He had remained after the war to take on the job of Economic Under Secretary of State, hoping to help rid the world of such things as tariffs, quotas, and exchange restrictions.

Clayton, the real formulator of the Marshall Plan, which he regarded as a temporary stop-gap, made the economic branch of the State Department something to conjure with, but his progress, which eventually led to the "Kennedy Round" of tariff-cutting at Geneva, was inevitably slow. House Republicans gave allegiance in the abstract to the free-enterprise philosophy, but when it came to concrete particulars they were anti-Clayton. Gearhart of California wanted an exception to be made for nut-growers, Knutson of Minnesota was in there pitching for the cheese makers, and Jenkins of Ohio demanded protection for watch manufacturers, glass blowers, and potters. The opposition abroad to the extension of reciprocal trade ideas was even more formidable. The Soviets, who were to deprive Eastern European countries of the benefits of the Marshall Plan, boycotted Geneva trade talks. As for the "social democratic" planned economies of Western Europe, even when they were prepared to give tariff concessions, they hung grimly to such things as quotas, exchange controls, subsidized exports, and trading by government boards.

Despite the obstacles to freeing up world trade, Clayton felt he had the future on his side. The U.S. was then exporting almost twice as much in dollar volume as it was importing, and its industrial efficiency made its capital goods and its advisory expertise definitely desirable products in economies that had been wrecked and starved by war. Because of the "dollar gap" created by our export balance, we had political leverage in those days that has long since disappeared. To get dollars needed for modernization, foreign nations should have been more than willing to make reciprocal trade deals that would have expanded world productivity and possibly have forestalled a few wars and revolutions.

Will Clayton, making skilled use of the Vandenberg Republicans in the

Senate, managed to keep the U.S. from sliding back into Smoot-Hawley high protective tariff thinking, but he could not stop his own party from piddling away U.S. advantage by uneconomic give-away diplomacy that applied Marshall Plan thinking where it was not appropriate. "Trade, not aid," never became a vibrant reality. So the "dollar gap" disappeared, and the time was to come when we would find ourselves with a huge domestic inflation that nobody abroad wants to find "exported" instead of the goods and services we might have continued to sell if the terms of trade had remained what Will Clayton expected them to be.

Because, despite Will Clayton's philosophy, our postwar aid was largely government-to-government, the idea that businessmen should do business directly with each other never really had the rebirth that is needed if a free international system is to prevail. In his extracurricular hours, Will Clayton supported Clarence Streit's movement to federalize the Atlantic democracies into a single viable political system, with one currency and no interstate barriers to exchange. There has been an approach to the Streit-Clayton idea in the Common Market area of Western Europe, which is now talking about a "European currency." If Clayton had lived, he would be disappointed to see the U.S. falling farther and farther behind in its ability to compete; when he was busy pushing his program, U.S. autos, electronic equipment, Baldwin locomotives, machine tools, and movies were all in high international demand. Now the only big things we have to sell are computers and jet planes. The Clayton work is threatened by the revival of the Smoot-Hawley spirit, supported by senators from the automobile state of Michigan in Will Clayton's own Democratic Party.

If Will Clayton was one bright spot in the Washington picture, Harry Truman's decision to keep the world from going by default to Joe Stalin was another. Unfortunately, Truman's grasp of the situation in the Far East was by no means as firm as his awareness of dangers in the eastern Mediterranean. China had not yet fallen to the Communists, but the propaganda that Mao Tse-tung was a mere "agrarian reformer" was strong enough throughout the U.S., and particularly in New York, to bring Ben Stolberg to Washington with an urgent plea that I get to know his good State Department friend Ray Murphy. Ray was a circumspect man who never talked for attribution even when he talked at all, but he was alarmed at the continuing popularity in his department of the theories of John Service and John Davies, who saw no reason to worry if the Chinese form of Communism were to win out over Chiang Kai-shek's shaky Kuomintang. When Ray discovered that we had mutual friends in Whittaker and Esther Chambers, the ice was broken. Ray had a particularly warm admiration for Esther Chambers, who was his ideal of a faithful and competent wife. Assured that there would be no public playback of our talks, which would have undermined his position as watchdog on the "agrarian reformer" clique in State, Ray finally gave me a chapter and verse outpouring on who and what was making the Far Eastern policy for the U.S.

After I had put Murphy's story into the form of an open letter to Assistant Secretary of State Robert Lovett, there was some argument at *Life* about the propriety of sending a message to a mere assistant. But Joe Thorndike, the managing editor, decided to let it go through. Actually, there was nothing in the "Open Letter" that might not have been gathered by a little judicious extrapolation from the books that Freda Utley had been writing about the Far East. It was enough to point out that John Service and John Davies were the carriers of a contagion that fed the U.S. will to believe that things must turn out hopefully even when Marxists take over. That is what Ray Murphy wanted to establish. The pity of it is that nobody could persuade Harry Truman, who let the Wedemeyer Report on China go unregarded while Mao Tse-tung's "agrarians" took over.

During my last months in Washington, Willi Schlamm had been busy working up a publication for Harry Luce that would, as Dan Longwell, the Chairman of the Board at *Life*, put it, have become "the biggest little magazine in the world" if it had ever reached the news stands. Willi wanted me to come back to New York to help him with his editing. Luce willing, I offered to spend the summer months at the job of turning a good prospectus into a backlog of articles, thinking to return to Washington in the autumn. October came, and we were still struggling with the magazine, this time with a triumvirate of editors that included Russell Davenport. We had a fine bank of articles ready, but Harry Luce, fearful of an economic downturn and preoccupied with other ideas (such as the one that became *Sports Illustrated*), suddenly decided to scrap what would have been his most intellectual publication.

By then my daughters had already been entered in a Cheshire, Conn., school. I returned to *Life* on a five-article-a-year basis that would have taken me to Washington without forcing me to live there, but before I had even finished a single article, I found myself shifted, as a "good soldier," into the chair that Jack Jessup was temporarily vacating as *Life's* editorial writer. This meant being Harry Luce's alter ego on any given week that he chose to become involved in affairs, a job of divination that had its charms and its drawbacks. I was never as good as Jessup at guessing what Harry had in mind before he had spoken, but I gave it a good try for an exciting two years.

Chapter 12

Writing editorials for Henry Luce was sometimes a delight and sometimes an ordeal. Luce thoroughly appreciateed my commitment to voluntarism and spontaneity; he laughed when I commended a young Governor of Illinois, Adlai Stevenson, for vetoing a bill that would have required putting collars and licenses on cats. But the year 1948 caused troubles. Luce had been a Vandenberg man—he had hoped against hope that the Michigan Republican Senator who had made a graceful transition from Midwest isolationism to thoroughly international bipartisan foreign policy would some day get the Republican nomination for President. But Tom Dewey was his party's 1948 choice, and Harry Luce went along.

I did not object, but I felt it somewhat unfair when, on the day after the late returns had certified that scrappy Harry Truman had edged the complacent Dewey in a "give-'em-hell" fight, Harry Luce grabbed me in the hall to tell me that "we have made a terrible mistake, and you are stuck with explaining it." In a coffee shop downstairs Luce instructed me on how to eat crow for Time, Inc. Though he never said he blamed me for *Life's* going-out-on-a-limb support of Dewey, I had the feeling that some of Luce's annoyance was projected at me for not having warned him that Truman had unsuspected virtues as a campaigner.

Maybe I was seeing things that weren't there. Harry Luce had always been understanding about differences in philosophy. When John Osborne, later to become famous for his "Nixon Watch" in the *New Republic*, came back from England to share the *Life* editorial-page duties with me, Luce fell into the habit of letting the two of us alternate in accordance with our predilections. It worked out well from the standpoint of editorial harmony, but it didn't suit my metabolism. The job of producing one editorial every other week left me with time on my hands. I took to making long midday subway trips to the Brooklyn Ice Palace for figure skating lessons from a real character, Bill Chase, who taught three-turns by making you follow through with tennis-stroke motions, and every so often I would duck downstairs to practice on the Rockefeller Center rink with Joe Purtell, the *Time* business editor. Luce didn't mind, but I felt that I wasn't giving him—or myself—full measure.

134

Besides, I shared with Henry Hazlitt, Don Levine, and others of the new breed of conservative, the feeling that there should be a more fundamental assault on the regnant liberalism if our intellectuals were ever to be reached. Fundamental change depends on the grassroots for corroboration, but it does not start at the grassroots. What had happened to make England "liberal" in accordance with trade-unionist tastes was one proof of the truism. Before there could be a Labour Party absorption of a majority of the old-fashioned Liberal Party, there had to be a Fabian Society. The Webbs, the George Bernard Shaws, and the H.G. Wellses had to weigh in with their collectivist basics before the pragmatic trades unionists were ready to abandon the old-fashioned liberalism of Cobden, Bright, and Herbert Asquith.

The same pattern had been followed in the America that finally went for Franklin Roosevelt's New Deal. If the *Nation* and the *New Republic* had not sold the intellectuals on the virtues of the planned economy in the '20s and early '30s, there would have been no Roosevelt Revolution.

In 1950 we had a good anti-Communist journalism, but it was limited to opposing the Soviet Union in foreign policy. Don Levine, bankrolled by the pertinacious Alfred Kohlberg, had been running an excellent anti-Communist magazine called *Plain Talk*. Kohlberg was a remarkable "angel." As an importer of Chinese-made fabrics, he naturally favored a foreign policy that would keep mainland China firmly pro-capitalist. He had been outraged that he had been played for a sucker as a supporter of the Communist-infiltrated Institute of Pacific Relations. But up to 1950, Kohlberg had not paid much attention to what Keynesians, Fabians, and Marxist fellow-travelers were doing to the American economy.

Sol Levitas's *New Leader* went right along with *Plain Talk* on foreign-policy issues. But it was a study in equivocation when it came to the question of maintaining a voluntary society at home. In a contribution which he gratefully accepted, I kidded Sol Levitas for running Walter Reuther's "Sixty Million Jobs" in the *New Leader*. If the government was going to guarantee capital to keep 60 million people employed, I wanted, so I informed Sol, to be cut in on the deal. I wanted capital to start a newspaper. "I demand," I said, ". . . a housing project for my staff. A bungalow for Ben Stolberg, my labor editor, with a mechanized kitchen designed by Mrs. Ralph Borsodi. I want a brick wall built between the houses that are to be occupied by my two educational columnists, Sidney Hook and Mark Van Doren. Of course, I demand a free hand editorially for my program, which is to knock the government all I damn well please."

What I was trying to tell Sol was that you can't have socialism and small business or individual access to government largesse at one and the same time. Sol would let me have my say, but it was tangential to argue my case in the *New Leader*.

The trouble with American business in the late '40s was that it had become timidly defensive. It wouldn't support its own journalism. Supporters of classical Henry Ford-type competition such as Garet Garrett simply had no place to write.

If it had been left to pusillanimous males probably nothing much would have happened. True enough, there was one valiant male, Leonard Read, who had made a libertarian reputation as head of the Los Angeles Chamber of Commerce and had come East to start his Foundation for Economic Education. But that was not journalism of a type that could spark a political movement, as the *Nation* and the *New Republic* had done for the '20s and '30s. We needed the Read Foundation, yes, and we also needed the Mont Pélérin Society which Friedrich Hayek, Milton Friedman, and other free-enterprise economists and publicists (including Leonard Read) had started on a Swiss mountain top to build up a backfire to the collectivism that was ravaging Western Europe and threatening the United States. But to give the gathering conservative and libertarian causes a forward thrust, a fortnightly journal of opinion was a sine qua non necessity.

It seemed to me significant that it was Isabel Paterson who gave me an introduction to Leonard Read. Returning from a labor-reporting assignment in Philadelphia, I had stopped off at the Biltmore to see Mr. Read in New York. I remember the occasion vividly because I had a Godawful stomach ache (my appendix burst the next morning when they were taking it out). Leonard and I hit it off right away, and we both agreed that Isabel Paterson was a phenomenon.

Indeed, it was three women—Mrs. Paterson, Rose Wilder Lane, and Ayn Rand—who, with scornful side glances at the male business community, had decided to rekindle a faith in an older American philosophy. There wasn't an economist among them. And none of them was a Ph.D.

I had already absorbed the message of Albert Jay Nock's *Our Enemy the State* and Hilaire Belloc's *The Servile State*, but it was Isabel Paterson's *The God of the Machine*, Rose Lane's *The Discovery of Freedom*, and Ayn Rand's *The Fountainhead* and (later) *Atlas Shrugged* that turned Nock's conception of social power into detailed reality. These books made it plain that if life was to be something more than a naked scramble for government favors, a new attitude toward the producer must be created.

Isabel Paterson began with physics, not economics. The individual was the dynamo: his creative activity set an energy current running. Capitalism was a "long circuit of energy," offering innumerable opportunities for hook-ups as new inventions and market developments came along. Rose Lane, an ex-socialist, had lived in Moslem countries and had been impressed with the inventiveness of classic Saracen civilization—an inventiveness that had been lost in the centuries of Turkish domination. As for Ayn Rand, she had lived in Russia and knew from personal observation as well as logic that the hand of the State was a deadening hand.

Isabel was particularly scornful of the "deckle-edged speeches" of the businessmen of the mid-'40s who had cravenly accepted the inevitability of a mixed, or Fabian, economy that kept edging toward socialism as compromise followed compromise. "I'd like to see them all hanged," Isabel said of the "go-along-to-get-along" business spokesman of the day. "But," she added with a whimsical gesture, "it would mean my own neck as well."

Isabel was the first to talk about the need of business to support its own press, its own electronic media, its own schools and universities. Advertising, she said, had two distinct functions. One was to sell the product, whether it was baby food or motor cars. The other was to help maintain a climate in which business could function without interruption.

To market something one had to have a marketplace. This meant a firm property base (you can't sell what you don't own.) It meant an acceptance of the idea of contract, with the state exercising its legitimate function of enforcing accepted terms. The maintenance of the marketplace called for a press that would not use the money derived from specific product advertising to sell out the whole idea of freedom for the individual enterpriser.

I found Isabel's analysis quite helpful, but to get a libertarian fortnightly going would require some subsidy at the start. The advertising support could come later. Don Levine, who proclaimed himself a "mutualist" when asked about his economic philosophy, had been listening to the "three women." But he, as I, couldn't see an opinion magazine starting on advertising alone. His own angel, Alfred Kohlberg, was willing to transfer the support he had been giving to the anti-Communist *Plain Talk* to a journal of wider scope. There were others who were willing to put up some money, including Jasper Crane, a duPont executive who had had a long correspondence with Rose Wilder Lane. So conversations got moving. It was finally decided that *The Freeman* (we wanted the old Albert Jay Nock title because we intended to stress social as against political power) would start as a fortnightly, but with an option to become a weekly. The editors were to be Don Levine, Henry Hazlitt, and I, each with a specific authority for certain sections of "the book."

A funny thing happened, however, on our way to publication. In one of the last issues of *Plain Talk*, Don Levine made a violent attack on Merwin Hart, a Right-wing publicist who had made some remarks that Levine considered anti-Semitic. The attack angered Jasper Crane, who thought the anti-Semitic charge nonsense. This led to some heated words, which Don Levine construed to mean that *The Freeman* could not count on a free editorial hand. So he withdrew from the enterprise, telling us to go along with the magazine if we chose to risk our editorial autonomy. Kohlberg, who was himself Jewish, thought that Don was seeing things under the bed; he would, so he told us, continue to give his *Plain Talk* money to *The Freeman*. The presence of other Jews on *The Freeman* board of directors—Leo Wolman, the labor expert, was one—seemed to Hazlitt and me ample reassurance that there would be no racial worries to contend with in our editorial conduct of the magazine. So, with the substitution of Suzanne LaFollette, one of Albert Jay Nock's old editors, for Don Levine, we were in business.

Advertising ourselves as a "fortnightly for individualists," we nailed a truly Nockian flag to our masthead. "True liberalism," we said, "rests on the common law, on clear and definite statute law, and on a government of limited powers." We were for "local autonomy and the decentralization of political power." Henry Hazlitt, who had been doing the "Business Tides" column for *Newsweek* and had written his challenging *Economics in One Lesson*, provided our statement of economic principles with a ringing declaration that "economic freedom, as embodied in the free market, is the basic institution of a liberal society." The recurrence of the word "liberal" in our policy statement was calculated: we intended to take the title back from the socialists and interventionists who had filched it and given it its totally unwarranted modern connotation.

Frankly, we were somewhat appalled by the task of finding contributors besides ourselves for a first issue. Libertarians were few and far between, and the new conservatism was still an import from England labeled T.S. Eliot. Russell Kirk had not yet published his *Conservative Mind*. The press, largely through *noblesse oblige*, printed three conservative columnists, Westbrook Pegler, David Lawrence, and George Sokolsky, but Pegler and Lawrence were strictly newspapermen and were not available for non-syndicate work. In the end we had to go with articles by Raymond Moley, John T. Flynn, and Sokolsky, who scrounged out the time to write for us despite his seven-days-a-week commitment to the Hearst papers. Isabel Paterson refused to write for us at two cents a word. The duPonts, she said, could afford more than that. She took it as an insult when I asked her twice.

Our first issue outraged my old friend and first night city editor Ed Klauber, who told me that I should see a psychiatrist. Another old friend who thought me daft was Royce Pitkin, head of Goddard College in Vermont. But our first issue provided a focus, and we quickly discovered that we were not alone. Hazlitt, with his Austrian economics school connections, drew a string of excellent economic contributors, headed by Ludwig von Mises (who became one of our directors), Friedrich Hayek, and Wilhelm Roepke, whose pupil Ludwig Erhardt had set West Germany on its free enterprise course in 1948. Sue LaFollette was responsible for bringing humorist Morrie Ryskind into the fold. We were offered reprint rights to a first-rate bank letter from St. Louis that bore the signature of Towner Phelan, and I was amazed to discover much later that Phelan's research had been done by a young woman named Phyllis Schlafly. The economics focus provided by Hazlitt and von Mises pleased Leonard Read, one of our directors who was chary of political articles that indulged in personalities. But no one objected at first to our insistence on pushing a lively journalism that featured attacks on the scandal-ridden Truman Administration.

Is it the mere egotism of a participant for me to say that our *Freeman* constituted a turning point in American intellectual history? The forces we tapped were already in existence, but in the 1940s they had had no focus. We had unpretentious offices in a building owned by Alfred Kohlberg on Madison Avenue near the Morgan Library, but we hadn't been in existence for a month before all sorts of people began beating a path to our door. There were those, such as Frank Meyer, who had been totally disillusioned by their early experiences in the Communist movement. There were the libertarians such as Frank Chodorov and a forgotten jokester named Harry Serwer, who contributed amusing papers on "signs of decay." Louis Bromfield, the novelist who was engaged in some exciting agricultural experiments on his showcase farm in Ohio, came East for lunch with us, with a project for attacking eggheads by a campaign of continued ridicule. We heard from the campus: Stanton Evans found our early issues a "revelation" when he encountered them at Yale, and two unknowns, Bill Buckley and Brent Bozell, who were allied as brothers-in-law as well as in conservative ideology, sent us contributions. Anthony Harrigan, a young South Carolina newspaperman who now issues a thought-provoking column from the Nashville headquarters of the United States Industrial Council, found his first outlet in our pages.

A high point for me was the periodic appearance in our offices of Garet Garrett, a holdover economist, philosopher, and novelist of the '20s. He had a gruff voice, the result, we were told, of a throat injury incurred in some sort of encounter with a hold-up man. As I knew from my *Fortune* studies of the automobile business, Garet Garrett thoroughly understood what Henry Ford had been up to when he raised wages in his plants to create incentives that would, paradoxically, lead to lower prices and more car sales. Garrett's *The Wild Wheel* should have been the bible for college students of productivity, but in the 1950s it had been forgotten.

Garrett had a theory, which he explained to us, that empire must pay for itself or be doomed to failure. He saw no sense in either lending or giving money to countries which had no visible prospects of repayment. Where the Roman Empire taxed its colonies, the United States bled itself to support a world that had no intention of unleashing its enterprisers to create conditions of prosperity. Henry Hazlitt, then engaged in questioning whether American dollars could save the world, drew telling support from Garrett.

The Revolution Was, said Garrett in a work that bore that title. Meaning, of course, that the New Deal had brought about a "revolution within the form." It had done this by stealing a whole vocabulary from the libertarians and traditional liberals. The "revolution" that "was" accommodated a socialist Reconstruction Finance Corporation in the name of saving Free Enterprise. And at the other end of the spectrum, it established "entitlements" that were supposed to tide helpless people over, but actually guaranteed their perpetual enslavement as "clients" of New and Fair Deal social workers.

Garrett's health was bad, but he said he was resolved to hold on until he had completed his *The American Story*, a history of the United States written from the point of view of what Leonard Read called the "freedom philosophy." "You can't die while you are still mad," he said one day. I had read Garrett's amazing novel, *The Driver*, which was roughly based on the career of E.H. Harriman, the stockbroker who had revived the Union Pacific Railway and made it profitable. Garrett was touched that I remembered a book that had appeared in the early '20s, and he brought me his other novels—*The Cinder Buggy*, a story of the erratic birth of the steel industry in a Pennsylvania that had been committed to iron, and *Satan's Bushel*, a dramatic novel of the Chicago wheat pit and the Western farmers who could not avoid raising that last marginal bushel of grain that could be counted on to break the price. I promised that I would do something about his novels in the book section of the *Freeman*, but we were out of business before I could get to it. The novels he brought to me were inscribed to his mother. "I give them to you with my heart in my mouth," he said. My only means of repayment after Garrett's death was to dedicate my *The Roots of Capitalism* to him along with Claude Robinson, who had commissioned the book.

Garrett had a faculty for touching people. An "Austrian" economist before we knew there were any such, he could make the philosophy of voluntarism a truly compelling imperative. He employed a young man named Richard Cornuelle for a time. Cornuelle went on to write *Reclaiming the American Dream* about the voluntarist approach to problem solving. Cornuelle, a doer as well as a theorist, had worked out a scheme with the bankers to provide loan money for boys and girls who needed it for college educations. But just when the Cornuelle scheme was gathering momentum, the federal government stepped in with its own system of educational support. There seemed to be no way of withstanding the government juggernaut, and Garrett died with a feeling that the American people had sold their birthrights for a mess of pottage. "The People's Pottage," Garrett called it in one of his last essays.

Frank Meyer, an ex-Communist who had gone into the silences of Woodstock, New York, along with Eugene O'Neill, Jr., to think things over, dropped in one day with the idea that he might return to the world of public discourse by doing an occasional unpretentious book review. Frank, a meticulous man, wanted to be certain of every step in forging a new philosophy of freedom for himself. He was, as he said, a chessplayer who felt diffident about making a commitment without seeing several moves ahead. Later, after a libertarian phase, Frank was to emerge as the great conciliator of the conservative movement; there could be a practical consensus on the political front, he said, once it had been accepted by various factions on the Right that freedom was the ultimate political end, leaving virtue to the individual conscience as tutored by traditions that were well understood in the West. The full articulation of Frank's thinking had to wait upon Bill Buckley's *National Review*, but it could be glimpsed in its embryonic form in conversations in the *Freeman* office.

There was nothing tentative about Willi Schlamm's contributions to the *Freeman*. When asked about his philosophy, Willi said he believed in "the Ten Commandments and Mozart," and that was enough. He had been thoroughly bored by Vermont rusticity, particularly after a project of writing a critique of the *New York Times* had fallen through. Willi had gone to Vermont with his wife Steffi partly because it had its obvious Tyrolean Alpine charm, and partly because he thought he would be sojourning among some of America's last true individualists. Alas, the Vermonters he came to know were just as eager for government hand-outs as any welfare "client" in New York City. When Henry Regnery, the publisher, visited Vermont on a ski expedition, Willi, hungry for literate conversation, kept him awake deep into the night, leaving an exhausted guest with only half the energy needed the next morning to conquer the slopes at nearby Pico Peak.

It was easy to lure Willi back to Manhattan on an "every other week" basis to cover his own proposed "Arts and Manners" back-of-the-book beat, which was subsequently imitated in a score of publications. There is hardly a Sunday section in America today without an "arts and leisure" page. But in between writing about such topics as Jimmy Durante's nose, Willi made our front-of-the-book paragraphs noteworthy for their exuberance. For a nickel Willi offered to take over an expensive study of freedom of the press in Argentina, there being no such phenomenon worth even the expenditure of a dime.

Helping to edit the *Freeman* made one quickly aware that there were depths within depths in the political maneuvering that goes on in Washington. The great Joe McCarthy polarization was in full press when the *Freeman* got under way. One day Freda Utley came into the office with a "deadly parallel" compilation of what Owen Lattimore had said either just before or just after Joe Stalin had said the same thing. She had made the compilation for McCarthy, but had carefully refrained from calling Lattimore a Soviet agent or even a fellow-traveler. But McCarthy, flaunting the parallels, proceeded to designate Lattimore as the head and fount of the Communist conspiracy in America. This, of course, could be only a surmise.

It so happened that we had just commissioned Forrest Davis to do a study of General George Marshall's post-World War II statecraft, particularly with reference to the Far East. Davis, a careful diplomatic reporter, had done notable work in explaining Roosevelt's "great design" for a peaceful world for the *Saturday Evening Post*; he thoroughly understood the differences between appearance and proof. Weeks went by, and the Marshall article never appeared. One day Forrest Davis burst into the

office with an exuberant, "John, I've betrayed you. The article has become
a book, and I've given it to Joe McCarthy to read on the floor of the Senate."

The book in question was *Marshall's Retreat From Victory*. It was a solid
job based on the most careful sort of research. Unfortunately, McCarthy, in
contributing his own introduction to the material, chose to portray George
Marshall as a conscious conspirator against America's interests. That was
not what Davis had said.

The McCarthy behavior, which was rooted in a most unsubtle character's inability to use the English language with any regard for finesse, posed
a problem for us. We knew there was genuine substance behind what the
Wisconsin populist Senator was trying to convey to a people who knew all
too little about Communist "disinformation" tactics. To repudiate McCarthy
when there was no one else in Washington who was willing to deal on any
basis whatsoever with such misleaders as Owen Lattimore seemed a
chicken-livered thing to do. So Suzanne LaFollette, in commenting on the
McCarthy speech on Marshall, held her tongue about McCarthy's unso-
phisticated verbalisms, and I commended McCarthy's own 1952 book
called *McCarthyism: The Fight for America*, which had its "sober cita-
tions" as well as what Bill Buckley and Brent Bozell, in their *McCarthy and
His Enemies*, admitted to be "egregious blunders." After all, I had listened
to Ray Murphy of the State Department tell me about Communist infiltration of the government. It was surely there, even though Joe McCarthy may
have erred in trying to reduce the penetration to a matter of specific
figures.

It was my conception of a political fortnightly that we had to take sides
involving personalities on the issues of the day. Sue LaFollette certainly
agreed, and Harry Hazlitt, though he was primarily interested in economics, for the most part went along. But there were questions of tone involved,
and it soon became apparent that our directors had their own often-
conflicting ideas. If Alfred Kohlberg had had his way, we would have run
anti-Communist exposure articles in every issue, with special emphasis on
the Maoist takeover of mainland China. Indeed, Alfred wanted to write
most of the articles himself. Nobody told us to go slow on the anti-
Communist theme, but the free marketers on the board—Jasper Crane,
Lou von Mises, Lawrence Fertig, and Leonard Read, among others—
wanted more space for the type of article that would make positive economic points. Leo Wolman, whose speciality was labor, hoped to see
specific attention paid to the unions. There was nothing in all this that could
not have been handled, and as long as it was a matter of training editorial
guns on Harry Truman, whose better qualities we failed to appreciate,
there was no particular objection from our board even when we became so
immoderate as to call on Truman to resign.

The real trouble came when personalities were superimposed on the
quarrel, then heating up in the Republican Party, between the supporters of

Bob Taft and Ike Eisenhower. Sue LaFollette and I were in Taft's corner, and Harry Hazlitt was certainly not anti-Taft. He did, however, object to Sue's sometimes strident way of expressing herself, particularly on behalf of Joe McCarthy. I had thought things were going along swimmingly (I was having fun editing the back-of-the-book sections and doing my own lead review), and I was flabbergasted when Harry suggested one day that we must "do something" about Sue's choice of articles for the body of the magazine. I know that I convinced Harry Hazlitt that it would not be understood in our little conservative community if Sue LaFollette were to be replaced. She represented continuity with the original *Freeman* of Albert Nock (as a talented and beautiful young woman she was one of his favored editors), and she had made a gallant attempt in the early '30s to revive the Nockian tradition with a journal called the *New Freeman*, which she edited with Sheila Hibben. As the author of a pioneer book called *Concerning Women*, she had a feminist following that resisted the sillier manifestations of the women's "lib" of a later day. And as the editor who had pulled together the findings of John Dewey's asylum-for-Trotsky committee, she helped bring a big segment of the anti-Stalinist socialists into our subscriber orbit, where, conceivably, they might catch a bit of free-market contagion.

Sue also happened to be a workhorse who was willing to sit up all night distributing semi-colons in refractory copy. She was not easy to face down: she hated my non-ideological taste for some of the reviews of Ed Dahlberg, author of *Bottom Dogs*, which I printed simply because I liked his way of writing. If she overdid the intransigence when backing political articles against economic, I felt it was the business of Harry Hazlitt and me to outvote her. Harry, however, wanted smoother inside-the-office sailing. Overburdened with the work of writing for *Newsweek* and doing a radio stint in addition to *Freeman* editorials, he finally agreed to a course of action that would give him more personal freedom and bring another voice into *Freeman* affairs. We would seek a "fourth" editor.

It so happened that Forrest Davis, who had come to New York from Washington to work on a project for Herbert Hoover, was at loose ends and willing to join the *Freeman*. He had already done some work for us. Forrest, an able journalist and a diplomatic historian of note (his *The Atlantic System* remains a most canny reminder of the need for the West to maintain a coherent policy), was a person of infinite but sometimes deceptive charm. He had done excellent work as far back as the '20s, when he covered the Scopes trial in Tennessee for the *New York Herald-Tribune*; and he had gone high in the Scripps-Howard organization until he could no longer abide what he thought of as "banishment" to the sticks in Denver, Colorado. I had known Forrest and his wife Toni in New York in the '30s when he was writing a book on Wall Street, and later in Washington during and after the war when he was shuttling between representing the *Saturday*

Evening Post and doing work for government officials. He had been a hard drinker in the '20s, but that part of a typical reporter's career was behind him.

To the *Freeman*, Forrest Davis brought many talents. But he was a Taft partisan who had little concern for the pro-Eisenhower sentiments of some of our board members who shared Hazlitt's distaste for stridency. There were motives within motives in the board fights that followed after an impolitic Davis had clashed with Harry Hazlitt over some bit of office protocol. To this day I have no clear conception of what Davis thought he might get by provoking an argument. He had his rough side, as I came to know when he called me "Peter Pan" when I refused to make a motion to fire Kurt Lassen, our business manager, who had been a Hazlitt choice and turned up as a Davis enemy. But, along with Sue LaFollette, I had to side with the pro-Taft directors on our board. They were Davis partisans as well as being Taft partisans, and the merging of personalities with political passions made for some extremely ugly meetings in which Davis managed to maintain a majority of one. I hated those meetings where, as the presiding officer, I felt trapped between two sets of friends who refused to understand each other.

What was particularly disconcerting to Sue LaFollette and me was the story, brought to our office by a Chicago lawyer who was a friend of Sue's, that the "duPont" element on our board was dead set against allowing us to state a preference for Taft. The "duPonts," according to the lawyer, were very much afraid that a Bob Taft in the White House would support a trust-busting Department of Justice in forcing the duPont company to divest itself of its big block of General Motors stock. (As it turned out, Eisenhower, when elected, did nothing to stop the divestiture.) Whether there was any basis to the lawyer's story we could not know. But we didn't like the idea that we might be the subject of a hidden manipulation.

In the end, Forrest Davis lost his majority of one among the directors. Alex Hillman, a Davis friend, pointed out to us that an almost-evenly divided board was worse than no board at all. The reason: nobody would raise any money for us while board bickering went on. Since we weren't being paid full salaries anyway, Sue LaFollette and I resigned, and Davis quit. Though the magazine, as a political fortnightly, continued to be published for a year or so more in its original format, I felt that it had lost its ability to fly on the two wings represented by anti-Communism on the one hand, and pro-free market theory on the other. Leonard Read, who had deplored the whole controversy, eventually bought what was the shell of a magazine and took it up the Hudson to his Foundation for Economic Education, where it had a rebirth as a monthly commentary on economic philosophy. Since I was never an enemy of economics, I later rejoined the monthly *Freeman* as its staff reviewer, a job in which, for 20 years, I have had the benefit of Ed Opitz's and Paul Poirot's editorial counsel. But we still needed a general journal of opinion, and it was a shame that we had muffed the chance to maintain *The Freeman* with its original objective, which was to fight the Leftist intellectual weeklies—the *New Republic* and the *Nation*—on their own ground.

In the longer perspective it did not matter that *The Freeman*, as an intellectual fortnightly, disappeared. For it was reborn in a couple of years in Bill Buckley's *National Review*.

The agent of rebirth was Willi Schlamm, who had gone back to Vermont after the *Freeman* shake-out. Willi's project for writing a book about the *New York Times* could not be retrieved, and the appointment of Clare Boothe Luce as Ambassador to Rome made it "inadvisable" for him to continue with a biography of Clare that might have offended diplomatic sensibilities. Accepting a commission from Henry Regnery to write an introduction to a manuscript called *McCarthy and His Enemies*, Willi had several sessions with Bill Buckley, who, with Brent Bozell, was responsible for a most controversial work that supported McCarthy without making him out to be a saint. Observing that Bill had access to funds, Willi broached the idea for an opinion magazine that, in an original prospectus, was called *National Weekly*. Willi's suggestion was that Bill should publish the magazine, own the voting stock, and also act as editor-in-chief. The failure of *The Freeman*, where editorial responsibilities were diffused among four co-equals and nobody controlled the voting stock, had impressed Willi with the need for a much tighter organization. He was confident, of course, that he could maintain his influence over a young man who was all of 28 years old and just feeling his way amid the complexities of a Stalin-dominated world.

The early mastheads of *National Review* were proof enough of *Freeman* continuity. But there were differences. Where the *Freeman* had been wholly secular in its tone, *National Review*, with three Catholics among its editors (Buckley, Bozell, and the incomparable Willmoore Kendall), was visibly concerned with religious and philosophical traditions which we, at the *Freeman*, had taken for granted and let go at that. Where we, at the *Freeman*, had combined the anti-Communist approach of Don Levine's *Plain Talk* with the free-market emphasis of Leonard Read's Foundation for Economic Education, *National Review* added the traditionalist interests of Russell Kirk, then emerging as America's chief exponent of Burkean conservatism, and Erik von Kuehnelt-Leddihn, the European monarchist. Buckley found himself compelled to ride herd on libertarians such as Frank Chodorov, ex-Trotskyites (James Burnham, Max Eastman), and assorted ex-radicals such as Freda Utley, Ralph de Toledano, and Frank Meyer. The job of handling tandem reins was certainly not beyond Bill, particularly after Frank Meyer had emerged as the great conciliator of the various conservative-libertarian factions, but Willi Schlamm, who had assembled the staff, became the sticking point.

Bill Buckley has told the story of his break with Schlamm with great magnanimity. Looking for steady support, Bill found it in James Burnham, whose style, soberly analytical, certainly contrasted with Willi Schlamm's exuberance and crusading inclinations. The curious thing about it was that Schlamm and Burnham held identical opinions on practically all things related to what Burnham called the "suicide of the West." The differences between the two personalities on whom Bill Buckley had come to rely were tactical and temperamental. One trouble was that Willi had an intense hunger to run his own magazine, where Burnham was content to be a faithful lieutenant. Willi had had too many disappointments: Harry Luce had let him down after staking him to buy 50 articles for the projected literary monthly to be called *Measure*, and the Hitler takeover in Prague had ousted Willi from his editorship of Ossietsky's famous *Weltbühne*. Willi had always pressured us for more responsibility on the *Freeman*. He was not born to serve.

Unfortunately, just as *National Review* was hitting its stride, Willi had a momentary blackout that he interpreted as a minor stroke. Sent to Florida to sit on a beach while he recovered, Willi brooded. He thought the staff he had assembled for Bill Buckley might have been more sympathetic about his mishap and more concerned with holding things in line at the office during his absence. But magazines have deadlines, as Bill Buckley quickly learned. And Bill, though inexperienced, was quite used to assuming authority on his own. He quickly discovered that Willi was not indispensible.

As Willi's oldest American friend, I had to hold his hand during the period of office tension that preceded his inevitable resignation. Willi made things more difficult by assuming that Patricia Buckley, Bill's wife, was against him, and his fulminations on this point cost him the sympathies of Sue LaFollette, who took the woman's side in a muted quarrel. My own difficulty in l'affaire Schlamm was that I thought Buckley was quite right in following his own take-charge impulses. When Willi said one day of Bill that he was "like a father to him," it struck me as laughable. After all, Willi came from Vienna, where Sigmund Freud had written extensively about father-son relationships that could only have one conclusion. Willi failed to see the humor of my remark that he should have been the last to trust to filial gratitude, especially when other "fathers"—Willmoore Kendall as well as Burnham—had a claim on Bill's affections.

Disappointed in America, Willi Schlamm went back to Europe, where he wrote excellent books on East-West relations. Eventually he came into his own as proprietor and editor of a magazine, *Die Zeitbühne*, in which he accurately predicted the troubles that continued to beset the West as it mistakenly pursued policies of détente that allowed the Soviets to win their many flanking victories in Asia, Africa, and Latin America. Willi was a genius, and it is enough to his credit that he set Bill Buckley on a path that proved to be indispensible to a conservatism that, in 1981, gave promise of a real turnover in the nation's course.

Bill Buckley has always been fantastically generous in acknowledging help in a career that would have happened even if Willi Schlamm had never lived. Not too long ago Bill credited me with changing the course of his life by writing an introduction to his first book, *God and Man at Yale*. The implication is that if I had not acted out of "reckless generosity" (his phrase) and stood sponsor for him in 1951, he would never have become a public figure. Of course, neither Willi Schlamm nor I had anything of a truly definitive nature to do with the development of Buckley as a publicist, a master of elegant letters, or a magazine editor. If I had not done the introduction to *God and Man at Yale*, somebody else—a Max Eastman, a Felix Morley, or a Henry Hazlitt—would have volunteered to do it. And while Willi Schlamm did persuade Bill to start *National Review*, it happens that Bill had all along been considering a magazine career on his own.

The point is that Buckley was in full control of his destinies even as an undergraduate at Yale. In his latter-day excess of generosity, he remarked that I had tried to invert the true order of benefactions by thanking him for the privilege of letting me introduce *God and Man at Yale* when it was I that was doing him the favor. The truth is that I, along with Henry Hazlitt, Sue LaFollette, and Frank Chodorov, had a shrewd notion that Bill was a good bet to make the conservative movement both respectable and fashionable. We at the *Freeman* had watched him and tagged him, along with his brother-in-law Brent Bozell, as someone who was going to be important. To understand our feelings about nurturing Bill Buckley, one has to realize the pariah status of conservatism in the early '50s. We needed a young champion with the insouciance, the faith, the public presence, and above all the wit, to carry on a fight that would ultimately redeem the conservative and libertarian movements from charges of antiquarian crack-pottism. It should be quite understandable that I considered it a favor on Buckley's part to be allowed to do him a favor. He, more than any single figure, has made conservatism a respectable force in American life.

I was not part of *National Review*'s administrative board, for I had made other commitments. But for several years I contributed the lead book review and spent two days every other week in the office writing editorials. The high point of this was the opportunity to renew a friendship with Whittaker Chambers, who, for a year in 1957, came to New York from his farm in Westminster, Maryland, to take part in editorial deliberations and write paragraphs and longer leaders as only he could write them. We shared a cubicle in the *National Review* office at 150 East 35th Street, and our conversations were anything but portentous. What the world never knew was that Whit had lightness and a gorgeous sense of humor. Economics bored him as it has never bored me. His prime reason for writing *Witness*, one of the truly great books of our time, was religious; he wanted to move people not only to reject Communism and its flabby "liberal" allies but also to rejoice in the Christianity that has made the Western tradition. As a practicing Quaker, Whit was willing to teach by example; he did not indulge in lapel-grabbing proselytizing, but he was always willing to be a "witness" to his faith. He and Esther brought their children, Ellen and John, up on the Maryland farm to recite a simple prayer before meals that went:

> God made the sun
> And God made the tree.
> God made the mountain
> And God made me.

> I thank thee, O Lord,
> For the sun and the tree
> For making the mountain,
> And for making me.

That was the essence of Whit's religion—the glad acceptance of the sacredness of human life. It was an Albert Schweitzer theology.

Knowing that I understood his deeper purposes and that there was no need for argument, Whit and I shared many lighter moments discussing the past that we had known at Time, Inc., before the Hiss case had dragged him from the journalistic and farming careers that he would have preferred to pursue. We usually ended up a discussion of Bill Buckley's editorial requirements by getting on to subjects that had no political relevance, such as ways to cook squash, which Wilt said was an unappreciated American vegetable. When Whit discovered a melon seed that would produce a ripe watermelon small enough for an ordinary refrigerator, he was ecstatic. He brought me a packet of the seed for trial in my Cheshire, Connecticut, garden, where the growing season couldn't match the season in Maryland. It pleased him when I reported, some months later, that the seed was everything he had claimed.

The Left has always tried to make it appear that Chambers was out to "get" Alger Hiss. This was never Whit's motive; indeed, a salient part of Whit's character was a disinclination to hurt anything. He did have a prejudice against cats because, as he said, they would kill anything that moves.

If the Nazi-Soviet pact had not disturbed Whit in 1939, he would never have gone to the government with Isaac Don Levine to warn Adolf Berle of "Marxist study groups" and Soviet "sympathizers" in the State Department. He did not want to implicate Alger Hiss, an old friend, as a "spy." During all of his years on *Time*, Whit's chief pride was that, unlike other "ex's" who had been in the Communist underground, he refused to make a living as a literary informer. Rebecca West might, as an author, be preoccupied with the "meaning of treason," but when Whit wrote about her for *Time*, he took a special satisfaction in talking about Miss West's love for her Buckingham farm and her herds of cattle.

I was a personal witness to Whit's first reaction to the word that he might be subpoenaed to testify on Soviet spying before the House Committee on UnAmerican Activities in Washington. A *New York Sun* reporter, Ed Nellor, had dragged out the old story of the Chambers-Levine 1939 visit to Berle. I was in Whit's office when the afternoon papers were delivered, and what I saw, as Whit leaped at the Nellor story, was a study in blue funk. Knowing nothing about Whit's actual experiences as a Communist courier who had worked with Hiss in the '30s, I said carelessly that Whit had nothing to fear about a Washington probing. "Just go there and tell them what you know," I said. Whereupon a distracted Whit looked down the corridor toward the desk of managing editor Tom Matthews and said, "Have you ever heard the word 'informer'? People don't like informers." Later on he said with a reconciled sigh, "Oh, well. I always feared I'd have to cross this bridge sometime, and now it's here."

Whit knew that he would be subjected to the full force of the Left's anger if he told the truth about Communist penetration of the State Department. He correctly predicted that he would become the butt of innuendo, his family would be made to suffer, and he would have to find ways of making a livelihood all over again if he was to keep his mortgaged Maryland acres. Whit was always prophetic, in both big things and small. Looking at a map of North Africa in 1945, he said there would be a Soviet grab for an encircling position south of Europe in the Mediterranean. But his most astounding prediction was that there would be a Soviet-American competition to control access to the moon. The earth, he said, was a "shore of space," and the first power to apply the Admiral Mahan doctrine of sea power to "stratosphere power" would dominate the globe.

What Whit knew earlier than the rest of us was the transcendent ability of the Communists to use the liberals to further their own "dis-information" tactics. When a few of us in the Time, Inc., Newspaper Guild became aware of the Left machinations, we followed a young Catholic named Larry Delaney in organizing an anti-Communist unit. But none of us—John Davenport, Calvin Fixx, Robert Cantwell, Jim Agee—had any sense about ways of combatting the fellow-travelers until Whit Chambers joined our group. Sitting in the rear at meetings, he would warn us about the probable course of voting action after two or three suburban Guild members had departed to catch the latest train to Mamaroneck or Princeton. With Delaney as the organizer and Chambers as the prophet, we soon learned how to deal with the Communist caucus. At *National Review* we had none of these organizational worries. But Whit's presence meant that Bill Buckley would never be an innocent victim of the Left.

Whit, who had a heart condition that caused him recurrent trouble, had to give up coming into New York to *National Review* on a steady basis. But his influence on *National Review* continued to his death, and even beyond it to this day. He set a tone for the magazine. I would not have written as he did about Ayn Rand's *Atlas Shrugged*, which I consider a great fable that embodies an enduring truth about releasing human energy. But there is much value in Whit's contention that Ayn Rand's insistence on 100 percent loyalty from her disciples, even to making a profession of atheism, distorted her efforts and spoiled her persuasiveness. What Whit established, with Bill Buckley's blessing, is that doctrine is often best promoted by seeming to be undoctrinaire and that compassion is not to be derided even though the Hubert Humphreys and the Fritz Mondales of this world try to patent it as something peculiarly their own.

Chapter 13

I f anyone in the '30s had said I would spend part of the '50s working with a couple of generals, I would have called him crazy. The "military mind," in the interwar period, vied with the businessman as an object of derision. But, as the drums began to play, it was quickly evident that there were generals and generals. My new friend, General Bonner Fellers, who had come down from West Point to protest our first draft of the *Fortune* article on the Philippines that treated General Douglas MacArthur as a pretentious actor, made a case for MacArthur's strategic sense that was thoroughly borne out in both the Pacific and the Korean wars.

We at the *Freeman* were particularly outraged when, on April 12, 1951, Harry Truman fired MacArthur for the indiscretion of telling Americans there was no substitute for victory. Truman had the technicalities on his side; it was not the business of a general in the field to question his Commander-in-Chief in public, particularly in a letter addressed to the leader of the opposition party. But there are times in the history of republics when the technicalities of protocol should be waived. MacArthur was so obviously right when, faced with the truce in Korea that let the Red Chinese off the hook, he said, "This is the end of Indochina."

In the late '40s, at the instigation of a lively literary agent named Gertrude Algase, I had taken on the job of revising and amplifying Stanislas Mikolaczyk's *The Rape of Poland*, which had originally run in the Hearst press. Mikolaczyk, a leader of the Peasant Party, had been the last non-Marxist premier of Poland, a brave man who had hung on until it became all too transparent that neither Washington nor London had the slightest intention of holding Stalin to the terms of Yalta that guaranteed self-rule to Eastern European nations. Mikolaczyk had originally dictated his story to Bob Considine, by all odds the most versatile, if not the greatest, reporter of his time. It tickled Mikolaczyk's democratic sense of proportion that his story should have been presented in the newspapers by an old-time sports writer, and he wanted the enlarged book version to be completed by the same hand. Unfortunately, Bob Considine had conflicting assignments in addition to his five-times-a-week syndicated column. So Mikolaczyk reluc-

tantly consented to accepting me as a substitute. In between writing for
Life I spent some fascinating hours listening to an authentic hero tell about
the fast footwork that enabled him to remain in Poland as long as he did.
Mikolaczyk, who escaped to the British zone in Germany, was luckier than
Czechoslovakia's Jan Masaryk, who was pushed out of the window by the
Stalinists in Prague.

As a literary agent, Gertrude Algase was an anomaly: she specialized in
handling manuscripts that would scarcely appeal to the average "liberal"
publisher of the early '50s. Her trouble, as she explained to me, was finding
writers who could help her—the talent, even for rewriting and revising,
seemed to be all on the Left. After the success of the Mikolaczyk project she
was after me for one thing or another. I couldn't take on anything extra in
the first days of the *Freeman*, but when it became obvious that our magazine was doomed as a wide-angle political fortnightly, I told her that I was
available. Coincidentally with the final *Freeman* collapse, she asked me if I
would be willing to collaborate with General Charles Willoughby, MacArthur's G2, in boiling down into a single, readable book the millions of words
in MacArthur's headquarters "histories," done by scholars in some ten
volumes.

The contract was a good one, with an extra promise of five personal
papers by MacArthur himself explaining key decisions in the Pacific wars.
Ben Hibbs, the editor of *Saturday Evening Post*, committed himself to
publishing several selections from the condensed histories provided the
words contributed by MacArthur could be clearly indicated. So I set to
work on a tedious but fascinating job of excerpting, inserting, and joining
with paraphrases enough of the so-called MacArthur papers to make a
magazine series and a book. I worked from the front end of the story,
beginning with a chapter called "The War of Distances" that dealt with the
forbidding problems that confronted MacArthur after his retreat from
Bataan in the Philippines to Brisbane in Australia. Willoughby took over the
back end, contributing his own reminiscences of the Korean War and the
MacArthur years as America's pro-consul in Tokyo, where MacArthur, a
thoroughly accomplished master of theatre, had to out-majesty an Emperor
who had only recently relinquished his claim to godhead.

It was a great experience, and I think we produced an important book.
Military critic Hanson Baldwin, reviewing it in the *New York Times*, called
it "the first comprehensive and authoritative account of MacArthur's
decade of glory . . . a headquarters story" of "greatest value" in emphasiz-
ing the "high command" point of view. Unfortunately we ran into difficulties with Ben Hibbs and the *Post*. MacArthur had originally given his
personal accounts of command decisions to Willoughby with no strings
attached. But, after prodding from his legal counsel General Courtney
Whitney, who had a future MacArthur autobiography in mind, MacArthur
shocked Willoughby by telling him we would have to put his words into the

"third person," inventing an absurd "observer" who could divine exactly what the General was telling himself at critical points in the war. Ben Hibbs concluded that if the series could not be presented as MacArthur's own story it would not suit *Post* readers. We quickly took the manuscript to the editor of *Collier's*, who accepted it on condition that MacArthur would put his name to it in some fashion. But that was not to be. Willoughby, who thought Courtney Whitney was an evil genius who contemplated getting special preference for his own book no matter what MacArthur might do about an autobiography, never got over the disillusionment. He kept the money from the *Post*, using it to build himself a retirement home on Massachusetts Avenue in Washington, D.C. But this was small compensation for an embittered man who had been a true hero-worshipper and a most understanding student of MacArthur's strategy. In his odd hours Willoughby amused himself by superimposing MacArthur's battles on similar battles of the Napoleonic wars. The "double-envelopments" and the flanking operations of MacArthur and Napoleon were the same, allowing for the substitution of air bombing for artillery and the movement of men over much vaster distances.

Despite Ben Hibbs, our book made the best-seller lists. Moreover, it earned accolades from spokesmen for the common reader who might have welcomed the story in the *Post*. The *New York Daily News* said editorially that it hoped the book would have a tremendous sale. "For our money," said the *News*, "the high spot in the volume is the passage concerning entry of the Chinese Reds into the war late in 1950, after MacArthur's men had chewed the North Korean Red forces to bits and had sent spearheads to the Yalu River border between North Korea and Manchuria. MacArthur had enough air power to smash every major supply depot and munitions plant in Manchuria."

Willoughby was convinced that the Red Chinese entered the war only because they had been assured, presumably by pro-Communist "moles" inside the British intelligence services, that President Truman would not permit any attack beyond the Yalu on the Manchurian Communist sanctuary. Said Willoughby, "That the Red Chinese commander apparently knew such a decision would be forthcoming, while General MacArthur did not, represents one of the blackest pages ever recorded."

Ben Hibbs was subsequently quoted as saying his decision to reject our story was a serious mistake. Even so, the "third person" version of MacArthur's own descriptions of his decisions would have forced the *Post* to make some silly explanations. The same MacArthur descriptions turned up later in the "first person" in MacArthur's own story.

I could take MacArthur's behavior with some equanimity, for I knew he was caught between promises to two friends. The whole experience of working with Willoughby, who had a reputation for a cantankerousness that he never showed to me, was vastly instructive. Even before Vietnam, I knew what the United States was in for simply because the otherwise sensible Harry Truman decided to play for a tie in Korea.

Later, in a long essay called "Douglas MacArthur: the Last General" which I wrote for *Human Events*, I tried to sum up what I had learned. I took off from Brent Bozell's despairing comment that the conservative movement in America had collapsed into "total irrelevance" because of the abandonment of four propositions; anti-statism, nationalism, anti-Communism, and constitutionalism. Anti-statism had been symbolized by Bob Taft, who had been side-tracked for the well-meaning Ike Eisenhower, who made no effort to build a conservative Republican organization; anti-Communism had been discredited with the humbling of Joe McCarthy; constitutionalism had lost out with the defeats of Strom Thurmond and Senator Bricker; and nationalism had been repudiated with Douglas MacArthur.

I couldn't agree with Brent Bozell about the abandonment of anti-statism, anti-Communism, and constitutionalism, for there were plenty of exponents of Leonard Read's "freedom philosophy" who were willing to fight on. But the "nationalism" bit was another story.

We had not yet decided to lose in Vietnam, but I could see the handwriting on the wall. I wrote in *Human Events* for April 12, 1969, that "no great nation—and no spirit of nationalism—can long survive if its elected leaders persist in engaging in wars in which generals are denied scope for practicing the art of successful generalship. Other things—national élan, the will to persist—must fail if a war, once entered upon, can't be brought to a conclusion that is sufficiently definite to keep it from breaking out again, under circumstances more favorable to the enemy."

This was the insight that MacArthur had tried, with such eloquence about "duty, honor, country," to bring home to the American people.

I never saw MacArthur in front-line action, but in the course of working with Willoughby, I met with "the presence" himself on several occasions at New York's Waldorf Astoria. In a group of three, MacArthur was thoroughly relaxed. He liked to project himself as a spiritual descendant of the early Wisconsin Progressives, who wanted to save the Republic for small competitive businessmen and farmers. Phil LaFollette had reciprocated by becoming his fervent disciple. He joked about his own theatricality. "Speaking among ourselves," he said, "we don't have to measure our words. But in a crowd one must be a bit of a ham." The hamminess, in Japan, had been calculated to enforce the authority of a conqueror who had exposed the fraudulence of the Emperor's claim to divinity yet was prepared to be magnanimous in bringing democracy to a people who would be happy with the results of embracing constitutionalism and such Western concepts as habeas corpus.

Above all, MacArthur hated waste, whether of effort or of men. Korea, he told Willoughby, was a wasted opportunity, for our failure to cripple the

Red Chinese by destroying their Manchurian sanctuary would merely shift the locus of the war to other areas. This happened, of course, when Kennedy and Lyndon Johnson were lured into fighting a more difficult land war in tropical Southeast Asia.

My generation had hated World War I because of its stupid attrition. The British had wasted an opportunity for an early breakthrough with massed tanks, their own particular invention. A second opportunity had been missed when the British fleet was called back from its effort to force the Dardanelles just when the Turkish shore batteries were running out of ammunition. If Lydell Hart's and Churchill's concepts of maneuver had been adopted, and the necessary preparations made, the war could have been ended in 1916, with republican traditions still sufficiently healthy to keep Lenin and Trotsky submerged. Making peace with the Kaiser would not have been difficult; after all he was European and a gentleman. Again as Max Nomad has said, "The Kaiser and Czar were liberals."

Delving into MacArthur's past, and forgetting the theatrics of the dispersal of the bonus army in Washington, our generation had discovered that the legend of "Dug-out Doug" was nonsensical. MacArthur had been gassed in battle in 1918. He had come out of World War I with a firm resolve never to be responsible for wasting lives on futile efforts to force strong points directly. He studied the Napoleonic flank attacks, the ball player's philosophy of Willie Keeler, who liked to "hit 'em where they ain't." As chief of staff in the '30s, he tried to build up the mobile units of the army, and he accepted the airplane not as a solo performer but as a form of flying artillery.

The pay-off came in the Pacific, where MacArthur, with Napoleonic patterns in mind, jumped 500 miles behind the Japanese on occasion. The capture of Hollandia in New Guinea, following a plan drawn up by Bonner Fellers, was a capital instance of his method. General Willoughby superimposed Napoleon's Battle of Eylau on Hollandia, demonstrating the theory of the double envelopment. The MacArthur formula was to control the air and sea, then to grapple for the opponent's rear and cut off his supply. After that the enemy could be left to "die on the vine." The same formula was later applied to Korea, to effect the critical Inchon landing. It was never tried in Vietnam, where Lyndon Johnson, no student of war, refused to touch enemy sanctuaries.

The enlightening experience of working with the MacArthur "histories" and General Willoughby made me jump at the chance of helping General Albert Wedemeyer with his book, *Wedemeyer Reports*. I had met Wedemeyer and his wife, the sprightly Dade, at Washington parties, and had hit it off with him because of our similar views on a number of things. He was a willing, though sometimes off-the-record, helper on *Life* articles. It was in his Pentagon office, where I had gone to learn something about the "polar concept" of air defense, that I got a call from Harry Luce to come to New

York on a hurry-up basis to do *Life* editorials. (Jack Jessup was being sent from *Life* to *Fortune* to renew its vitality.) "Good soldier," I remember Luce saying as he hung up the phone. I don't know whether he was commending the General or me.

Wedemeyer, after a period in business, started on his memoirs, but he was soon having difficulties with his collaborator, Freda Utley. Freda had her own pronounced opinions about the war in China, and she insisted upon their inviolability in rewriting the General's scripts. "She keeps putting words in my mouth," Wedemeyer said. It became too much when she put a tinge of malevolence into Wedemeyer's portrait of Ambassador Pat Hurley, with whom the General had always maintained friendly relations even when they differed. Wedemeyer said that forebearance with Pat Hurley usually paid off; he could be counted on to turn up on the right side wherever the Communists were involved.

After a number of bitter arguments with Freda, the General asked me if I would be willing to help him finish a book that was less than half-completed. I agreed on condition that I would work with his papers and tapes as I had done with the MacArthur histories, limiting my role to paraphrasing, cutting, and rearranging. The Wedemeyer words would be his own, minus the repetitions that inevitably creep into dictated copy.

It all worked out well, though I don't think the reviewers, aside from Joseph Evans in the *Wall Street Journal*, caught the full tragic implications of what Wedemeyer was saying. Wedemeyer, a Nebraskan who recalled all too vividly that the Versailles Treaty had turned out badly, had no desire to see America in the war in the first place. He had been sent by the army to study in Germany, and he considered us badly prepared to take on Hitler. But, like any good soldier, he waived all that once he had his orders. A favorite with General George Marshall, he became "Marshall's planner."

As such, he found himself enmeshed in a subtle politics that he could not possibly control. He had made a thorough study of Mediterranean logistics, and was convinced that any attempt to flank the Axis powers by thrusts through the Balkans or up the Italian peninsula would fail because of inadequate port facilities at the unloading end. In brief, the "soft underbelly" of Europe was not particularly soft. Meanwhile the clock was running in Russia. Hitler, reaching for Stalingrad, had his own logistical troubles. The Soviets were clamoring for a second front out of desperation. Wedemeyer concluded that 1943 was the year to accommodate them, but for reasons that Stalin might find offensive if they were explicitly set forth. The Wedemeyer idea was that a successful cross-Channel invasion of Western Europe should be timed to coincide with the deepest Nazi penetration of Russia. Committed at the Volga, Hitler would not be able to pay full attention to his western flank. Mechanized thrusts from France and Belgium might enable our Pattons to reach far into Europe before Hitler could properly react. We would thus be the liberators of Czechs, Austrians, and even Poles and Hungarians. There would have been no need for a capitulation to Stalin at Yalta.

The catch in this prospectus was manpower. With Allied troops and ships committed to North Africa and Sicily, there could be no realistic second front in northern France until 1944. Wedemeyer would have scratched the North African and Italian campaigns, concentrating every-thing on a master blow in northern France and the Low Countries. Mar-shall, whose logistical education was gained in northern France in 1917-18, supported the logic of his "planner," but was unable to carry the day with Franklin Roosevelt. The plain truth was that Churchill, thinking of Empire communications as well as of defeating Hitler, considered a 1943 Channel crossing premature. The strategy of clearing the perimeter and nibbling at extremities had worked for Britain in Napoleonic times, when Spain and Russia had bled Napoleon. Why wouldn't it work once more?

Wedemeyer's answer was that Stalin would be uncontrollable in the peace if he could reach Warsaw, Prague, and Berlin before the Western Allies. We no longer lived in a Metternichean world. If Wedemeyer had had support in Washington, the British might have been prevailed upon to change their tune. But the man whom Churchill called "Lord-Root-of-the-Matter," Harry Hopkins, didn't care. Hopkins was convinced that the Soviets were going to play a strong part in post-war Europe anyway. And Roosevelt, as Hopkins' patron, had his own illusions about handling "Uncle Joe."

Having lost his usefulness to Marshall, Wedemeyer could only acquiesce in his "banishment" to the Orient. As a replacement for "Vinegar Joe" Stillwell, who had made himself persona non grata to Chiang Kai-shek, Wedemeyer was a great success. But he was fated to lose in the post-war what he gained in the war in continental China against the Japanese. His warning to Harry Truman that, without more support from Washington, Chiang would be defeated by Mao Tse-tung, was never heeded. Marshall, arguing for a Chinese "coalition," thought his old "planner" had grown "too big for his britches."

Working with Willoughby, MacArthur and Wedemeyer led me to reflect on the danger of relying on old shibboleths, such as "War is too important to leave to the generals." A third general, Truman Smith, who had been our military attaché in Germany, also helped open my eyes to untrustworthy aspects of the conventional wisdom.

Hal Horan, the *Time* correspondent in Washington, had introduced me to Smith, then a colonel, in front of the Munitions Building in the early days of the war. The Nazis had just invaded Norway, and I remarked that the German general in charge of the operation must be pretty good. Where-upon Smith exploded with a statement that the Nazis had 20 generals who were even better, and that if the blankety-blank American liberals didn't wake up, they were going to lose their own country.

Smith, like Wedemeyer, was one of Marshall's trusted men. Because he called the shots about German strength as he saw them, the liberals whom he excoriated jumped to an unwarranted conclusion that he must be pro-Nazi. They linked him to Colonel Lindbergh in this respect. They even suspected Smith of writing Lindbergh's America First speeches.

Smith, as I soon found out, was close to Lindbergh, but not in any way the liberals supposed. Angered at the effectiveness of Lindbergh's campaign to keep America out of the war, Roosevelt and his Secretary of the Interior Harold Ickes had slandered him where they did not dare slander Norman Thomas or Chester Bowles, or Yale's Kingman Brewster. Ickes thought Lindbergh wanted to become the American *Fuehrer*; Roosevelt called him a Copperhead. The White House let it be supposed that Lindbergh had made his several trips to Germany on his own and had become a willing transmitter for Nazi propaganda.

The facts, however, were that Lindbergh had undertaken his trips at American and French government instigation.

One trip was at Truman Smith's special request. As an infantryman, Colonel Smith, though an accredited attaché, had encountered some difficulty in getting a line on Nazi aircraft production. He felt that Lindbergh, as a flyer, could use his expertise either to elicit new information or to make some shrewd guesses based on his practiced eye.

A subsequent Lindbergh trip had been made at the request of the U.S. State Department on behalf of German Jews. The proposal, as outlined for Lindbergh, was to play upon the sympathies of Hermann Goering, who was not personally an anti-Semite. Lindbergh was to present a plan to Goering for allowing Jews to leave Germany with some of their property. It was to be presented to Hitler as a cheap way of solving the "Jewish problem."

In the course of his mission, Lindbergh had the Goering medal pinned on him. Taking one horrified look at it, Anne Lindbergh whispered, "the albatross." Yet Lindbergh could not have turned it down without ruining his mission.

Truman Smith told me that he had written a full account of the Lindbergh trips in a manuscript which he had deposited in the Yale Library. When the controversy broke out over the publication of Lindbergh's war journals and his wife's diaries and letters of the interwar period, I got Smith's permission to read his manuscript. It was a revelation, and it allowed me to get a news beat which was lifted from a *National Review* book review and printed on the front page of the *New York Times*.

Lindbergh, as it turned out, was wrong about British staying power in the war, and Roosevelt and Ickes were right. But this does not excuse wanton attacks on an honest man's character. In the same opportunistic way, Roosevelt later tried to pin the blame for Pearl Harbor on Admiral Kimmell, whose autobiography I helped to edit. When Roosevelt was condemning Lindbergh, he was himself violating the neutrality laws by supplying the British with an American pilot and an American plane to help track down the German battleship *Bismarck*, then loose on the high seas on a commerce-destroying mission. The unconstitutional act resulted in the cornering of the *Bismarck*, which may have been all for the best. Nevertheless it was an impeachable act.

I got to know Lindbergh after the war through my wife, who taught modern dancing to his two talented and charming daughters, Annsie and Reeve, and to Anne Lindbergh herself. I found him to be a man of almost prickly rectitude. He would have been quite willing to admit with his wife Anne that the big British secret of the war, which consisted of a foolproof method of breaking any and all Nazi codes, had transformed the conditions of judgment about relative national staying power. Hitler spent four years telegraphing his punches. But Lindbergh always insisted that no matter what the circumstances, a negotiated ending for the war would have been vastly better than the total victory that let Stalin into central Europe. It is a horrifying thought that Lindbergh could turn out to be a better long-term prophet than Roosevelt.

Not that he would have wanted any such vindication. He ended his life as a believer in the Schweitzerian doctrine of the sacredness of life. As an environmentalist he went around the world crusading for the safety of the blue whale, the lions of the Serengeti, and a bird life which he considered more important than the airplane which had made his own life and reputation. The odd thing is that he hoped to win his ecological victories in secret. When I wrote a column on his war against the extinction of the blue whale, he lectured me severely about the impropriety of bringing his name into it. He felt, he said, that he could work more effectively behind the scenes.

When he died, leaving money for a LIndbergh fund to honor those who best combined environmental care with modern technology, he had to admit that names count for something. The name of Charles Lindbergh will always count.

Chapter 14

After quitting the *Freeman* I got a telephone call from John Davenport, who had left *Fortune* magazine to take over the editorship of *Barron's Financial Weekly*, then a weak and struggling Dow Jones Company publication of far less distinction than its lively sister, the *Wall Street Journal*. John had convinced Bill Grimes, the *Journal's* editor who had been charged with "doing something" about *Barron's*, that what we needed in New York was an American version of the *London Economist*. John's own personal contribution to the upgrading of *Barron's* was a weekly front-page editorial that was as carefully crafted as any of his brother Russell's business-and-government essays in *Fortune*. But where Russell had groped for a free-market point of view, John had worked his way through John Maynard Keynes to a final rejection of Keynesianism as it had become popularly understood. The Davenport editorials had an authoritative ring, but John was still having trouble building a staff for the inside of his magazine. He had one promising reporter, Bob Bleiberg, who later succeeded him as editor, but he needed more manpower.

My answer to his offer of a job had to be conditional, for I was already at work on the MacArthur project with General Willoughby. John agreed to taking me on a part-time basis. It was a most congenial arrangement, for it got me out into the world for two or three days in the week, which is something I have always needed for stimulation while engaged in more bookish pursuits.

The *Barron's* work let me pick up where I had left off as a *Fortune* and *Life* writer. I had always liked industrial reporting, and there was plenty of that. But John Davenport, with the ideal of the *London Economist* in mind, wanted page-three articles that would not be strictly financial. He had always thought of himself as a political economist, which meant that business matters must be dealt with in political and social settings. So, for me, it was back to Washington for an occasional assignment. I remember one Washington trip vividly—it was to interview Vice President Richard Nixon on the subject of Indo-China, where French soldiers had just been overwhelmed in the fortress of Dienbienphu.

Nixon had correctly diagnosed the nature of French troubles in Indo-China. With 200,000 French volunteers and Foreign Legionnaires and 200,000 native Vietnamese under arms, the French government had numerical superiority over the insurgent Communist Ho Chi Minh. But Paris had lost all appetite for the war. The problem, as Nixon saw it, was to draw a line somewhere in the world against a Stalinist aggression that included the use of Communist-provoked and Communist-manipulated civil uprising. The Nixon 1954 proposals for taking American leadership in an effort to save the French in Indo-China were not acted on, and are of purely historical interest today. What remains in memory about the interview was the tribute Nixon paid to "Uncle Whit"—meaning, of course, Whit Chambers. Whit had not only helped Nixon understand the ramifications of Communist infiltration in the United States as exemplified in the Hiss case, but he had started Nixon thinking about the long-term objectives of Moscow foreign policy. When Chambers told Nixon that the Korean War was a war about Japan, Nixon got the idea. In a subsequent trip to the Far East, Nixon, with Chambers' overview in mind, could see that the "civil" war in Indo-China was not only a struggle for Indo-China, but for everything from Tokyo to Melbourne. It was Chambers who helped Nixon to become a geopolitical thinker—and the education was to have important consequences. Nixon was destined to lose in Indo-China because of Watergate, and his willingness to play the China card without consideration for either Taiwan or Japan was insensitive, to say the least. Nevertheless, it was important to play balance-of-power politics in Asia, and the fact that Republicans today are aware of the duplicity with which the Communists pursue their foreign-policy objectives is due to a wisdom that can be traced back to the man whom Nixon called "Uncle Whit."

Davenport's admiration for the *London Economist* pattern of mixing general-commentary articles with those more specifically aimed at market subjects was never wholly shared by Bill Grimes, who thought some of the things printed in *Barron's* belonged more properly on the *Wall Street Journal* editorial page. It could have been a tacit signal to Davenport when, one day after an early-in-the-week editorial conference, Grimes suggested that I move across the street to the *Journal's* editorial offices to do articles and book reviews. It could be part-time or full-time, as I wished, which would leave me with an elasticity after I had finished with MacArthur. Since Bill Grimes, who did not like to be crossed, could lay down a most forbidding law (he once promised to hit anybody over the head with his crutch if he were called a Senior Citizen), I felt it the better part of valor to make the change. I would have felt disloyal about leaving *Barron's* if I hadn't had a feeling, gathered from talks with Kurt Bloch, *Barron's* omniscient editorial researcher, that Davenport might be considering a return to *Fortune*. As it turned out, the premonition was right—Luce made Davenport an offer that he couldn't turn down. Davenport left his mark on

Barron's, for Bob Bleiberg picked up his knack of writing effective free-market editorials with the precision of a sonneteer. For his own part, Bob, an ex-Marine who had been raised in Wall Street journalism, was more willing than Davenport to make *Barron's* a "market" publication. Bob's devotion to the market is best exemplified by his statement that when the atom bombs begin to fall on New York he will be on the phone short-selling in San Francisco.

Working for the *Journal* editorial page meant taking assignments from a soft-spoken North Carolinian who bore the strange name of Vermont Connecticut Royster. Roy, who had been a destroyer officer in World War II, was too much of a gentleman to be anything more than a mild disciplinarian, but he generally had his way. If he wanted changes in copy, he would make a couple of suggestions and hand it back, saying "run it through your typewriter again." As a result of this sound way of editing, staff-written articles on the editorial page always seemed tonally intact. Tone was one of Royster's fetishes—he often said he admired the substance of that most rambunctious of writers, John T. Flynn, but considered it a great mistake to write like Flynn, who had a faculty for alienating readers by his scorn for the ingratiating approach.

The *Journal*, under Grimes and Royster and Chief Executive Officer William Kerby, hadn't come around to the idea of having a board of eminent editorial contributors, but it was experimenting with a diversified opinion page. William Henry Chamberlin, writing out of his extensive knowledge of Soviet Russia as well as out of a generally conservative background, did one or two center-page articles each week. Bob Novak, from the *Journal* Washington staff, was the authority on Republican politics. Joe Evans, the assistant editor, was mostly anonymous, but occasionally he would take off on a long trip to Russia or Africa, contributing brilliant articles that would have been prelude to a memorable career if he had lived. Dick Whalen, who sometimes annoyed Royster with a hard-line foreign policy approach, did amenable editorials on domestic subjects before leaving the *Journal* to write his fascinating study of Old Joe Kennedy for *Fortune Magazine*. Expanded to book length, Dick submitted the manuscript to Arthur Krock of the *Times*, who came up with a truly inspired title, *The Founding Father*.

Royster's gentle humor made it a pleasure to come to work in the *Journal's* editorial room. Bill Fitzpatrick, one of the editorial writers, amused all of us with his parodies of Damon Runyon. The atmosphere was at once mildly acerbic and genial. Roy would come to the office, look at the headlines, and say of Ike Eisenhower, "He ain't done nothing good and he ain't done nothing bad. What'll we write about today?" But even in the placid mid-'50s, there was always plenty to say. Believing in the conversational approach, Roy would send Ed Roberts, his bright young protégé, out to some distant spot in Nebraska or wherever with instructions to get a drive-yourself car and go out and talk to people. It was a better technique than telephone polling. Ed developed an original approach that was later to win him a Pulitzer Prize as an editorial commentator for the short-lived Dow-Jones Sunday publication, the *National Observer*; he now is editorial-page director for the *Detroit News*. Henry Gemmell, who had quit the managing editor's job to write editorials for Royster, and John Bridge were other *Journal* editorialists who went to the *National Observer*. Gemmell's most famous crack, before he departed, was, "It's nice to work for a paper that doesn't give a damn." Meaning, of course, that Royster had let him have his say.

Royster liked the arts, and he pointed the *Journal* editorial page toward a general coverage of the theatre and books. He let me balance my week's grist with a column called "Reading for Pleasure." He also had an abiding concern for American education. At his direction I spent a fascinating month going back to school, "auditing" classes in suburban Connecticut, in urban Indianapolis and Washington, D.C., and in prep schools in New England. What impressed me was the ferment in school districts that were taking seriously the attack made in *Why Johnny Can't Read* on the so-called look-say method of teaching the art of reading. In schools with independent-minded citizen boards, the phonic approach to reading was staging a real come-back. Mortimer Smith's Council for Basic Education was having its effect. In Washington, D.C., a first-rate superintendent, Carl Hansen, had established a track system of education that let bright students go ahead at their own pace. Languages—French and Spanish—were being taught in the third grade in suburban Connecticut communities such as Fairfield and Glastonbury. And in Indianapolis you could get Latin, Greek, and even Hebrew in high school. This was in the '50s, before the drive for integration messed things up. Bowing to the victory of sociology over education, Carl Hansen had to relinquish the track system in Washington schools in favor of a "mainstreaming" that inevitably hurt the gifted while not markedly helping anybody. The grassroots urge to better education was seriously damaged by concentration on busing and by an inane preoccupation with racial quotas at the expense of trying to spread the good teaching of fundamentals everywhere.

Another series I did for the *Journal* was a survey of the economics textbooks used in American schools and universities. Ralph Husted, a power-company executive who was a Board of Education member in Indianapolis, put me on to this. The Keynesian approach—the macroeconomics of "aggregates"—dominated in all of the textbooks, from Samuelson on down. The Austrian idea that it is the marginal choices of individuals that set prices and determine investment opportunities was conspicuous by its absence. "Aggregate demand" explained everything; the enterpriser's hunch was immaterial.

Working for the *Journal* as an article writer and book reviewer allowed me to keep the double focus that I had always found congenial. It was good to go out into the world, to look at actual business practices, while at the same time reading the economic literature that failed utterly to make connections with reality. The theory of oligopoly was having a big run in academia in the '50s; everyone from Professor Edward Chamberlin to John Kenneth Galbraith held that large units could, in tacit collusion, force an industry to accept what amounted to a posted price. Galbraith, who as a fellow *Fortune* writer had liked to boast that he was a "Rumanian" economist where John Davenport and myself were "Puritans," was busy elaborating his idea that the business "techno-structure" had made free pricing an anachronism. But my own experience in writing about the automobile market confuted this.

The automation of the production line, with Cross Company machines in football-field-length extension turning out cylinder blocks with only a controller's hand at work, knocked pennies off the price at the very start. The system of trade-in allowances made posted prices at the retailer's end a purely nominal thing. Every possessor of a used car was both a potential buyer and seller. I did a study of Detroit called "The Big Two-and-One-Half" which, running in *Barron's*, turned out to be prophetic of some of Chrysler's troubles. But the idea that the disappearance of Chrysler would change an American automobile "oligopoly," or "few to sell," into a "duopoly," or "two to sell," was ridiculous. There were plenty of foreigners—Volkswagen, Fiat, etc.—waiting to invade the American market even before the Japanese had begun to send us their Hondas and Toyotas.

Distrustful of "models," I was impressed by F.A. Hayek's statement that "imperfections" in the market were to real competition what gasoline is to an automobile. It is the "imperfections"—special advantages in resources and know-how—that make things go. "Perfect" competition, with absence of trade secrets and free access to the market by anybody who had a uniform product to sell, had never existed—economic competition had always been a matter of product differentiation that proceeded from the inequality of the entrepreneur. Fashion would explain much, but fashion was always fickle. In Jane Austen's *Northanger Abbey*, a character objected to the "odious gigs" she saw at the fashionable resort of Bath. She would, at a later date, have said "Oh, those odious tail-fins," which were already on their way out when Ken Galbraith was hailing them as eternal monuments to capitalism's bad taste.

I made myself plain on the subject of the "true perfection of competition" on the *Journal* editorial page—and got a grudging letter from Galbraith about my ability to turn up significant material. But the theorist of the "technostructure" and the "affluent society" had dug himself in too deep ever to relinquish a preconception. Ken Galbraith has never pondered the nature of his own success. It is the differentiated product—the famous Galbraith style—that makes his books saleable in the first place. But it is the paperback and the second-hand bookstore that keeps the market churning.

It is no different in essence with automobiles and washing machines.

As an enemy of price-fixing by the "technostructure," Galbraith would substitute price-fixing by the state. He assumes, against all the evidence, that technostructures, with their allies on Madison Avenue, are powerful enough to control the consumer. But the top is always slippery. Who, a generation ago, would have predicted the losses of General Motors and Ford, let alone Chrysler? It was a sequence of accidents, unforeseeable in the 1950s, that wrecked the American car "oligopoly." With cheap gas and wide-open roads, the big car had become a "must" for the average American suburban family. But in the old countries of Europe and in Japan, constricted space and medieval alleys dictated a different type of car—and jealous governments compounded the troubles of automobile owners by taxing engine size and the fuel itself. The Europeans and the Japanese never "planned" to take over the American car market. They merely lucked into things when the Arabs cut off the oil supply as a prelude to jacking prices sky-high. The foreign car, with its cramped interiors and its politically-dictated fuel conservation, was fortuitously ready for export when the gas crunch came. Now, like Westbrook Pegler, we can all feel like worms emerging from chestnuts. We have had product differentiation by accident. The Galbraithian "technostructure" as applied to Detroit transportation tumbled in a hurry, for reasons that Ken Galbraith had never foreseen.

While working at the *Journal* I had met a remarkable public-opinion pollster named Claude Robinson. Claude worked out of Princeton, New Jersey, which had become a center of opinion testing. Dissatisfied with the low estate of public economic intelligence, he conceived the idea of assembling a "Princeton Panel" of authors who would be subsidized to write a series of books—a "library" of American capitalism—that would make the case for a profit-and-loss system. He himself proposed to start things going with a book on the idea of profit, with Murray Rothbard, one of Ludwig von Mises's more brilliant students, as his guide and researcher. He wanted me to follow up with a general book descriptive of capitalism.

I don't know what Claude expected, but the last thing I wanted to do was a "primer" on the subject. What I proposed was to take each principle or institution of economics and examine it in terms of its origins in time, place, and the personalties involved in its articulation. I began with Adam Smith and the concept of the freely choosing man. But choice implies possessions with which to bargain and a platform on which to stand, so I had to jump back of Smith by a full century to present John Locke as the philosopher who had made the case for the sanctity of the property base. Following on, there had to be a political framework for an open society of buyers and sellers operating from fixed bases, which meant that the founders of the American republic—Jefferson, Hamilton, Madison, and the rest—had to be considered as prime contributors to economic theory.

Trading, projected into the future, meant that promises had to be honored, which involved us once more in law. This led me to Sir Henry Maine, who defined progress as a change from a society of status to a society of contract.

It was by a long detour through Locke, the Founding Fathers, and Sir Henry Maine that I finally got around to classical economic theory, which, in its early formulation of "iron laws"—the law of wages, the law of rent—seemed to me all wrong. Ricardo, the stock broker, and Malthus, the parson, had their points, but they did not reckon with the resiliency of man. The "wage fund" obviously expands or contracts with productivity—if more goods can be produced in an hour with less work, there is obviously going to be a bigger income for the worker and the capitalist to share. As for land, though acreage is finite, its cultivation can be intensified with every advance in chemistry, genetics, and the use of machinery.

I think my book took a truly original turn when I wrote about Robert Owen, not as a socialist, but as a forerunner of Henry Ford. At the New Lanark mills in Scotland, Owen hit upon the basic postulate of "consumer capitalism," which needs a well-heeled working class if it is to find a mass market for its goods. Owen supplied schools and good housing for his workers, and lured productivity out of them by paying good wages. Somehow Owen, as an old man, missed the import of everything he had practiced at New Lanark. He became a socialist, the forerunner of the Fabians, which led to disaster in England even as Henry Ford was discovering the validity of New Lanark by buying up the most productive workers in Detroit with his offer of $5 for a real day's work.

John Stuart Mill was to refute the "iron laws" in England, but the clearest exposition of a "motivated" capitalism came from a 19th-century Yale professor, Francis Amasa Walker. It was Garet Garrett who led me to Walker as the man who had "unstiffened" economic theory in a way that was peculiarly relevant to the development of the American system. Walker stressed qualitative factors. When James Mill divided a wage fund by the number of available workers to arrive at an "average" wage, Walker said "nonsense." He knew that individual workers differed among themselves. In his observation New England Yankees were, for cultural reasons, better at using machinery than East Indians, Russian peasants, or Bengalees. A man who could do 30 times as much work as the next man would certainly command more for the job, whether there was an "iron law" of wages or not.

Walker's emphasis on qualitative factors led naturally to the idea of "working smarter." So I came to the idea of "contrived fecundity," which involved exploring the various theories of shop practice. Marginal analysis explained much about pricing and investment, but it was the man who changed the margin, by devising ways of putting the marginal producer out of business, who really accomplished things. Such figures as Eli Whitney, Frederick Taylor, and Henry Ford were not economists. But they contributed more to American economic theory than any academic with the exception of Francis Walker who proved that "natural price" was whatever the enterpriser could make it by rearranging his tools and expanding his production and sales.

Without being boastful about it, I think most of "supply-side" economics can be found in the book I turned into Claude Robinson and his young editor Dick Cornuelle as *The Roots of Capitalism*. The book is still in print as a Liberty Press Classic. I certainly anticipated much of Milton Friedman's *Capitalism and Freedom*, and some of George Gilder's *Wealth and Poverty*. Congressman Jack Kemp paid me the compliment of presenting *The Roots of Capitalism* to his son as a high school graduation present to steer him right when he came to studying economics at Darthmouth. And Jude Wanniski, the supply-sider who wrote *The Way the World Works*, called me the first neo-conservative. It is sheer vanity, however, to claim originality for supply-side theory—it's all in J.B. Say's famous *Law of Markets*, which holds that production, if considered apart from the "money illusion," creates its own purchasing power. John Stuart Mill said it best of all when he remarked that "the means of payment for commodities is simply commodities. . . Could we suddenly double the productive powers of the country, we would double the supply of commodities in every market; but should we, by the same stroke, double the purchasing power... everyone would have twice as much to offer in exchange."

This is what the New Dealers, with their theories of crop limitation and inflationary tinkering with the money supply (the "money illusion" that did not fool either J.B. Say or John Stuart Mill), forgot. After 50 years of wandering in the Keynesian wilderness, we are now rediscovering Say's Law. That is what Ronald Reagan and Jack Kemp hope to establish as a basis for return to the American way.

Claude Robinson died before he could arrange for any additional Princeton Panel titles. If he had lived, the theoretical underpinning of the Reagan Revolution might have been more detailed. But Robinson's ideas percolated even without his entrepreneurial guidance. I am eternally grateful to him for providing me with the opportunity for extensive reading in the whole subject of economics. When I was finished with *The Roots of Capitalism* in 1959 I was ready for my next book-length venture, which was to write a history of American business for *Fortune Magazine*, ultimately completed as *The Enterprising Americans*.

Chapter 15

W hen, over the luncheon table in 1960, John Davenport, then an assistant managing editor of *Fortune*, complained that one of his daughters couldn't find anything to use in a school paper to counter the "robber-baron" approach to American business, it struck a responsive chord with me. I had been voicing my own complaints about Arthur Schlesinger, Jr., and other American historians for viewing the American story through wholly political lenses. Even Garet Garrett's *The American Story*, which was thoroughly respectful of what great business innovators such as Andrew Carnegie and Henry Ford had done to change the patterns of American life, had put its emphasis on politics. I wasn't much help to John Davenport in finding something for his daughter, but our conversation had planted a seed.

In addition to being a poet, an economist, and an authority on Winston Churchill, John Davenport has been one of America's more creative editors. He had also had a sure hold on his philosophy. Less flamboyant than his brother Russell, or "Mitch," who once frightened a *Fortune* staff group by bringing "Kitty"—an uncomfortably large lion cub—into an editorial gathering in the country, John could always be counted on to give a Rightward tug to *Fortune* story-scheduling sessions. It wasn't long after our lunch that I had agreed to do a history of American business for *Fortune* that would concentrate on the creative energies of the country, relegating government to its place as the provider of a legal framework in which men of action and imagination could move without fear of confiscation. I don't know what *Fortune* expected of me, for a business history could take many shapes. But Duncan Norton-Taylor, the managing editor, and assistant publisher Brooke Alexander gave me my head, with Alexander supplying the title, *The Enterprising Americans*. Provided with a competent researcher, Mireille Gerould, I felt free to treat the American business story as a dramatist might have treated it, concentrating on its adventurous side and on the key items—an invention here, a bit of cross-education there, or the intrusion of chance as embodied in an unusual personality—that shaped specific epochs. I wanted a minimum of statistical tabulations, of piling up

168

data relating to GNP or other abstractions. Harry Luce, when informed that a business history would be serialized in 13 issues of his favorite publication, entered only one stipulation—he didn't want an "economic interpretation" of history that would ignore the role that religious faith had played in unsettling Europe and settling America. I assured him that it was the workings of the Protestant Ethic with which we were dealing, and there could be nothing anti-religious in that.

What had always struck me was the unexpectedness of the events that really change history. When Samuel Colt, as the story had it, was spinning the wheel of a ship and meditating on the uses of the ratchet catch, it planted an idea that led at a later date to the adaptation of ratchet action to a revolver chamber. This meant a new business, one that could make use of Eli Whitney's mass production of interchangeable parts. But it was sheer serendipity that the invention and manufacture of a revolving gun chamber came in time to supply Texas Rangers with a weapon needed to deal on the wing with Comanche Indians. The frontier, in a sense, created the American factory. It was juxtapositions like this that impressed me as I plunged deeply into the story of American enterprise. The strange turns that invention took also fascinated me: by what provision of fate did Alexander Graham Bell get his telephone blueprint to the patent office a few hours before Elisha Gray's similar plan? The biggest wonder of all was the fact that America, at the outset, was practically a land without capital. If ever a country needed a Marshall Plan or a Point Four program, it was the young United States. But, thanks to New England skippers who traded Columbia River furs to Canton merchants for tea, it made it on its own where the Russia of the Czars, with the whole Siberian frontier at their disposal, did not. I did what I could to make this sink home—and I can say with some satisfaction that the book I wrote is still selling after 20 years.

I fully intended to return to full-time work at the *Wall Street Journal* (Royster willing, of course) after finishing my business history. But George Sokolsky, one of the country's few conservative columnists, had just died, and Bill MacLearn, the editor at King Features Syndicate, needed a hurried replacement for the man who, with Westbrook Pegler, had given the Hearst organization an op. ed. conservative one-two punch. I was tempted by the offer of Sokolsky's job, but it was a six-day-a-week proposition. When I said I'd do it on a three-day basis, Bill MacLearn said no, it would have to be six or nothing. I knew this would mean no more book writing for a while, but the prospect of filling the right-hand column on the *New York Journal-American* page was too enticing to turn down. So I capitulated.

Columning has had its good and bad features. I was disappointed when the *Journal-American* went out of existence, for it meant tht I was no longer writing for friends in New York. But the great thing about columning was that it opened up a whole new world of travel, including *carte-blanche* tickets to political conventions. There was freedom to go and see, to select one's own subjects, and to deal with them without anyone's blue pencil hovering over the product. The three editors I have had at King, Louis Messolonghites, Granville McGee, and Mary Joe Connolly, were always zealous in protecting me from mistakes, but they never tampered with a column's plan or meaning. I had good sources in Washington; one of them, geologist Julian Feiss, who worked for the Department of the Interior, knew practically everything.

Only once, in 19 years, did King Features kill a column on me. I had read a book, *Trujillo: The Last Caesar*, by the Dominican Republic's dictator's intelligence officer General Arturo Espaillat, published by Henry Regnery. The book seemed to me a proper peg on which to hang a column saying that if our CIA was going to send guns to foreign countries to assassinate their leaders (as was the case in the Trujillo assassination), then President John F. Kennedy might expect a reprisal. The column would have gone out a few days before the Kennedy assassination in Dallas, but the King libel lawyers killed it on what appeared to me specious grounds that it libeled the CIA. I didn't like what seemed wanton censorship at the time, but if the column had appeared as scheduled on the day of Kennedy's death, it would have put me in the uncomfortable position of having said, "I told you so," in a moment of harrowing national sorrow. The King lawyers had done me an unwitting good turn.

My years spent in writing columns spanned the rise and fall of Barry Goldwater, and the subsequent spectacular conservative recovery that has put Ronald Reagan in the White House. When I started columning it looked as if we were doomed to a long succession of Kennedys, not merely the 1,000 days of Camelot celebrated so nostalgically by Arthur Schlesinger. When it was proposed that the Republicans should run Senator Goldwater against Kennedy in 1964, it seemed too good to be true. Barry's *The Conscience of a Conservative*, written with the help of Brent Bozell, made him the obvious choice of conservatives and libertarians to attempt the job of upending Camelot. Barry would have entered the lists with the zeal of a Sir Lancelot if his opponent had been J.F.K. But the assassination spoiled things for him. It was not a duplicitous Lyndon Johnson that he wanted to take on.

The Goldwater enthusiasts at the Cow Palace in San Francisco in 1964, however, were quite oblivious to the fact that their champion was a most reluctant tiger. I was swept up in the excitement as Rockefeller was booed from the galleries and the liberals—Bill Scranton and the rest of the Eastern Establishment—were sent packing. The Republican Party seemed transformed, and the famous line given to Goldwater by Karl Hess—extremism in defense of liberty is no crime—did not immediately impress one with its time-bomb quality. It sounded more like Patrick Henry than an invitation to McCarthyism.

So we had victory celebrations in San Francisco that were certainly premature. Phyllis Schlafly was positively glowing when she said we had a choice, not an echo. Walter Winchell, then on his last legs as a columnist, was particularly exuberant. He asked me to get out of his car at two in the morning after a long Cow Palace session to watch a fire in a downtown San Francisco street. When a policeman recognized him, asking rhetorically, "Aren't you Walter Winchell?," Walter grinned and said to me, "That's me public."

The convention week was topped off for me with a dinner at the Omar Khayyam restaurant, hosted, as I remember, by Bill White of Emporia, Kansas, and by Hobart Lewis of the *Readers' Digest*. The dinner gave me the opportunity to exchange reminiscences with John Dos Passos. We had had the same sort of "two lives." Once we had seen capital as a fount of evil. But the Communists, in the mid-'30s, had proved worse than the capitalists. We had had comparable disillusionments about Spain. And we had turned "Right"—if Jeffersonian philosophy can properly be called "Right"—at the same moment. We had met on occasion at the Century Club during the '50s to talk about the difficulty of dealing with "reactionary" labels at a time when I was reviewing Dos's labor novel *Midcentury* and his idyllic *Chosen Country* for the *Wall Street Journal*. And my wife and I had visited with him and his charming second wife, Elizabeth Holdridge, at his tidewater Virginia home. We could agree, as the champagne flowed in San Francisco, that a change was coming in America.

And then we departed to face the bitter reality of the most unfair campaign in modern American history, with the Democratic Party of Lyndon Johnson damr ing Barry Goldwater as a warmonger, a killer of little girls who plucked daisy petals in an unconscious countdown to atomic devastation.

We conservatives—or libertarians—had to endure the years of the Counter-Culture, when so much in America seemed to go so wrong. I felt myself hobbled as a commentator by my feeling that Lyndon Johnson and Richard Nixon had no business drafting young men to fight a war they had no intention of really winning. For that matter, as a verbal purist who thinks words should have precise meanings, I had always considered the draft a patent infringement of the Thirteenth Amendment, which categorically prohibits involuntary servitude save as punishment for the commission of a crime. But, draft or no draft, there was no excuse for what went on in the colleges as the New Left took to throwing deans downstairs and setting off explosions in laboratories. The drug scene seemed the ultimate in perversion. Things seemed to be picking up under Richard Nixon, so it was particularly galling to have to live through the Roman orgy of Watergate, which the *Washington Post* and the *New York Times* turned into a circulation-building circus that was out of all proportion to anything that Richard Nixon (as distinct from the Watergate conspirators) had actually done. Of course, Nixon did little to help his own cause. The climax to the

Woodward-Bernstein book, *All the President's Men*, came not with any revelation from the mysterious Deep Throat, who was always a big dud, but with the exclamation that, with the news that certain tapes existed, "Nixon has bugged himself." If Nixon had claimed rights to the tapes as his personal property and had burned them, the liberal press would have screamed bloody murder but no impeachment charges would ever have been made and no resignation would have been forthcoming.

In pursuing a career as columnist through the disappointing '70s, which were at their worst in the Carter years, I tried to follow two lines of thought. One was to press the need for electing politicians whose aims would, paradoxically, be to de-politicize American life. The other was to search out the developments in technology and market practice that would enable people to solve productive problems on their own without running to Washington for special help. Though I have spent a lot of time in Washington, I have always regarded myself as an anti-Washington columnist, and have found New York more congenial to the job of tracking market developments that make political solutions to our problems an unnecessary waste of energy.

Membership in the Mont Pélérin Society has been of inestimable help in pursuing my second line of thought. The Mont Pélérin Society, named from the Swiss mountain where it had been set up by a handful of free-enterprise economists and philosophers in the late 1940s, struggled in obscurity for a time, but two of its early presidents, F.A. Hayek and Milton Friedman, were destined to become Nobel Prize winners, and Ludwig Ehrhard, the man who set the so-called German miracle in motion in 1948, always acknowledged his debt to Mont Pélérin advice. Over a period of years extending from 1965 to 1980 I managed to attend Mont Pélérin annual meetings in Stresa (Italy), Tokyo (Japan), Vichy (France), Aviemore and St. Andrews (Scotland), Brussels (Belgium), Munich (Germany), Caracas (Venezuela), Madrid (Spain), Montreux (Switzerland), Hongkong (with side trips to Taiwan and Portuguese Macão), and Hillsdale College and Palo Alto (the Hoover Institute) in the United States. Meeting in such cosmopolitan places, with participants from all countries, one could hardly avoid learning a great deal about the conditions of freedom throughout the world. After listening to a British president of Mont Pélérin, Arthur Shenfield, or a British secretary of the society, Ralph (now Lord) Harris, the meaning of Margaret Thatcher's victory comes clear, both as to its accomplishments and its troubles. And nobody who has been to Mont Pélérin meetings has been able to avoid instruction in monetarism (Milton Friedman), or in the counterclaims of the Gold Standard (Jacques Rueff, as interpreted by John Exter and others who believe that the paper Federal Reserve note is, quite simply, an "I owe you nothing").

Mont Pélérin meetings were invariably the excuse for more extended traveling. To get to the Tokyo Mont Pélérin meeting in 1966, my wife

Ernestine and I had literally to go around the world. An airline strike in the United States forced us to go to Tokyo by way of Athens, Beirut, Bangkok, Hongkong, and Taiwan. Stopping off in Beirut, we made a sidetrip to the Jordanian section of Jerusalem to visit with Ernestine's good friend, the Abbess Tamara, who ran the Eastern Orthodox convent on the Mount of Olives. Ernestine had known the Abbess in Geneva, in the Russian émigré circles of the 1930s. The Abbess happened to be a Romanoff, second cousin of the last Czar. When her husband died and her children married, she decided that she had a religious calling. She took the veil, and with her inborn administrative ability she soon became an Abbess. She told delightful stories of circumventing the attempt of the Soviet-infiltrated Moscow Greek Orthodox patriarchate to plant KGB spies on her. King Hussein of Jordan, she said, always backed her in her refusal to accept doubtful help from Russia.

I did an amused column on her that ended with a snapper conclusion that her success in avoiding infiltration was the only instance in history in which a Romanoff had gotten the better of the Bolsheviks. When I returned to New York I discovered that the last line had been dropped in a paper that had been saved for me, rendering it utterly pointless. I remembered a warning passed on to me by Jim Bishop never to risk an O. Henry ending in a newspaper.

It was disappointing not to be able to cross the line from the Jordanian Mount of Olives to the green areas ruled by Israeli Jerusalem, but if we had done it we could not have returned to Beirut under our Arab permits. Later, on a subsequent archaeological junket to Israel, I visited Megiddo, where scripture holds that the last big world battle of Armageddon will be fought. The "tel" at Megiddo happens to be at a point on the West Bank that dominates the north-south Israeli route that had been taken by Assyrian invaders in Biblical times. With the Mediterranean only 15 or so miles to the west, it was easy to appreciate Israeli worries that if the Palestinian Liberation Organization were ever to control Megiddo, a surprise Arab tank thrust from the Jordanian West Bank to the sea would cut Israel in two.

The prediction of Armageddon was all too realistic. The Palestinian Arabs who have been exiled from the West Bank have their legitimate grievances, but realpolitik must tell any objective observer that the Israelis will never give up control of north-south routes in Israel without fighting for Megiddo. If ever the flash point comes at this ancient archaeological site, it could detonate World War III, with atomic destruction everywhere.

On to Bangkok on that memorable 1966 round-the-world trip, we had the luck to be entertained by Thanat Khoman, the Thai foreign minister whom I had known in New York. Thanat Khoman had learned all about Soviet machinations during a long stay in Austria. When I wrote several columns in which I interviewed a mythical foreign minister of Ruritania, a gentle cynic, I got an invitation from Anand Panyarachun, the Thai ambassador to the UN, to meet Thanat Khoman. I shortly discovered that my foreign minister of Ruritania was Thanat Khoman's intellectual twin in every respect.

Mont Pélérin kept the idea of the free market alive through some dark years, and I, to the extent that one can do it in op. ed. columns, have tried to pass its wisdom along.

It was hard going at first. I wrote columns to help Dan Mahoney and Kieran O'Doherty get their New York Conservative Party on the ballot, but the party's stated objective, which was to force the Republicans to purge themselves of the influence of Nelson Rockefeller and Jake Javits, seemed light years from any possible fulfillment. In New York City even the Republican *Herald-Tribune* seemed incorrigibly wedded to Leftist notions—it threatened to fire its financial editor, Don Rogers, if he were to accept membership on the Conservative Party board. The journalistic picture in New York City was generally hopeless—and when we tried to start a new tabloid size *Trib* a few years later, we couldn't make a go of it financially. (I did have fun doing its book reviews for three months.) Conservatism, of course, did have its lively weekly and monthly press. But it often seemed as though we were talking to ourselves. We read and wrote for *Human Events*, or Bill Buckley's *National Review*, or Leonard Read's monthly *Freeman*, or such scholarly quarterlies as *Modern Age*, but conservatives were usually dismissed as ultra-Rightists and compassionless monsters in the big press. Larry Fertig had a good weekly free-enterprise column in the *New York World-Telegram*, but for the daily pages there were only David Lawrence, Ralph de Toledano, Holmes Alexander, and me. We were tolerated for reasons of a token fairness. The reinforcements—Jack Kilpatrick, Bill Buckley (as a columnist), Joe Sobran, Pat Buchanan, John Lofton, Bill Rusher, Kevin Phillips, George Will, Jeffrey Hart, and the rest—had yet to entice the syndicates with a type of commentary that now dominates op. ed. pages everywhere.

As a columnist I dutifully fought the New Left, but I had more fun trying to correct the excesses of the new breed of environmentalists who, in the name of a good ideal, seemed bent on stopping expansion before the blacks, the Puerto Ricans, and the Chicanos of the Southwest could move into the middle class along with the older ethnic minority groups. As I said in a speech, "Wanted: A Journalism That Understands Technology," made at Anthony Harrigan's instigation at a National Issues Seminar in Washington held by the United States Industrial Council, I believed with the environmentalists that "we must find ways of sharing the earth with the caribou and the bald eagle, the lion and the kangaroo." But I noted that we had been taken for quite a ride by idiots in the name of such things as ecology and consumerism. We lived, I said, in a New Age of Fable. Too many of us believed that a pipeline from the North Slope oil fields of Alaska would wreck the tundra and be the ruination of the caribou. Nobody looked at the map to see that crossing the top of Alaska from east to west was like going from New York to the Mississippi, and that a pipeline bisecting this stretch would be a mere sliver, a thread to guide bush pilots over a howling wilderness that would be essentially undisturbed by the passage of oil. With their anti-business bias, the ecological fanatics stopped the Alaska pipeline for five years, with deleterious effects on our ability to face the Arab nations and the OPEC monopoly that has done so much inflationary damage to our economy.

As one who wanted to give a hopeful cast to columning, I was happy to quote the Smithsonian Institute reporter who had returned from Alaska with the news that the caribou, far from resenting the pipeline builders, enjoyed huddling on the raised right-of-way to get away from the mosquitos.

My willingness to take on the phony ecologists may have lost me papers, particularly in the Pacific Northwest, but it attracted the attention of the Heritage Foundation in Washington, whose dynamic Hugh Newton signed me on to do special articles to counter Ralph Nader's anti-business Big Business Day. Heritage, under the smiling Ed Feulner, simply proclaimed its own Growth Day, scheduling it to coincide with Nader's call for anti-business demonstrations. The pieces I wrote about all the new things that business, both little and big, was doing made the *Washington Post* and the *Washington Star* in a curious reversal of editorial policy that must have had Nadar gasping. I said that if Jehovah could ask Job if he could make a horse, we were entitled to ask Nader if he could make a carburator, and the thrust struck home.

My Heritage articles owed a good deal to the sort of story I liked to report in columns. I watched the unveiling of a promising gas-from-coal experiment in Windsor, Connecticut, and listened to Gulf and Western's presentation of a zinc-chloride battery capable of running a car for 200 miles without recharging. Putting many things together, I was convinced that the country would be able to survive the disappearance of the Age of Oil. "What we need," I said, "is a journalism that knows how to look for the technological signs. We have had enough of scares, which only succeed in giving environmentalism—which ought to be a worthy-'ism'—a bad name."

Columning involves causes, and when causes are embodied in individuals one takes one's chances. I was struck by the promising figure of Dr. Tom Matthew, a black neurosurgeon who opened a hospital on a shoestring, with the idea of creating supporting companies to manufacture hospital supplies and, incidentally, to give employment to blacks from the Harlem and Bedford-Stuyvesant slums. Alas, Tom Matthew couldn't enlist enough interest to get his venture in black free enterprise off the ground. He made an appeal to Richard Nixon's brain trust, but the association backfired. Though he never received any tangible help from the Nixonites, he got himself known as "Nixon's Nigger," which was the kiss of death in liberal New York. Some years later, two excellent black economists, Walter Williams and Thomas Sowell, started proselytising for the Matthew idea. And Ronald Reagan, in an address to the NAACP, urged blacks to get themselves a new dray horse—i.e., black free enterprise. Maybe the idea will take hold this time.

Another cause into which I was reluctantly drawn (though this had no connection with columning) was that of Dr. Arthur James Kraus. Kraus, a Polish immigrant, had been fired as an instructor from New York's City College in the early '30s for conducting a march on the Polish consulate to protest some Fascist enormity in Europe. He had permission to lead his students in the march, but when it got adverse publicity he was unceremoniously bounced from the faculty and, indeed, slugged over the head during the course of a supposed psychiatric examination. It always seemed something of a waste to me that a man would spend 30 years of his life trying to get strict justice for himself in a world of alternative opportunities, but Kraus had been a victim of academic sadism. That was something that should be exposed. I chaired an investigative meeting in which John Harlan Amen, the Nuremberg prosecutor, acted out of the goodness of his heart as Kraus' attorney of record. Eventually we got a pension for Kraus, through a bill signed by Governor Nelson Rockefeller, along with a belated apology from the New York Board of Higher Education. Justice had at last been done.

Kraus, however, was not satisfied. He was restless and disoriented without his cause. Eventually he went on a hunger strike to bring attention, as he said, to his ideals. It seemed to me a hopeless business of picking the wrong means to achieve a most cloudy end. As Kraus wasted away on his hunger strike, I kept thinking of Rexford Tugwell's humorously expressed query, "Who expects justice?" To me, one lesson of the "Kraus case" was: "Don't pay evil people the compliment of caring what they may have done to hurt you. It will only divert God-given energies to sterile uses." But Kraus had been so grievously wronged that he would have had to be a veritable saint to turn the other cheek.

Taking on a job of starting a school of journalism at Troy State University in Alabama was a cause of a different sort. I did this at the invitation of a remarkable man, Dr. Ralph Adams, the president of the university. Adams, going against the academic tide, was intent on bringing conservative scholars to his campus when other college presidents were bowing to the shibboleths of the New Left. He hired California's Max Rafferty to head his department of education. Pat Buchanan came often to talk about politics. Edward Teller, the so-called father of the H-bomb, was a frequent Troy State lecturer. So was Russell Kirk. Tony Kubek, an academic who had displeased the liberal establishment by standing out against the Red seizure of China, brought his famous Far Eastern library to Troy. And Jack Carroll, who had won a Pulitzer for completing Douglas Southall Freeman's life of Washington, was a Troy professor.

I thoroughly enjoyed a seminar in investigative journalism which I ran every third week for four years at Troy. My aim was to stack the modern investigative breed of reporter up against the real pioneers of muckraking (Lincoln Steffens, Ida Tarbell, Ray Stannard Baker, and others) who did much deeper digging in the early years of the century.

My idea was to make the Troy School of Journalism a magnet for distinguished conservative journalists from all over the country, and to this end we held a seminar in which Bob Tyrrell, the editor of the *American Spectator*, radio commentator Jeffrey St. John, publicist and p.r. man-extraordinary Hugh Newton, Reed Irvine, the editor of *Accuracy in Media*, and others took part. John Hamner, a Florida editor, backed me as assistant dean. But Troy, after all, was a state university, and the idea of making its school of journalism a national school could only be pushed so far. Jim Hall, the university Director of Communications, wanted the school to be pitched more directly to the needs of local journalism. So it was decreed. But as a partial concession to the national idea, Washington writers Stan Evans and Ken Thompson have been making weekly pilgrimages from Washington to Troy to lecture on their own cosmopolitan specialties.

My trips to Troy gave me some insight into Alabama politics. Once I was invited, along with visiting lecturer Erik von Kuehnelt-Leddihn, to a dinner at the Governor's mansion in Montgomery. When Kuehnelt-Leddihn, a convinced Austrian monarchist, said to George Wallace, "Governor, what you need in America is a king," the governor cannily refused the gambit. No doubt he could see the headlines, "Wallace is for an American king." Someone broke the silence by saying, humorously, that Alabama already had a king named George Wallace. The governor, with a twinkle in his eye, let it go at that.

One of the last by-products of my tenure at Troy State was a trip over the Georgia border to Jimmy Carter's home town of Plains, where I met Jimmy's mother and was accused of being a dude because I wore a coat and tie. The contrast between Plains and the Kennedy compound at Hyannisport, Massachusetts, or even the L.B.J. ranch, did much to explain some of Jimmy's presidential troubles. Jimmy simply couldn't cope with cosmopolitan dazzle.

During the long interval between the Goldwater defeat and the Reagan victory of 1980, I did what I could to keep Reagan in the limelight as the conservative heir-presumptive. Ever since meeting him at a party in the hills above the San Fernando Valley near Los Angeles, where I listened to him tell some of his experiences in fighting the Left in the Screen Actors Guild, I have trusted Reagan to be himself. It was obvious, during the L.B.J., Nixon, and Ford years, that the ideas of the Right were merging more and more with the changing ideas of the Center, and that eventually there would be a big break-through in politics to challenge the Left's ascendancy. Where the early conservatives and libertarians—Frank Hanighen at *Human Events*, the group at *National Review*, the libertarian Frank Chodorov, and the religious Whittaker Chambers—talked, a new breed of conservative activist was coming into existence. Our cause was getting organized for action. New think tanks were a-borning: the American Enterprise Institute, the enlarged Hoover Institution, the Institute of Humane Studies, the Institute for Liberty and Community and, finally, the Heritage Foundation were attracting both scholars and doers. The American Conservative Union pushed its propaganda. The neo-conservatives—Irving Kristol, with his *Public Interest* magazine—began to give two cheers for capitalism. Young Americans for Freedom carried on. The National Tax Limitation Committee pushed the spirit of California's Proposition 13 in statewide campaigns. There were the conservative foundations—Olin, Koch, Bechtel, Coors, Scaife, Lilly, and J. Howard Pew—ready to finance a variety of projects. And there were the sympathetic colleges, Hillsdale, Rockford, Grove City, with their newsletters and journals.

The Old Right emerged from its magazines and its narrow lecture circuits to take over column space, to appear on Spectrum programs and to dare the Firing Line, and to infiltrate even the faculties of the Ivy League. The New Right—Paul Weyrich of the Committee for the Survival of a Free Congress, Terry Dolan of the National Conservative Political-Action Committee, Reed Larson of the Right-to-Work-Committee, Howard Phillips of the Conservative Caucus—started going for the jugular in politics, making use of the direct-mail capabilities of the amazing Richard Viguerie, who had learned his trade from Marvin Liebman of the Old Right in New York City and who had perfected his use of lists in a campaign to raise the money needed to pay off George Wallace's political debts.

It all came together, at least for a shining moment, in the Reagan victory that carried with it the domination of the U.S. Senate. Whether Reagan will be able to change the country 180 degrees around with a trillion-dollar debt hanging over its head is obviously conjectural, but he will give it the old college try. He has the voluntaristic spirit of the old American republic in his bones, he learned his economics in the pre-Keynesian era, and he is a personally secure individual who will continue to support his beliefs without worrying in any crippling way about the glory of winning a second term.

For myself, I hope to live to add a chapter or two to prove that the Reagan revolution in attitude has staying power. There may be fumbles as "gypsy moth" Republicans and "boll weevil" Democrats shift their grounds. But what the experience of my own dissident pilgrimage among the "scribblers" who have set the intellectual fashions of the past half-century tells me is that the Left has nothing more going for it beyond its willingness to use force or deception in order to stay in power. It can suppress, but it has never managed to revive the spirit of innovation anywhere.

Jack Kemp has had some sharp words about a Republican Party whose symbol is the elephant. The elephant should remember what happens when it identifies itself with a big business whose CEOs, managerial rather than entrepreneurial in psychology, compromise with the spirit of socialism in order to "get along." If the Republicans fail Reagan, we could be in for a long period of trouble. But the American people will find voluntaristic ways of doing things. They will turn to barter, to ingenious personal solutions, and, if necessary, to an underground economy that will not be considered as any more law-breaking than taking a drink in prohibition times.

We did not unsettle the Old World merely to reestablish its repressive ways in the New.

Index

N

Nader, Ralph, 175
Nash, Odgen, 51
Nation, 11, 144
National Review, 21, 28, 112, 141, 145, 174
Nazaroff, Alexander, 32
Nearing, Scott, 55
Nellor, Edward, 149
Nevin, Judge Parker, 18
Nevins, Allan, 50
New Freeman, 143
New Masses, 55, 65
New Republic, 22, 60, 145-50 passim
New York Herald Tribune, 12, 23, 174
New York *Morning World*, 23
New York *Sun*, 18
New York *Times*, 18-35 passim, 79, 93, 108-14, 119
New York *Times Sunday Book Review*, 11, 42-43, 50
New York *World*, 22, 107
New Yorker, 18
Newell, William, 86
Newhall, Professor Richard, 9
Newton, Hugh, 175, 177
Nicholas II, 67
Nichols, Dudley, 22
Nichols, Lewis, 21
Niebuhr, Reinhold, 66
Nixon, Richard M., 160-61, 171-72, 175
Noble, Hollister, 24
Nock, Albert Jay, 60, 80, 96, 136-138, 143
Nollen, Emmeline, 76-77
Nomad, Max, 33, 155
Norton-Taylor, Duncan, 168
Noüy, Lecomte du, 66
Novack, George, 54
Novak, Robert, 162

O P Q

O'Doherty, Kieran, 174
O'Flaherty, Liam, 11
O'Hara, John, 22, 25, 62
O'Neill, Eugene, 36
O'Neill, Eugene, Jr., 140
Ochs, Adolph, 18, 23, 52, 65, 109, 111, 113
Ogden, Rollo, 52, 109
Oliva, John, 1, 4
Opitz, Ed, 144

Osborne, John, 67-68, 134
Ossietsky, Carl, 90
Otten, Al, 94
Oulahan, Dick, 26
Owen, Robert, 166
Owen, Russell, 18, 23
Paine, Ralph D. (Del), 87, 93
Paley, William, 20
Panyarachun, Anand, 173
Pareto, Vilfredo, 60
Parker, Dorothy, 34
Parrington, Vernon, 33
Paterson, Isabel, 35, 96, 136-38
Pearce, Cap, 44, 54
Pearson, Drew, 123
Pegler, Westbrook, 24, 40, 103, 138, 169
Pendray, G. Edward, 76
Percy, Charles, 80
Perkins, Frances, 100
Perkins, Harold, 77
Perkins, Maxwell, 35
Peyton, Green, 74
Phelan, Towner, 138
Phelps, William Lyon, 10, 16, 28, 34
Phillips, Kevin, 174
Phillips, Howard, 178
Phillips, Osmund, 18, 19, 23
Phillips, Ruby Hart, 112
Pickford, Mary, 15, 26
Pinckney, C.B., 123
Pitkin, Royce, 138
Plato, 13
Poetry, 36
Poirot, Paul, 144
Politics, 73
Porter, Cole, 9, 61
Porter, Katherine Anne, 62
Porter, Russell, 18
Prescott, Orville, 93, 107
Progressive, 87
Proust, Marcel, 11
Purtnell, Joe, 134
Putnam, Jim, 35
Quang, Thich Tri, 95

R

Rae, Bruce, 18
Rafferty, Max, 176
Rand, Ayn, 97, 136, 150
Rascoe, Burton, 11, 34
Raskob, John H., 28